AN INTRODUCTION TO
VATICAN II AS AN ONGOING
THEOLOGICAL EVENT

SACRA DOCTRINA SERIES

Series Editors

Chad C. Pecknold, *The Catholic University of America*

Thomas Joseph White, OP, *Dominican House of Studies*

AN INTRODUCTION TO VATICAN II
AS AN ONGOING THEOLOGICAL EVENT

Matthew Levering

 The Catholic University of America Press
Washington, D.C.

Copyright © 2017
The Catholic University of America Press
All rights reserved
The paper used in this publication meets the minimum requirements of American
National Standards for Information Science—Permanence of Paper for Printed
Library Materials, ANSI Z39.48-1984.
∞

Cataloging-in-Publication Data available from the Library of Congress
ISBN 978-0-8132-2930-0

 To Robert Imbelli

CONTENTS

Acknowledgments   ix

Introduction   1

1. Persons and Propositions: *Dei Verbum* in Context   20

2. Active Participation: *Sacrosanctum Concilium* in Context   50

3. True and False Reform: *Lumen Gentium* in Context   81

4. Nature and Grace: *Gaudium et Spes* in Context   134

5. Vatican II as an Ongoing Theological Event: The Way Forward   174

Conclusion   207

Bibliography   223

Index   239

ACKNOWLEDGMENTS

My first thanks go to my dear friend Fr. Thomas Joseph White, OP, for suggesting that I write an introductory book on this topic. During the writing process, I was aided by two speaking invitations for Fall 2015: from Christopher Ruddy and Robert Miller to speak at the Catholic University of America to a conference devoted to *Dei Verbum*, and from Fr. Antonio López, FSCB, to speak at the Pontifical John Paul II Institute for Studies on Marriage and Family at the Catholic University of America to a conference devoted to *Gaudium et Spes*. In a very different form, parts of chapter 4 will appear as "Nature and Grace in *Gaudium et Spes*: The Status of the Theory of the Natural Desire for the Supernatural" in a book edited by Antonio López (Grand Rapids, Mich.: Eerdmans, forthcoming). Many thanks to these good friends for the invitations to speak and for their gracious hospitality.

The process of revising the manuscript was a difficult one. I owe particularly extensive thanks to my colleague Fr. Scott Hebden and to Fr. Innocent Smith, OP, both of whom read the draft in its roughest form and made incisive and wide-ranging corrections. Fr. Robert Imbelli, Andrew Meszaros, and Fr. Thomas Guarino read and corrected portions of the manuscript and also merit my deep thanks. To others who helped me during the revising of the manuscript, I extend my warm thanks. Christopher Ruddy graciously read a penultimate draft of the introduction, chapter 5, and the conclusion, and his superb corrections and insights enabled me to make some crucial last-minute additions and deletions. My research assistant and friend David Augustine, now a doctoral student at the Catholic University of America, did the bibliography and helped me with the book in a variety of other ways.

A short, introductory book such as this one pursues various goals at once and can achieve only some of them! Fundamentally, the book seeks to be of service to a movement of renewal in Catholic theology, rooted in a strong sense of divine revelation and of the transformative power of Jesus Christ.

At the Catholic University of America Press, John Martino ably steered the manuscript to publication. I received helpful corrections from Gavin D'Costa and from an anonymous peer reviewer. Anne Needham, who copyedited the book for the Catholic University of America Press, suggested a number of corrections that improved the book greatly. I owe a major debt to Mundelein Seminary, especially to its Rector Fr. John Kartje and its Dean Fr. Thomas Baima, and to James and Mary Perry who generously endowed the chair that I hold.

To my beloved wife, Joy, I "give thanks to God always for you" (2 Thes 2:13) and for our children. You are such a treasure! Scripture truly describes you when it praises the person who is "temperate, sensible, dignified, hospitable, an apt teacher, no drunkard, not violent but gentle, not quarrelsome, and no lover of money" (1 Tm 3:2–3). You embody the "still more excellent way" (1 Cor 12:31).

This book is dedicated to a true man of the Council, whose formative years as a seminarian took place in Rome in the very midst of the Council, and who has zealously sought ever since to embody its letter and spirit in word and deed in the service of Jesus Christ: Father Robert Imbelli. I and many others studied at Boston College under Fr. Imbelli, who also preached beautifully at the parish Joy and I attended. "Let the elders who rule well be considered worthy of a double honor, especially those who labor in preaching and teaching" (1 Tm 5:17).

INTRODUCTION

In his Address at the Solemn Opening of the Second Session of the Second Vatican Council (September 29, 1963), Pope Paul VI observed: "The starting point and the goal [of the Council] is that here and at this very hour we should proclaim Christ to ourselves and to the world around us: Christ our beginning, Christ our life and our guide, Christ our hope and our end."[1] In the same vein, in his 1964 encyclical *Ecclesiam Suam*, Paul VI exhorts the whole Church "to make a conscious, generous, whole-hearted act of faith in Jesus Christ our Lord."[2] Warning against those who "imagine that the Church should abdicate its proper role, and adopt an entirely new and unprecedented mode of existence," he argues that the crucial evangelistic task, presently being undertaken by the Council (in 1964), consists in the Church's contemplation of its divinely given constitution and mission. As he explains, "The Church must get a clearer idea of what it really is in the mind of Jesus Christ as recorded and preserved in Sacred Scripture and in Apostolic Tradition, and interpreted and explained by the tradition of the Church under the inspiration and guidance of the

---

1. Pope Paul VI, Address at the Solemn Opening of the Second Session of the Second Vatican Council, September 29, 1963, §3.3, at www.vatican.va (Latin); see the English translation in *Council Daybook: Vatican II, Session I, 1962, and Session II, 1963*, ed. Floyd Anderson (Washington, D.C.: National Catholic Welfare Service, 1965), 143–50. For discussion, see Jared Wicks, SJ, "Vatican II's Turn in 1963: Toward Renewing Catholic Ecclesiology and Validating Catholic Ecumenism," *Josephinum Journal of Theology* 19 (2012): 1–13, at 5–8.

2. Pope Paul VI, *Ecclesiam Suam*, Encyclical Letter, August 6, 1964, §23, at www.vatican.va.

Holy Spirit."³ The heart of everything that the Council does, therefore, must be the Church's "renewed discovery of its vital bond of union with Christ."⁴ The purpose of this "renewed discovery" is not solely to enrich the Church's unity in Christ, but to enrich the unity of the whole world. As Pope John XXIII put it in his Address at the Solemn Opening of the Second Vatican Council on October 11, 1962, the Church, "illumined by the light of Christ," seeks to spread charity and to enable all human beings "to thoroughly understand what they themselves really are, what dignity distinguishes them, what goal they must pursue."⁵

Meeting twenty years after the Council's conclusion, the 1985 Extraordinary Synod of Bishops—gathered to assess the implementation of the Council twenty years after its conclusion—joyfully affirmed the Council "as a grace of God and a gift of the Holy Spirit."⁶ At the same time, the

---

3. Ibid., §26. Thus Paul VI aims to combat "the errors we see circulating within the Church itself and to which people are exposed who have only a partial understanding of the Church and its mission, and who do not pay close enough attention to divine revelation and the Church's Christ-given authority to teach" (ibid., §27). As he observes, "Obviously, there can be no question of reforming the essential nature of the Church or its basic and necessary structure. To use the word reform in that context would be to misuse it completely. We cannot brand the holy and beloved Church of God with the mark of infidelity.... [W]hen we speak about reform we are not concerned to change things, but to preserve all the more resolutely the characteristic features which Christ has impressed on His Church. Or rather, we are concerned to restore to the Church that ideal of perfection and beauty that corresponds to its original image, and that is at the same time consistent with its necessary, normal and legitimate growth from its original, embryonic form into its present structure" (ibid., §§46–47). In the same context, Paul VI cautions against the notion that "the reform of the Church should consist principally in adapting its way of thinking and acting to the customs and temper of the modern secular world. The fascination of worldly life today is very powerful indeed, and many people regard conformity to it as an inescapable and indeed a wise course to take. Hence, those who are not deeply rooted in the faith and in the observance of the Church's laws, readily imagine that the time is ripe to adjust themselves to worldly standards of living, on the assumption that these are the best and only possible ones for a Christian to adopt" (ibid., §48).

4. Ibid., §35.

5. Pope John XXIII, "Gaudet Mater Ecclesia," Address on the Occasion of the Solemn Opening of the Most Holy Council, October 11, 1962, §17 (Latin text available at https://w2.vatican.va/content/john-xxiii/la/speeches/1962/documents/hf_j-xxiii_spe_19621011_opening-council.html; English translation at https://jakomonchak.files.wordpress.com/2012/10/john-xxiii-opening-speech.pdf). The Lutheran scholar Oscar Cullmann, an invited observer at the Council, points out that "John XXIII, to whom today has been incorrectly assigned a radicalism, something foreign to him, desired a *Catholic renewal* in a *Catholic framework*" (Cullmann, *Vatican Council II: The New Direction*, trans. James D. Hester [New York: Harper and Row, 1968], 68).

6. The Synod of Bishops, "Final Report," December 7, 1985, in *The Extraordinary Synod—1985: Message to the People of God* (Boston, Mass.: St. Paul Editions, 1986), 37–68, at 38.

bishops fault their reception of the Council for "speaking too much of the renewal of the Church's external structures and too little of God and of Christ."[7] They propose to read the Council afresh by giving "[s]pecial attention ... to the four major constitutions of the Council, which contain the interpretative key for the other decrees and declarations."[8] In their view, only by attending to the central conciliar teachings, which flow from a desire for a more perfect union with Christ, can the Church truly have something to offer the world and thereby meet the challenge posed by John XXIII at the outset of the Council and by Paul VI in *Ecclesiam Suam*: "The Church must enter into dialogue with the world in which it lives. It has something to say, a message to give, a communication to make."[9]

With a similar emphasis on Christ and evangelization, Pope Francis's 2013 apostolic exhortation *Evangelii Gaudium*—published fifty years after the promulgation of the first document of the Council—begins with a personal call to faith. Pope Francis states, "I invite all Christians, everywhere, at this very moment, to a renewed personal encounter with Jesus Christ, or at least an openness to letting him encounter them; I ask all of you to do this unfailingly each day. No one should think that this invitation is not meant for him or her."[10] This invitation to the whole world to

7. Ibid., 41. 8. Ibid.
9. Paul VI, *Ecclesiam Suam*, §65.
10. Pope Francis, *Evangelii Gaudium*, Apostolic Exhortation, November 24, 2013, §3, at www.vatican.va. For the Christological and ecclesiological links between Benedict XVI and Pope Francis, see Robert P. Imbelli, "Benedict and Francis," in *Go into the Streets! The Welcoming Church of Pope Francis*, ed. Thomas P. Rausch, SJ, and Richard R. Gaillardetz (New York: Paulist Press, 2016), 11–27. Imbelli argues that both popes are significantly influenced by Henri de Lubac. He concludes, "What intimately supports and sustains the ecclesial vision of Benedict and Francis is this conviction: if the center who is Jesus Christ is secure, one can venture courageously to the farthest peripheries without losing the Way" (Imbelli, "Benedict and Francis," 24). In the same volume, by contrast, Gerard Mannion argues that "Both [*Evangelii Gaudium*] and so much of Pope Francis's subsequent actions and statements have demonstrated a clear and dramatic break with the agenda and perspectives of his two immediate predecessors on many fronts" (Mannion, "Re-engaging the People of God," in *Go into the Streets!*, 57–75, at 59). Mannion suggests that the previous two pontificates (John Paul II and Benedict XVI) had encouraged Catholics to "resist the vision of the Council" (Mannion, "Re-engaging the People of God," 59). After this rather divisive assertion, Mannion relates that Pope Francis "accentuates what people share in common rather than what divides them" (Mannion, "Re-engaging the People of God," 60). For Mannion, Pope Francis "has certainly appeared to take a stance on the Council's attempts to affirm a greater sense of episcopal collegiality throughout the church" (Mannion, "Re-engaging the People of God," 61), and I agree that this is so, even if the contributions of the African bishops at the 2015 Synod were disparaged

encounter Christ personally is at the heart of the Second Vatican Council. As Karol Wojtyła (the future Pope John Paul II) remarks in his 1972 book *Sources of Renewal*, which he wrote after taking an active part in the Council's deliberations, "The enrichment of faith is nothing else than increasingly full participation in divine truth. This is the fundamental viewpoint from which we must judge the reality of Vatican II and seek ways of putting it into practice."[11]

Inspired by the words of the present pope and his predecessors, as well as the words of the bishops who gathered twenty years after the Council to reflect upon its implementation, the present book engages Vatican II as an *ongoing theological event*. Drawing upon the use of the term "event" in historiography and sociology, Joseph Komonchak defines "event" as "a 'noteworthy' occurrence, one that has consequences.... In almost all of the literature, the assumption is that an 'event' represents novelty, discontinuity, a 'rupture,' a break from routine, causing surprise, disturbance, even trauma, and perhaps initiating a new routine, a new realm of the taken-for-granted."[12] I agree that Vatican II was an "event" in the sense of "a 'note-

---

and the Synod's participants and outcome were shaped decisively by Vatican intervention. For a generally appreciative evaluation of Pope Francis's steps toward increasing episcopal collegiality, see Christopher Ruddy, "The Local and Universal Church," in *Go into the Streets!*, 109–24. Mannion repeats the standard warning against "the juridical and institutional discourse of the late eighteenth and especially nineteenth and early mid-twentieth centuries" (Mannion, "Re-engaging the People of God," 63), but I find Mannion's essay to be itself overly focused on juridical and institutional power distribution and not sufficiently attentive to the actual demands of the gospel of mercy with its universal call to holiness. Juridically—since he focuses upon power relationships rather than upon evidences of faith, hope, and love—Mannion argues that under the past two popes, "Slowly but surely the image of the church as people of God was challenged and then supplanted by the official *communio* ecclesiology. Many of the gains of Vatican II that were grounded upon the ecclesiology of the people of God were therefore also challenged—for example, the sense of co-responsibility in the church and a more egalitarian understanding of collaborative ministry.... The emphasis in Francis's papacy thus far upon greater consultation and dialogue, alongside increasing hints toward a radically more participatory style of teaching authority, suggests there may also be a revolution in the understanding and exercise of magisterium in this papacy" (Mannion, "Re-engaging the People of God," 65, 69).

11. Karol Wojtyła, *Sources of Renewal: The Implementation of the Second Vatican Council*, trans. P. S. Falla (San Francisco: Harper and Row, 1980), 15.

12. Joseph A. Komonchak, "Vatican II as an 'Event,'" in *Vatican II: Did Anything Happen?*, ed. David G. Schultenover, SJ (New York: Continuum, 2007), 24–51, at 27. Komonchak, however, argues that the interpretation of the Council promoted by Henri de Lubac and Joseph Ratzinger "plays down the eventful character of the council as a break or rupture with tradition" (ibid., 29). I think, on the contrary, that de Lubac and Ratzinger fully recognize the "event" character of

worthy' occurrence, one that has consequences," and in my view it remains today—in and through the sixteen conciliar documents—an ongoing "event." Continuity in the Church's teaching does not mean no change, no "break from routine," no "disturbance," no discontinuity whatsoever. In the hands of Yves Congar, Henri de Lubac, Joseph Ratzinger, Avery Dulles, and others upon whom I model my approach to Vatican II, the term "continuity" means that the enduring cognitive content of divine revelation has been and continues to be faithfully handed on by the Church; it is in this sense that Vatican II's teaching does not constitute "rupture" or "discontinuity." In describing Vatican II as an "ongoing theological event," I should also note that I intend no separation between the "event" and the actual texts of the Council's documents, since it is the latter that must govern the ongoing theological event.[13]

In order to introduce Vatican II, my book focuses upon the four

---

the Council; they are well aware of the Council's boldness and new directions. At the same time, like Yves Congar and Avery Dulles, they emphasize doctrinal continuity. See also Ormond Rush, *Still Interpreting Vatican II: Some Hermeneutical Principles* (New York: Paulist Press, 2004). For Rush, agreeing with Komonchak (and with John O'Malley), "a retrospective interpretation of the Council along the continuum of church history does indeed show that it constitutes an 'event,' in that it marks a radical break beginning a new epoch. Retrospectively, and seen within the context of two thousand years of church history, the Council can now be seen to constitute a deliberate break with particular elements of the tradition (variously named Constantinian, Gregorian, Counter-Reformation, Pian, etc.), now judged to be impeding continuity with the great tradition and impeding a more effective *receptio/traditio* of the Gospel in the contemporary world" (Rush, *Still Interpreting Vatican II*, 75). All agree that the Council broke deliberately with some "Constantinian, Gregorian, Pian, Counter-Reformation" elements; de Lubac and Ratzinger themselves sought and welcomed this kind of break. The question however is whether a rupture occurred in definitive doctrinal teaching. Rush assumes that there is something called "the Gospel" whose content is knowable insofar as we can make judgments today about how to receive and hand it on in "a more effective" way, but it is precisely the existence of "the Gospel" (as a reality mediated faithfully through Scripture as interpreted by the Church) that is at stake in the question of doctrinal rupture, unless one is a biblicist. Rush holds that Ratzinger rejects "'rupture' theories of any kind," but in fact Ratzinger accepts certain kinds of breaks and ruptures while rejecting (on Christological and pneumatological grounds) the possibility of other kinds. Rush argues: "A pneumatology of *aggiornamento* is needed that incorporates discontinuity along with continuity" (Rush, *Still Interpreting Vatican II*, 75). In fact Congar worked his whole life to develop just such a pneumatology, but he still insisted upon doctrinal continuity (in terms of definitive doctrine about the content of the gospel). For Congar, as for Newman, enduring truth is not opposed to historical contextualization. See my *Engaging the Doctrine of the Holy Spirit: Love and Gift in the Trinity and the Church* (Grand Rapids, Mich.: Baker Academic, 2016), especially chapter 7.

13. See also Andrew Meszaros, "Vatican II as Theological Event and Text according to Yves Congar," forthcoming in the *Josephinum Journal of Theology*.

Constitutions that the Council produced: the Dogmatic Constitution on Divine Revelation (*Dei Verbum*, which I treat first because divine revelation is the absolute *sine qua non*), the Constitution on the Sacred Liturgy (*Sacrosanctum Concilium*), the Dogmatic Constitution on the Church (*Lumen Gentium*), and the Pastoral Constitution on the Church in the Modern World (*Gaudium et Spes*). I highlight four doctrinal and pastoral themes by which the Council sought to increase "full participation in divine truth" and to make possible "a renewed personal encounter with Jesus Christ." These four themes are divine revelation as a personal and cognitive-propositional encounter with Christ, active participation of the laity in the liturgy, reform of the Church's human aspects so as to make the divine gifts more visible, and the orientation of human nature to fulfillment through the grace of Christ. Each of these themes was hotly debated during the conciliar era and remains central to theological and pastoral discussions today.

In accord with the four themes I have chosen, each of the first four chapters surveys one cutting-edge book from the conciliar era that highlights one of these four themes, so as to contextualize the conciliar Constitutions in their era. Each chapter then gives a detailed summary of one of the four Constitutions, concluding with some reflections drawn from today's ongoing theological debates about the theme that I highlight in the chapter. My goal is to exhibit not only the content of Vatican II's Constitutions but also their emergence from complex theological discussions and their ongoing importance in today's theological discussions and debates. Gabriel Flynn has rightly observed that "the documents of the Second Vatican Council ... are, for the most part, unread, even by students of theology."[14] I hope to stimulate interest in reading the Council's Constitutions by indicating their relationship to the theological debates of our time and by echoing their call to a deeper and more personal worship of Christ.[15]

In their recent introduction to Vatican II, *Keys to the Council: Unlock-*

---

14. Gabriel Flynn, "Epilogue: Yves Congar's Theology in the New Millennium," in *Yves Congar: Theologian of the Church*, ed. Gabriel Flynn (Leuven: Peeters, 2005), 459–61, at 460.

15. See the essay by Christopher Ruddy, "'In my end is my beginning': *Lumen Gentium* and the Priority of Doxology," *Irish Theological Quarterly* 79 (2014): 144–64.

ing the Teaching of Vatican II, Richard Gaillardetz and Catherine Clifford acknowledge that "the sheer volume of the council documents can overwhelm the reader."[16] Their solution is to focus on "twenty passages from the council documents that we believe provide interpretive 'keys'" and that "can lead the reader to a greater appreciation for the larger vision of the council."[17] Fourteen of their twenty passages come from the four Constitutions on which I focus: *Sacrosanctum Concilium* §§6, 7, 14; *Dei Verbum* §§2, 8; *Lumen Gentium* §§1, 4, 7, 10, 13, 23; and *Gaudium et Spes* §§40, 43, and 48. Their other six passages come from *Christus Dominus* §11; *Dignitatis Humanae* §2; *Unitatis Redintegratio* §§3, 6, and 11; and *Nostra Aetate* §2.[18]

---

16. Richard R. Gaillardetz and Catherine E. Clifford, *Keys to the Council: Unlocking the Teaching of Vatican II* (Collegeville, Minn.: Liturgical Press, 2012), xvii. John W. O'Malley, SJ, puts the matter more bluntly (and, surely, accurately): "The verbosity of the documents of the Council often makes them boring to read, almost impossible to teach, and further complicates their interpretation" (O'Malley, "Vatican II: Historical Perspectives on Its Uniqueness and Interpretation," in his *Tradition and Transition: Historical Perspectives on Vatican II* [Wilmington, Del.: Michael Glazier, 1989], 19–31, at 28). For O'Malley, this verbosity is a positive sign of "the growing awareness of the participants of the complexity of the issues, of the wide variety of positions possible concerning them, and of the necessity of not bringing them to a premature closure" (O'Malley, "Vatican II: Historical Perspectives," 28). I think that the documents simply cover a lot of moral and doctrinal ground, in addition to treating a number of practical matters. O'Malley also observes that "the documents have a kind of detached quality to them, suspended somehow above the historical situations that they were aimed at changing. Since enemies and abuses are not named as such, the documents have a vagueness that opens them to a variety of interpretations, especially by persons untrained in the exegesis of theological texts. Since they are committee documents, moreover, they evince a flaccid quality that, at least at the distance of over twenty years, weakens the dramatic punch many of them in fact in their substance delivered" (O'Malley, "Vatican II: Historical Perspectives," 27). O'Malley approves, as I do, of the dialogic style of the Council's documents, although he exaggerates the ecclesiological "horizontalism" implied by true dialogue: "Dialogue is horizontal not vertical, and it implies, if it is to be taken seriously, a shift in ecclesiology more basic than any single passage or image from *Lumen gentium*" (O'Malley, "Vatican II: Historical Perspectives," 27–28).

17. Gaillardetz and Clifford, *Keys to the Council*, xvii–xviii.

18. These six texts engage teachings on religious freedom, ecumenism, interreligious dialogue, and the distribution of power between the bishops and the pope and Curia. The grounding for each of these texts is found in the four Constitutions. For recent valuable studies of *Dignitatis Humanae* and *Nostra Aetate*, see David L. Schindler and Nicholas J. Healy, Jr., *Freedom, Truth, and Human Dignity: The Second Vatican Council's Declaration on Religious Freedom: A New Translation, Redaction History, and Interpretation of* Dignitatis Humanae (Grand Rapids, Mich.: Eerdmans, 2015); and Gavin D'Costa, *Vatican II: Catholic Doctrines on Jews and Muslims* (Oxford: Oxford University Press, 2014). See also my essay on *Christus Dominus* and its reception, in *The Reception of Vatican II*, ed. Matthew L. Lamb and Matthew Levering (Oxford: Oxford University

I agree with Gaillardetz and Clifford's privileging of the four Constitutions and with their view that an introductory book on the Council cannot and should not try to cover all the documents. Nonetheless, as they recognize, crucial passages from the four Constitutions are missing from their selections. Consider, for example, the eschatological and evangelizing notes of *Sacrosanctum Concilium* §§8–9, or *Sacrosanctum Concilium* §10's crucial teaching that the liturgy is the source and summit of the Church's work. Consider likewise *Dei Verbum* §1's stirring citation of 1 John 1:2–3 to express its desire for the whole world to hear the call to salvation; *Dei Verbum* §§3–7's exposition of the economy of salvation, the obedience of faith, and the nature and transmission of divine revelation; and *Dei Verbum* §§9–12's presentation of Scripture, Tradition, the Magisterium of the Church, and the inspiration and interpretation of Scripture.

Also missing from Gaillardetz and Clifford's book are *Lumen Gentium* §§2–3 on the Father's sending of the Son and Spirit and on the eucharistic upbuilding of the Church in unity; *Lumen Gentium* §§5–6 on the Church as the inauguration of the kingdom of Christ and on the Old Testament images of the Church; *Lumen Gentium* §8 on the unity of the hierarchical Church with the heavenly Church and on the truth that Christ's Church "subsists in the Catholic Church, which is governed by the successor of Peter and by the bishops in communion with him"; *Lumen Gentium* §12 on the proper meaning of the *sensus fidei*; *Lumen Gentium* §§18–22 on the hierarchical constitution of the Church; and *Lumen Gentium* §§30–42 on the work of the laity and on the universal call to holiness. Their book is also unable to include *Gaudium et Spes* §§1–10 on the need to communicate the gospel of Christ to the whole of humankind, in dialogue with the problems and aspirations of the modern world, with Christ as the key and the center and the goal of history; *Gaudium et Spes* §§12–21's reflections on humans as created to know and love God, yet afflicted by atheism; and *Gaudium et Spes* §22's teaching that Christ reveals

---

Press, forthcoming), as well as the essays in that volume by Nicholas J. Healy Jr. ("*Dignitatis Humanae*"), Gavin D'Costa ("*Nostra Aetate*"), and Matthew Ramage ("*Unitatis Redintegratio*"). For further historical background to Catholic ecumenism, see Jerome-Michael Vereb, CP, *"Because He Was a German!" Cardinal Bea and the Origins of Roman Catholic Engagement in the Ecumenical Movement* (Grand Rapids, Mich.: Eerdmans, 2006).

humankind to itself, because only Christ reveals the meaning and goal of the mystery of human life by showing us the path of self-sacrificial love and the goal of resurrected life as adopted sons in the Son. They also leave out *Gaudium et Spes* §§23–32 on how Christ fulfills the social or communal vocation of humanity, rather than offering a merely individualistic salvation; and *Gaudium et Spes* §45 on Christ as the alpha and omega and on the Church as the sacrament of salvation.

Although they are not explicit about it, Gaillardetz and Clifford's introductory book belongs to a particular stream of contemporary theology. Their perspective can be seen when they argue, for example, that today (in 2012) "much of the council's teaching is being minimized, dangerously reinterpreted, or altogether ignored," and so "an authentic and informed understanding of the council is more important than ever."[19] In saying this, they indicate their deep concern about the ways in which then-Pope Benedict XVI (and his predecessor John Paul II) implemented Vatican II. By analyzing twenty key passages from the Council's documents, Gaillardetz and Clifford hope to "unlock a vision of the church that remains both challenging and liberating, a vision capable of guiding our church in the decades to come."[20] Thus their book is an effort to introduce Vatican II in a manner that cautions against specific ways in which Vatican II was, in their view, "being minimized, dangerously reinterpreted, or altogether ignored" during the pontificate of Benedict XVI.[21] Their selection and analysis of twenty key passages from the documents of Vatican II is guided by this theological viewpoint.

My own theological viewpoint appears clearly in this book, since although I survey the whole of each conciliar Constitution, I do so by focusing on conciliar-era theological debates that remain contested. Let me reiterate the four theological themes that guide my engagement with the four Constitutions: (1) the relationship in divine revelation between persons (personal encounter) and propositions (cognitive judgments[22]);

---

19. Gaillardetz and Clifford, *Keys to the Council*, xviii.
20. Ibid.
21. Ibid.
22. A "proposition" is language that conveys cognitive content that is true or false. As Mats Wahlberg points out: "Maybe the most common misconception about propositional revelation is

(2) the active participation of all believers in the liturgical enactment of Christ's sacrificial self-offering, with reference to whether the priest should face the people in the Eucharistic prayer; (3) true and false reform in the Church, and thus the question of what is irreformable and what is reformable; and (4) the need of created human nature for fulfillment through graced communion with Jesus Christ in the Holy Spirit.

Specifically, in surveying the paragraphs of *Dei Verbum* (chapter 1), I have in view "persons and propositions" and René Latourelle's *Theology of Revelation*. In surveying the paragraphs of *Sacrosanctum Concilium* (chapter 2), I have in view "active participation" and Louis Bouyer's *Liturgy and Architecture*. In surveying the paragraphs of *Lumen Gentium* (chapter 3), I have in view "true and false reform" and Yves Congar's *True and False Reform in the Church*. Lastly, in surveying the paragraphs of *Gaudium et Spes* (chapter 4), I have in view "nature and grace" and Henri de Lubac's *The Mystery of the Supernatural*. Latourelle's and de Lubac's books were published during the Council on the basis of research done prior to the Council (although the translated edition of Latourelle's book includes some new material and appeared in 1966); Congar's book was published in 1950 with a revised edition appearing shortly after the Council; and Bouyer's book appeared in 1967 and generally reiterates historical points that he had made prior to the Council, although he is also responding to the postconciliar situation.

---

that it is incompatible with the metaphorical and symbolic character of much biblical language" (Wahlberg, *Revelation as Testimony: A Philosophical-Theological Study* [Grand Rapids, Mich.: Eerdmans, 2014], 37). Since metaphorical and symbolic language can convey cognitive content that is true or false, it is a mistake "to think that only *literal* speech can express propositions" (ibid.). Wahlberg notes that it is possible that some propositions "can *only* be expressed by metaphorical or symbolic speech" (ibid., 38), and he gives the example of the metaphorical affirmation of God as our father. He adds that the allegorical and spiritual cognitive content in biblical texts (whether in psalms and hymns, narratives, poetry, or other genres), even if it cannot be stated in literal language, can be propositional. Furthermore, not all propositions need express truths, since a proposition "can be *expressed* without being *asserted* (claimed to be true)" (ibid., 38). The key point is that anything is propositional that conveys information. Wahlberg concludes that "revelation indeed is more than a transmission of information. The crucial point is that it cannot be less. If the goal of the transformation [brought about by revelation] is something that the subject is supposed to consciously affirm and pursue, then information about that goal must somehow be involved in revelation. And there is absolutely no incompatibility between viewing revelation as life-transforming and as information-providing" (ibid., 41).

In highlighting these theological themes and sources, I hope to shed light upon the very heart of the Council's dogmatic and pastoral contributions: namely, its insistence upon the centrality of Jesus Christ within the modern pluralistic, technologically advancing, and historically conscious world. Put succinctly: We can encounter Christ personally and know him cognitively (propositionally) as our Savior today, two thousand years after his Pasch (*Dei Verbum*). We are called to actively participate liturgically in Christ's holy self-offering on the Cross to the Father through the Holy Spirit (*Sacrosanctum Concilium*). As members of Christ's eschatological people and his mystical Body, we receive the holy gifts of Christ's teaching, sacraments, and hierarchical order that enable us, in a manner that is ever in need of renewal and reform, to share in his priestly, prophetic, and royal mission (*Lumen Gentium*). Lastly, in the midst of the unique pastoral developments, challenges, and opportunities of the modern world, we attain in Jesus Christ to the graced fulfillment of the world's highest aspirations (*Gaudium et Spes*).

The first four chapters are arranged to show the interrelatedness of the four Constitutions with respect to Christ and the Church. *Dei Verbum* comes first, because without God's self-revelation in Christ nothing else would follow; then comes *Sacrosanctum Concilium*, since the Eucharist builds the Church by uniting us in and through Christ's Pasch; then *Lumen Gentium* on the Church as participating in Christ's offices of priest, prophet, and king, and finally *Gaudium et Spes* on the Church in the modern world that (often without knowing it) yearns for the fulfillment that Christ brings.[23] In this order, the four chapters engage with fundamental theology (*Dei Verbum*), liturgical theology (*Sacrosanctum Concilium*), ecclesiology (*Lumen Gentium*), and theological anthropology (*Gaudium et Spes*). I devote a fifth and final chapter to reflecting upon

---

23. Other authors order the four Constitutions differently; I defend my ordering further in chapter 5. I use the translations of *Dei Verbum* and of the first part of *Gaudium et Spes* that are found in *Vatican Council II*, vol. 1, *The Conciliar and Post Conciliar Documents*, rev. ed., ed. Austin Flannery, OP (Northport, N.Y.: Costello Publishing, 1996); while for *Sacrosanctum Concilium*, *Lumen Gentium*, and the second part of *Gaudium et Spes*, I use the translations found in *Decrees of the Ecumenical Councils*, vol. 2, *Trent to Vatican II*, ed. Norman P. Tanner, SJ (Washington, D.C.: Georgetown University Press, 1990). I have chosen to employ both of the two standard compendiums of the documents of Vatican II in English (although I also consult the Latin texts directly).

contemporary scholarly orientations to the Council and its texts. In this fifth chapter, I focus upon two representative, but contrasting, perspectives on the Council set forth by Robert Imbelli and Massimo Faggioli.[24] I argue that Imbelli's perspective accurately unfolds the Council and its reception, because Imbelli emphasizes the centrality of Christ for the whole Council and for the ongoing theological debates that surround it. In this way, Imbelli's perspective is attuned to the centrality of personal and cognitive-propositional revelation of Christ, active participation in Christ's liturgical self-offering, true reform of the Church so as to allow Christ's enduring gifts to shine forth, and the orientation of human nature to graced fulfillment in Christ. Latourelle, Bouyer, Congar, and de Lubac would have recognized and approved Imbelli's approach, which succeeds by refusing to float free of the actual theological soil in which Vatican II germinated.

The four theological themes highlighted in my book inform the other twelve documents of the Council, which I do not have space to treat. Thus, the relationship of person/encounter and cognitive-propositional knowing is an underlying issue in *Inter Mirifica*, *Gravissimum Educationis*, and *Optatam Totius*; true and false reform is an underlying issue in *Orientalium Ecclesiarum*, *Perfectae Caritatis*, and *Unitatis Redintegratio*; active participation is an underlying issue in *Christus Dominus*, *Presbyterorum Ordinis*, and *Apostolicam Actuositatem*; and the relationship of nature and grace, or Church and world, is an underlying issue in *Ad Gentes*, *Nostra Aetate*, and *Dignitatis Humanae*. These four theological themes (or, better, realities) converge in broader themes or realities, such as the universal call to holiness, the history of salvation, ecumenical and interreligious reconciliation, and the communion that God wills for his people in Christ and the Holy Spirit. Holiness and communion in history are another way of speaking of the Person and work of Jesus Christ, in whom all the themes of Vatican II have their center: "when the Counselor comes, whom I shall send you from the Father, even the Spirit of truth, who proceeds from the Father, he will bear witness to me, and you also are witnesses" (Jn 15:26–27). The Council's

24. Imbelli was a seminarian at the Gregorian University in Rome during the four years of the Council, and among his teachers was Latourelle. Both Imbelli and Faggioli are well known scholars who also publish frequently in popular venues such as *Commonweal*.

ecumenical passion, its affirmation of religious liberty, its love for the Jewish people, its respect for other religions, its commitment to a historically conscious faith that does not fear the modern world, its effort to enhance participatory communion within the Church, its universal call to holiness, its Mariology, its insistence upon evangelization—all these follow from the Council's proclamation of Jesus Christ, no mere abstraction but a living Person.[25]

According to the four Constitutions, Jesus reveals God to us: he is the human face of God, and he reveals God in a manner suited to our mode of knowing, since he teaches us by words and performs deeds that are intelligible to us (though mystagogically inexhaustible). We receive divine revelation within the communion of a people (Israel and the Church) called and gathered to share in Christ's Paschal offering to the Father by the Holy Spirit, and God's revelatory words and deeds are never separated from the interpretative matrix of this liturgical people, who are guided by the ascended Lord and his Spirit. Jesus Christ is the measure of true reform of the Church: true reform always deepens the relationship of the whole body of Christ to its head. True reform refines and renovates the merely human elements and limited perspectives that, however useful at an earlier time in history, now impede believers from attaining to their full unity and stature in Christ. The active participation of the laity in

25. For eighteenth-century background to Vatican II, relevant for almost all the domains described in this paragraph, see Shaun Blanchard, "'Proto-Ecumenical' Catholic Reform in the Eighteenth Century: Lodovico Muratori as a Forerunner of Vatican II," *Pro Ecclesia* 25 (2016): 71–89. Blanchard sums up Muratori's contribution: "First, his theology succumbed neither to Enlightenment rationalism nor to Catholic movements that were ultimately suppressed, he approached problems with historical consciousness, and he had a 'proto-ecumenical' spirit. Second, Muratori was deeply Christocentric, and in this he anticipated the Council and especially *Dei Verbum*. Third, he was a forerunner of *Sacrosanctum Concilium* by advocating lay liturgical participation and comprehension. Fourth, Muratori critiqued devotions to Mary and the saints that obscured Christocentrism, scandalized Protestants, and encouraged superstition. In this he also anticipated Vatican II, and particularly *Lumen Gentium*" (ibid., 89). As Ulrich L. Lehner has demonstrated, Vatican II should be read in light of the Tridentine reform as mediated by the Catholic Enlightenment, without thereby neglecting the contributions of the Baroque scholastic theologians. See Lehner's *The Catholic Enlightenment: The Forgotten History of a Global Movement* (Oxford: Oxford University Press, 2016); Lehner, *On the Road to Vatican II: German Catholic Enlightenment and Reform of the Church* (Minneapolis, Minn.: Fortress Press, 2016). See also Paola Vismara, "Lodovico Antonio Muratori (1672–1750): Enlightenment in a Tridentine Mode," in *Enlightenment and Catholicism in Europe: A Transnational History*, ed. Jeffrey D. Burson and Ulrich L. Lehner (Notre Dame, Ind.: University of Notre Dame Press, 2014), 249–68.

the liturgy and in the Church has as its purpose full configuration to the Passover of Christ, the members with the Head, so as to share in Christ's Resurrection. The profound relationship between nature and grace flows from the fact that Christ, as the eternal Word, is the Creator of the world and the world was made for fulfillment in Christ. In Christ, fallen human nature, wounded and subject to death, finds its true meaning and attains its true expression in self-giving love for the sake of the world's communion with God. Thus the four theological themes highlighted in this book illumine, in various ways, the Christ-centered reform and renewal of the Church undertaken by the Second Vatican Council in the context of the modern world.[26]

For a succinct introduction to the content and background of all sixteen of the documents, I recommend *Vatican II: Renewal within Tradition*, but there are many other helpful one-volume or multivolume introductions to the contents of the sixteen documents.[27] For exposition and analysis of the behind-the-scenes debates and controversies among drafters, as well as for the speeches on the floor of the Council and the role of Popes John XXIII and Paul VI, readers should see detailed scholarly studies such as Jared Wicks's writings on *Dei Verbum*, or multivolume works such as the historical and theological commentary on the Council edited by Herbert Vorgrimler (1966–1968), the five-volume history of the Council edited by Giuseppe Alberigo (1995–2006), and the five-volume commentary edited by Peter Hünermann and Bernd Jochen Hilberath (2004–2006).[28] A readable short history of the Council's main events is John

---

26. See the important essay of Jean Galot, SJ, "Christ: Revealer, Founder of the Church, and Source of Ecclesial Life," trans. Leslie Wearne, in *Vatican II: Assessment and Perspectives; Twenty-Five Years After (1962–1987)*, vol. 1, ed. René Latourelle, SJ (Mahwah, N.J.: Paulist Press, 1988), 385–406. After detailing the Christocentrism of *Dei Verbum*, *Lumen Gentium*, *Sacrosanctum Concilium*, and *Gaudium et Spes*, Galot concludes: "There is no christomonism here, for the Council is careful to place Christ within the divine plan of salvation. The Son is sent by the Father and acts through the Holy Spirit. Moreover, his predominant action in the life of the Church does not curb the activity of the members of his body, but tends rather to develop it as much as possible" (ibid., 403).

27. See Philippe J. Roy, *Bibliographie du Concile Vatican II* (Vatican City: Libreria Editrice Vaticana, 2012).

28. Jared Wicks, SJ, "*Dei Verbum* Developing: Vatican II's Revelation Doctrine, 1963–1964," in *The Convergence of Theology: A Festschrift Honoring Gerald O'Collins, S.J.*, ed. Daniel Kendall, SJ, and Stephen T. Davis (New York: Paulist Press, 2001), 109–25. Jared Wicks, SJ, "Pieter Smulders and Dei Verbum," 5 Parts, *Gregorianum* 82 (2001): 247–97; 82 (2001): 559–93; 83 (2003): 225–67;

O'Malley's *What Happened at Vatican II*, although one should be aware of the theological perspective that informs O'Malley's work.[29] If one reads German, one has available the short history authored by Knut Wenzel or the lengthier work, with analysis of the postconciliar period, by Otto Hermann Pesch.[30] Numerous instructive diaries penned during the Council have also been published in recent years, including those of Gérard Philips,

---

85 (2004): 242–77; 86 (2005): 92–134. Jared Wicks, SJ, "*Dei Verbum* under Revision, March–April 1964: Contributions of Charles Moeller and Other Belgian Theologians," in *The Belgian Contribution to the Second Vatican Council*, ed. Doris Donnelly, Joseph Famerée, Mathijs Lamberigts, and Karim Schelkens (Leuven: Peeters, 2008), 460–94. Jared Wicks, SJ, "Six Texts by Prof. Joseph Ratzinger as *Peritus* before and during Vatican Council II," *Gregorianum* 89 (2008): 233–311. Jared Wicks, SJ, "Vatican II on Revelation—From behind the Scenes," *Theological Studies* 71 (2010): 637–50. Jared Wicks, SJ, "Scripture Reading Urged *Vehementer* (*Dei Verbum* no. 25): Background and Development," in *50 Years On: Probing the Riches of Vatican II*, ed. David G. Schultenover, SJ (Collegeville, Minn.: Liturgical Press, 2015), 365–90. Herbert Vorgrimler, ed., *Commentary on the Documents of Vatican II*, 5 vols. (New York: Herder and Herder, 1967–1969). Giuseppe Alberigo, ed., *History of Vatican II*, 5 vols, English version ed. Joseph A. Komonchak, (Leuven: Peeters, 1995–2006). Peter Hünermann and Bernd Jochen Hilberath, ed., *Herders theologischer Kommentar zum Zweiten Vatikanischen Konzil*, 5 vols. (Freiburg im Breisgau: Herder, 2004–2006). See also, for further theological and historical analysis, four recent edited volumes: *El Concilio Vaticano II: Una perspectiva teologica*, ed. Vicente Vide and José R. Villar (Madrid: San Pablo, 2013), with essays by Luis Ladaria, SJ, Salvador Pié-Ninot, and others; *La théologie catholique entre intransigeance et renouveau. La reception des mouvements préconciliaires à Vatican II*, ed. Gilles Routhier, Philippe J. Roy, and Karim Schelkens (Leuven: College Erasme / Universiteitsbibliotheek, 2011); *Erinnerung an die Zukunft. Das Zweite Vatikanische Konzil. Werweiterte und aktualisierte Auflage*, ed. Jan-Heiner Tück (Freiburg im Breisgau: Herder, 2013), with essays by Thomas Prügl, Marianne Schlosser, and others; and *Zweites Vatikanisches Konzil. Programmatik—Rezeption—Vision*, ed. Christoph Böttigheimer (Freiburg im Breisgau: Herder, 2014).

29. John W. O'Malley, SJ, *What Happened at Vatican II* (Cambridge, Mass.: Harvard University Press, 2008). For concerns about O'Malley's book, see John M. McDermott, SJ's erudite "Did That Really Happen at Vatican II? Reflections on John O'Malley's Recent Book," *Nova et Vetera* 8 (2010): 425–66.

30. Knut Wenzel, *Das Zweite Vatikanische Konzil: Eine Einführung* (Freiburg: Herder, 2014); Otto Hermann Pesch, *Das Zweite Vatikanische Konzil: Vorgeschichte—Verlauf—Ergebnisse—Nachgeschichte* (Ostfildern: Matthias Grünewald, 2001). See also Giuseppe Alberigo's less accurate *A Brief History of Vatican II*, trans. Matthew Sherry (Maryknoll, N.Y.: Orbis Books, 2006). Richard Schenk, OP, cautions: "Alberigo identifies his circle of friends and mentors with the majority. Freely awarded modifiers, bluntly separating 'fortunate' from 'unfortunate' developments at the Council, underline the personal stance behind the book, based on memories of personal involvement in the events by the late author and his wife, Angelina Nicora, whose journals are cited here at length as authoritative. The book presents the majority's successful interventions with the pope as something altogether positive. By contrast, the minority's occasionally successful interventions with the pope are portrayed as nefarious and opposed to the conciliar dynamic. Official and spontaneous subgroups of the majority are portrayed as pro-conciliar; those of the minority, as anti-conciliar" (Schenk, "*Gaudium et Spes*: The Task before Us," *Nova et Vetera* 8 [2010]: 323–35, at 325).

Otto Semmelroth, Pieter Smulders, Yves Congar, and Henri de Lubac.

For the purposes of this book, I presume that readers know the basic history of the Council: Pope John XXIII's decision in 1959 to call an ecumenical Council and its opening on October 11, 1962; the conflict, which especially marked the early stages of the Council, between Roman neo-scholastic theologians and (often younger) Belgian, French, and German theologians of the *nouvelle théologie*; Pope John's death on June 3, 1963, and the election of Pope Paul VI, who as Giovanni Montini had already been collaborating closely with Pope John; the debating and repeated re-drafting of each conciliar document by Commissions composed mainly of bishops assisted by theological experts (*periti*);[31] the gradual promulgation of the first five conciliar documents, starting with *Sacrosanctum Concilium*, between December 1963 and November 1964; the promulgation of the final eleven conciliar documents in late fall 1965; and the closing of the Council on December 8, 1965.

Speaking as a historian, John O'Malley sharply criticizes efforts to engage the teachings of Vatican II that "[s]tick to the final sixteen documents and pay no attention to the historical context, the history of the texts, or the controversies concerning them during the council."[32] As the son of an accomplished historian, I value historical work and historical-critical analysis of the contexts in which texts were written. In my view, theologians should integrate the fruits of historical work into properly theological modes of reflection on the Council. I consider that the Council best comes alive today through contact with its insistence upon the centrality of Christ and upon our Spirit-filled participation in Christ through Scripture, the liturgy, and evangelization. The centrality of Christ has ramifications for the distribution of power in the Church, as can be seen especially in the case of true reform.[33] Yet, in the Council's own focus on Christ,

---

31. On the role of the *periti*, see Jared Wicks, SJ, "Theologians at Vatican Council II," in Wicks, *Doing Theology* (New York: Paulist Press, 2009), 187–223. See also *Personenlexikon zum Zweiten Vatikanischen Konzil* ed. Michael Quisinsky and Peter Walter (Freiburg: Herder, 2012).

32. John W. O'Malley, SJ, "Ten Surefire Ways to Mix Up the Teaching of Vatican II," in O'Malley, *Catholic History for Today's Church: How Our Past Illuminates Our Present* (Lanham, Md.: Rowman and Littlefield, 2015), 109–13, at 112.

33. Summarizing the central thesis of his *What Happened at Vatican II*, O'Malley identifies "three issues-under-the-issues" that are determinative for understanding the sixteen conciliar documents: "(1) Under what circumstances is change appropriate in the church, and with what

power dynamics take a firmly secondary place, important though the distribution of power is. Along these lines, Marc Ouellet insightfully points out that "the Council is Christocentric, which immediately means Trinitarian. For Christ admits us into the Trinitarian communion. He comes in the name of his Father; he speaks in the name of the Father; he communicates to us the Spirit of his Father."[34]

There are a number of limitations with my approach. For example, by focusing on four distinct theological themes, I do not integrate the Constitutions with one another as clearly as I might. Nor can I give equal attention to all the themes about which the Council was passionate, such as ecumenism.[35] In addition, each of the first four chapters is inevitably

---

arguments can it be justified? (2) What is the relationship of center to periphery, which, put in its most concrete form, is the relationship between the papacy (including the curia) and the rest of the church, especially the bishops? (3) No matter how authority is distributed, what is the style or model according to which it should be exercised?" (O'Malley, "What Happened and Did Not Happen at Vatican II," in *Catholic History for Today's Church*, 115–32, at 118). All three of these underlying issues have to do with true reform, and most importantly with the reform of power in the Church. It seems to me that O'Malley thereby underestimates the importance of broader Christological and missiological dimensions of the Council.

34. Marc Cardinal Ouellet, *Relevance and Future of the Second Vatican Council: Interviews with Father Geoffroy de la Tousche*, trans. Michael Donley and Joseph Fessio, SJ (San Francisco: Ignatius Press, 2013), 57. For a similar emphasis on Christocentricity, focusing on part 1 of *Gaudium et Spes*, see Thomas Gertler, *Jesus Christus - Die Antwort der Kirche auf die Frage nach dem Menschsein* (Leipzig: St. Benno-Verlag, 1986).

35. For the ecumenical passion and fruitfulness of the Council, see for example Donald W. Norwood, *Reforming Rome: Karl Barth and Vatican II* (Grand Rapids, Mich.: Eerdmans, 2015); Yves Congar, OP, "Conquering Our Enmities," in *Steps to Christian Unity*, ed. John A. O'Brien (New York: Doubleday, 1964), 100–109; Timothy George, "*Unitatis Redintegratio* after Fifty Years: A Protestant Reading," *Pro Ecclesia* 25 (2016): 53–70; Jared Wicks, SJ, "Cardinal Willebrands's Contributions to Catholic Ecumenical Theology," *Pro Ecclesia* 20 (2011): 6–27. See also Karl Barth, *Ad Limina Apostolorum: An Appraisal of Vatican II*, trans. Keith R. Crim (Edinburgh: The Saint Andrew Press, 1969); as well as such analyses as G. C. Berkouwer, *The Second Vatican Council and the New Catholicism*, trans. Lewis B. Smedes (Grand Rapids, Mich.: Eerdmans, 1965); Cullmann, *Vatican Council II: The New Direction*; and George A. Lindbeck, "The Second Vatican Council," *Concordia Theological Monthly* 34 (January 1963): 19–24. Writing at the very outset of the Council, Lindbeck already observes that "there has been a revolutionary change in the ecumenical atmosphere," and he concludes that "when the council is viewed in the broad sweep of history, there is every reason to believe that it marks the conclusion of the Counter-Reformation epoch. For centuries Roman Catholicism has, from the Reformation perspective, been moving further and further away from its Christian foundations toward a more and more rigidly defensive authoritarianism, toward increased papal power and Roman centralism, toward greater Mariolatry. Since Leo XIII a countercurrent has intermittently flowed, leading to a greater freedom in the social and political spheres and—especially in recent decades in Europe—to theological, liturgical and biblical reviv-

somewhat diffuse, since in each chapter I provide a detailed survey of one conciliar Constitution and introduce an ongoing theological debate without resolving it in a systematic fashion. Although I tried to match an appropriate conciliar-era book with each of the four Constitutions, there can be no one-to-one link between the thematical focus of the conciliar-era book and the wide-ranging exposition that necessarily characterizes each Constitution. Lastly, the detailed surveys of the four Constitutions may put off advanced readers who are already well versed in the Council, and my attention to the theological discussions and debates of the conciliar era may put off introductory readers who simply want a brief analytical digest of the Council.

By engaging the Council through four ongoing theological debates, four cutting-edge conciliar-era books, and detailed surveys of the four Constitutions, I wish to invite readers to think theologically *with* the Council. Above all, I aim to draw the reader into the Council's goals of fostering encounter with the self-revealing God in Christ through the opening up of Scripture, active participation in Christ's self-offering, true ecclesial reform so as to intensify the communion in Christ of the whole people of God, and appreciation of the graced ordering of all creatures to fulfillment and unity in Christ in a manner that mandates a mutually enriching dialogue of the Church with the world. At the heart of all this is Jesus of Nazareth, who as the Messiah of Israel calls us to "come and see" and to abide with him (Jn 1:39), liturgically offers us his "blood of the covenant, which is poured out for many" (Mk 14:24), constitutes us "a royal priesthood, a holy nation, God's own people" (1 Pt 2:9), and frees the whole creation "from its bondage to decay" so that all things might share in "the glorious liberty of the children of God" (Rom 8:21). As Ouellet sums up the achievement of the Second Vatican Council: "The Church had to be redefined starting from Christ, not on the basis of a sociological model or of one particular state in the Church's history."[36]

---

als. The coming council, if it follows the lead of the preparatory work, will be basically on the side of this renewal" (Lindbeck, "The Second Vatican Council," 24). For summaries of the responses of leading Protestant theologians to the Council, though from a perspective quite suspicious of Catholicism, see Leonardo De Chirico, *Evangelical Theological Perspectives on Post–Vatican II Roman Catholicism* (New York: Peter Lang, 2003).

36. Ouellet, *Relevance and Future of the Second Vatican Council*, 38–39.

In short, I seek theological renewal, a new *ressourcement* in the spirit of the theologians whose work inspired the Constitutions of Vatican II and produced a rich *aggiornamento*.[37] Renewal (or true reform) must steer between two poles: an ahistorical extrinsicism, for which no reform is ever needed in the Church, and an atheological historicism, for which reform is merely a matter of adjudicating power within ever-changing human constructs.[38] Such renewal or reform is nourished by love for the living Person of Jesus Christ, whose personal presence is mediated liturgically and doctrinally by the Church of the Holy Spirit, and who calls us to share in his life and mission. As the Orthodox theologian Nicholas Denysenko remarks, "The Council envisioned a significant body of Christians participating in Christ's eternal liturgy offered to God; having partaken of God by hearing the proclamation of the Word and receiving Holy Communion, Christians return to the world to bear Christ and contribute to society's transformation and transfiguration into an icon of God's kingdom."[39] This deeply challenging and deeply rewarding work of renewal is the central task of the ongoing theological event that is the Second Vatican Council.

---

37. The contrast between *ressourcement* and Thomistic modes of thought has been exaggerated, to the detriment of both. For a corrective, see Thomas G. Guarino, "Analogy and Vatican II: An Overlooked Dimension of the Council?," *Josephinum Journal of Theology* 22 (2015), forthcoming. See also Thomas Joseph White, OP, "*Gaudium et Spes*," in *The Reception of Vatican II*, ed. Matthew L. Lamb and Matthew Levering, forthcoming; Yves Congar, OP, *Situation et taches présentes de la théologie* (Paris: Cerf, 1967), 53; Joseph A. Komonchak, "Thomism and the Second Vatican Council," in *Continuity and Plurality in Catholic Theology: Essays in Honor of Gerald A. McCool, S.J.*, ed. Anthony J. Cernera (Fairfield, Conn.: Sacred Heart University Press, 1998), 53–73.

38. On these two poles, see Maurice Blondel, *History and Dogma*, trans. Alexander Dru, in Blondel, *The Letter on Apologetics and History and Dogma* (Grand Rapids, Mich.: Eerdmans, 1994), 221–87.

39. Nicholas E. Denysenko, *Liturgical Reform after Vatican II: The Impact on Eastern Orthodoxy* (Minneapolis, Minn.: Fortress Press, 2015), 37. Denysenko goes on to point out, "*Ressourcement* aimed to illuminate a more holistic ecclesial history so that the contemporary Church would reform herself in light of her whole story. Vatican II did not inaugurate *ressourcement*, but the Council employed and encouraged it. At the same time, *ressourcement* was and remains an ecumenical endeavor" (ibid., 38).

CHAPTER 1

PERSONS AND PROPOSITIONS

Dei Verbum in Context

In his 1992 remarks announcing the promulgation of the *Catechism of the Catholic Church*, Joseph Ratzinger observes that the *Catechism* draws its answers to the basic questions of human life from "observations transcending the merely human, observations that transmit what was seen and heard by men who were in contact with God himself."[1] Defending the *Catechism* from the charge that its teachings fail to appreciate the timebound and contextualized character of all expressions of Catholic faith, Ratzinger emphasizes that the Church speaks about God (and about humanity) on the basis of God's self-revelation in Christ, as communicated faithfully in Scripture and Tradition. He states that "we can-

---

1. Joseph Cardinal Ratzinger, "What Can We Expect from a Catechism of the Catholic Church?," in his *Gospel, Catechesis, Catechism: Sidelights on the* Catechism of the Catholic Church (San Francisco: Ignatius Press, 1997), 9–22, at 14.

not speak rightly about God unless God himself tells us who he is," and he argues that the *Catechism* "is able to make all its affirmations about our moral conduct only in the perspective of God, the God who has revealed himself in Jesus Christ."²

Ratzinger had advocated for a universal catechism since the 1970s, and during the Extraordinary Synod of 1985, the assembled bishops voted to commission a universal catechism. In explaining the bishops' decision, Ratzinger recalls a conversation from the early postconciliar period in which Hans Urs von Balthasar advised Ratzinger: "Do not presuppose the faith but propose it."³ This advice was an awakening for Ratzinger, presumably because he had always lived in a strongly Catholic culture. What he learned from von Balthasar, he says, was that "[f]aith is not maintained automatically. It is not a 'finished business' that we can simply take for granted. The life of faith has to be constantly renewed."⁴

This insight seems surprisingly simple, but Ratzinger suggests that after the Council a number of bishops came in various ways to the same awakening that von Balthasar's letter had triggered for Ratzinger. He states, "The bishops present at the 1985 Synod called for a universal catechism of the whole Church because they sensed precisely what Balthasar had put into words in his note to me."⁵ In sum, the purpose of the *Catechism* was to "propose" the faith by instructing believers about the content of divine revelation as handed on in the Church under the guidance of the Holy Spirit through Scripture and Tradition, because the fundamental content of Catholic faith was in danger of being neglected, obscured, and forgotten.

The *Catechism*'s historical context, in which the bishops deemed that a propositional restatement of the content of Catholic faith was necessary, was largely the opposite of the context of the Second Vatican Council's Dogmatic Constitution on Divine Revelation, *Dei Verbum*. *Dei Verbum* has its roots in a widespread and salutary determination, shared by

---

2. Ibid., 14–15. For strong concerns expressed by leading Catholic theologians in America about a draft of the Catechism's text, as well as doubts that a useful Catechism could ever be produced, see *The Universal Catechism Reader: Reflections and Responses*, ed. Thomas J. Reese, SJ (New York: HarperCollins, 1990).
3. Ratzinger, "On the Meaning of Faith," in *Gospel, Catechesis, Catechism*, 23–34, at 23.
4. Ibid.
5. Ibid., 24.

the young Ratzinger and other leading theologians at the Council, to replace a propositionalist understanding of revelation (revelation as a set of revealed truths) with a personalist understanding of revelation as dynamic encounter with the living Lord and therefore as transformative of the whole person rather than solely engaging the intellect.[6] In critiquing propositionalism, they sought to highlight the central place of Scripture and its dialogue between God and his people as fundamental for the ongoing life of the Church. Thus, in his 1967 commentary on *Dei Verbum*, Ratzinger remarks that "[o]ne of the most important events in the struggle over the Constitution on Revelation was undoubtedly the liberation from this narrow [neo-scholastic] view and the return to what actually happens in the positive sources, before it was crystallized into doctrine, when God 'reveals' himself."[7] In the same place, Ratzinger bemoans "how little intellectualism and doctrinalism are able to comprehend the nature of revelation, which is not concerned with talking *about* something that is quite external to the person, but with the realization of the existence of man, with the relation of the human 'I' to the divine 'thou.'"[8] Against

---

6. See Joseph Ratzinger, "Dogmatic Constitution on Divine Revelation: Origin and Background," trans. William Glen Doepel, in *Commentary on the Documents of Vatican II*, ed. Herbert Vorgrimler, vol. 3 (New York: Crossroad, 1989), 155–66; Ratzinger, "Chapter 1: Revelation Itself," in *Commentary on the Documents of Vatican II*, 170–80. From the same time period see also the following two commentaries on *Dei Verbum*: Augustin Bea, *The Word of God and Mankind*, trans. Dorothy White (London: Geoffrey Chapman, 1967); Henri de Lubac, SJ, *La Révélation Divine*, 3rd ed. (Paris: Cerf, 1983), whose first edition appeared in 1968. For de Lubac's book, Jean-Pierre Torrell, OP, prepared the Latin text and French translation of *Dei Verbum*.

7. Ratzinger, "Chapter 1: Revelation Itself," 170.

8. Ibid., 175. Ratzinger's critiques of neo-scholasticism are balanced by his reflections about the postconciliar period in an essay written less than a decade later: "Boldly and certain of victory, we barricaded the door of a time that was past and proclaimed the abrogation and annihilation of all that lay behind it. In conciliar and post-conciliar literature, there is abundant evidence of the ridicule with which, like pupils ready for graduation, we bade farewell to our outmoded schoolbooks. In the meantime, however, our ears and our souls have been pierced by a different kind of ridicule that mocks more than we had wanted or wished. Gradually we have stopped laughing; gradually we have become aware that behind the closed doors are concealed those things that we must not lose if we do not want to lose our souls as well. Certainly we cannot return to the past, nor have we any desire to do so. But we must be ready to reflect anew on that which, in the lapse of time, has remained the one constant. To seek it without distraction and to dare to accept, with joyful heart and without diminution, the foolishness of truth—this, I think, is the task for today and for tomorrow: the true nucleus of the Church's service to the world" (Ratzinger, "On the Status of Church and Theology Today," in *Principles of Catholic Theology: Building Stones for a Fundamental Theology*, trans. Mary Frances McCarthy, SND [San Francisco: Ignatius Press, 1987], 367–93, at 393).

"intellectualism and doctrinalism," which imagine that divine revelation aims solely to deliver doctrinal truths, Ratzinger in 1967 states that "the purpose of this dialogue [made possible by revelation] is ultimately not information, but unity and transformation."[9]

Taken together, Ratzinger's remarks in 1967 and in 1992 underscore that both the personal and the cognitive-propositional dimensions of divine revelation are necessary. As Gerald O'Collins has shown (in accord with Ratzinger's own view), the latter dimension is enfolded within the former: "The interpersonal 'dialogue,' which is God's self-communication, says and communicates information. Through encountering the divine Truth in person, human beings know new truths."[10] O'Collins's formulation carefully unites the personal and cognitive-propositional elements of revelation, showing that they must be inseparable (as they are in Scripture) if in fact any real revelation has occurred. Just as one finds in Scripture itself, O'Collins gives primacy to the dimension of personal encounter: "Revelation [for *Dei Verbum*] primarily means meeting the Mystery of God in person and only secondarily knowing the divine mysteries (plural and in lowercase)."[11] O'Collins contrasts this position with Vatican I's *Dei Filius*, which (in his words) understands "divine revelation to be primarily God communicating the divine truths (plural)."[12] *Dei Filius*, of course, was responding in its nineteenth-century context to currents of thought that denied the existence (and even the possibility) of a cognitively knowable and necessary supernatural revelation, the existence of which O'Collins strongly defends.[13]

---

9. Ratzinger, "Chapter 1: Revelation Itself," 175.

10. Gerald O'Collins, SJ, *The Second Vatican Council: Message and Meaning* (Collegeville, Minn.: Liturgical Press, 2014), 142.

11. Ibid., 143. See also *Die Wahrheit ist Person: Brennpunkte einer christologisch gewendeten Dogmatik. Festschrift für Karl-Heinz Menke*, ed. Julia Knop, Magnus Lerch, and Bernd J. Claret (Regensburg: Verlag Friedrich Pustet, 2015).

12. O'Collins, *The Second Vatican Council*, 143.

13. See *Dei Filius* (Dogmatic Constitution on the Catholic Faith), chapters 2–3, in *Decrees of the Ecumenical Councils*, vol. 2, *Trent to Vatican II*, ed. Norman P. Tanner, SJ (Washington, D.C.: Georgetown University Press, 1990), 804–11, at 806–8. Following Vatican I, theologians and catechists worked intelligently to explicate and defend this teaching of *Dei Filius*. For the point that the historico-personalist conception of revelation is fundamentally coherent with the scholastic definition of revelation as *locutio dei*, see Andrew Meszaros, "Revelation in George Tyrrell, Neo-Scholasticism, and *Dei Verbum*," *Angelicum* 91 (2014): 535–68.

The question of the relationship of personal self-revelation and cognitive-propositional content governs further positions that theologians take today with regard to whether Scripture and dogma can adequately (even if not exhaustively) express divine revelation. We see this, for instance, in Lieven Boeve's 2003 argument that Christianity "constitutes a specific, always particular, context-determined and, in light of this context, irreplaceable witness to that which transcends its witnessing."[14] For Boeve, Christianity is a "witness" and thus a personal encounter with the Transcendent, but the truth-status of its cognitive claims can be evaluated only in terms of its own "particular narratives, concrete images and contextual thought patterns."[15] On this view, Christians bear a "witness" that cannot lay claim to describing reality in an enduring and definitive way for all humans prior to the eschaton, since divine Truth can be relationally encountered and pointed toward, but is fundamentally inexpressible in human words. Here Scripture functions as a springboard for Christians, but not as an inspired means by which God personally communicates trans-historical truth about himself for the purpose of human salvation.

The ongoing theological event of *Dei Verbum*, therefore, today consists centrally in the effort to understand how the personal and the cognitive-propositional relate in the revelation of the divine Mystery, a revelation that is faithfully communicated in Scripture and Tradition and that involves the action of God with his covenantal people, Israel, and the union of believers with Christ through the Holy Spirit.[16] In order to introduce *Dei Verbum* as an ongoing theological event, this chapter first explores René

---

14. Lieven Boeve, *Interrupting Tradition: An Essay on Christian Faith in a Postmodern Context* (Leuven: Peeters, 2003), 176.

15. Ibid.; cf. 175.

16. Only a deeper understanding of this relationship will enable scholars to meet the need identified by Brigid Curtin Frein, who remarks in a 1997 essay that "there is still need for a biblical scholarship that is distinctively Catholic.... Biblical scholars in the Church need to develop approaches and methods that rest on the presupposition of faith" (Frein, "Scripture in the Life of the Church," in *Vatican II: The Continuing Agenda*, ed. Anthony J. Cernera [Fairfield, Conn.: Sacred Heart University Press, 1997], 71–87, at 83). See also Joseph Ratzinger, "Biblical Interpretations in Conflict: On the Foundations and the Itinerary of Exegesis Today," trans. Adrian Walker, in *Opening Up the Scriptures: Joseph Ratzinger and the Foundations of Biblical Interpretation*, ed. José Granados, Carlos Granados, and Luis Sánchez-Navarro (Grand Rapids, Mich.: Eerdmans, 2008), 1–29; Ignace de la Potterie, SJ, "Interpretation of Holy Scripture in the Spirit in Which It Was Written (*Dei Verbum* 12c)," trans. Leslie Wearne, in *Vatican II: Assessment and Perspectives; Twenty-Five Years After (1962–1987)*, vol. 1, ed. René Latourelle, SJ (Mahwah, N.J.: Paulist Press, 1988), 220–66.

Latourelle's *Theology of Revelation*, published in 1963. A young French-Canadian professor of theology at the Gregorian University, Latourelle had earned doctorates in history and theology and was later to become dean of the Gregorian.[17] In his book, he highlights the primacy of the personal and existential dimensions of revelation, and he also underscores the central place of inexhaustible mystery in revelation. At the same time, he insists upon revelation's cognitive or propositional content, without which no true testimony to Jesus Christ would be possible. After presenting the main lines of Latourelle's book, I survey the twenty-six paragraphs of *Dei Verbum* with the relationship of personal-existential encounter and cognitive-propositional content in view.

René Latourelle's *Theology of Revelation*

René Latourelle's *Theology of Revelation* begins with God's Presence, and specifically with God revealing himself to us in Jesus Christ. Citing Hebrews 1:1 and John 1:18, Latourelle states: "God is not an absent Presence.... God broke the silence; God came out of His mystery; He addressed Himself to man and unveiled for him the secrets of His personal life; to man He communicated His unheard-of plan for a covenant with man, offering him a share in life. God, the living God, *has spoken* to humanity."[18] This speaking—like all speaking—has cognitive content. But perhaps even more important is the fact that "[t]he whole economy of salvation, in the order of knowledge, rests upon this *mystery* of God's self-manifestation in trust and love."[19] God's personal self-manifestation "is the original mystery" that "communicates every other mystery."[20] There is a distinction, though not a separation, between "the original mystery" (God's personal Presence, no longer hidden) and "every other mystery." The cognitive content of faith leads us back to the "original mystery" of the living God who personally comes to meet human beings.

---

17. See also the essays in the Festschrift presented to Latourelle on the occasion of his seventieth birthday: *Gesù rivelatore. Teologia fondamentale*, ed. Rino Fisichella (Casale Monferrato: Piemme, 1988).
18. René Latourelle, SJ, *Theology of Revelation* (New York: Alba House, 1966), 13.
19. Ibid.
20. Ibid.

This "original mystery" has the character of an event, and thus cannot be simply reduced to its cognitive expressions. Latourelle explains: "Scripture and tradition contain this word; the preaching of the Church transmits it; the liturgy celebrates and actualizes it. But all this derives from the original word spoken *through* God."[21] Revelation is one thing; the transmission and actualization of its cognitive content is another. Even if the cognitive content is the same, the experience of the event of revelation—especially in the earthly ministry of Jesus Christ—is distinguished by the existential directness by which God touched the humans to whom he revealed himself. In the strictest sense, Latourelle defines "revelation" as the "first intervention by which God comes out of His mystery, addresses Himself to humanity, and communicates His plan for salvation."[22]

Although this "first intervention" is existentially distinguishable from its written transmission, since it takes place fundamentally "under the form of an encounter between two people" (God and the human being), nonetheless revelation never lacks a cognitive-propositional aspect. For Latourelle, in the Old Testament "revelation is presented primarily as the experience of the activity of a sovereign power," but "this activity is not a brute display of power; it is always incorporated in words: this power is the dialogue, the announcement, the explanation, the manifestation of a plan."[23] For this reason, Latourelle argues that revelation in the Old Testament is consistently revelation of the word of God. It is a cognitive communication, even though as an existential experience it is certainly more than that—as for instance in Moses's experience of awe at Sinai.

This emphasis on revelation as communicating God's word fits with the cognitive communication that we find in Scripture, which is the word of God written down in a fixed form. Regarding the relationship of revelation and (Israel's) Scripture, Latourelle states: "This fixed format made it possible to read and meditate the word of God, to contemplate His faithful accomplishment of His promises. In its written form, the word of God takes on a quality of durability and eternity: it abides, irrevocable and infallible. On the other hand, in its fixed form, it runs the risk

---

21. Ibid., 15.   22. Ibid.
23. Ibid., 22.

of losing something of the dynamism that it had in the prophets."²⁴ This "dynamism" experienced by the prophets is what Latourelle has in view when he speaks of revelation in the strictest sense, as the event of personal encounter with the self-manifesting God. Yet revelation is always an experience with cognitive-propositional content, and therefore the cognitive content—written down in Scripture—is the word of God just as much as the original dynamic communication was. Latourelle remarks that the written word regains its dynamic dimension when it is "actualized and applied to new situations in history, by a constant re-reading, which is itself the key to a new depth of understanding."²⁵

Latourelle differentiates the cognitive content of the word of God from purely abstract, impersonal propositions. Citing a number of Old Testament texts that refer to God's word or *dabar*, he finds that God's word is "not the pure expression of abstract ideas; it is full of meaning, it has a noetic content, resulting from a man's concentration on an object or the rising up within him of thoughts which seize upon him, but at the same time it expresses a state of soul; something of his soul impregnates the spoken, articulated word."²⁶ This "state of soul" is characteristic of revelation as a personal encounter or event. For Latourelle, therefore, the investigation of divine revelation must aim not simply at determining the revealed truths found in the deposit of faith, but at identifying and participating in the existential energy produced by the event of revelation. He explains: "For Israel, the word possesses a double force: *noetic* and *dynamic*.... [T]he word is an active force whose dynamism is rooted in the very dynamism of the person who pronounces it. It is hardly distinct from the person whose mode of being and activity it represents."²⁷ To apprehend *God's* personal revelation, then, one must apprehend cognitive content (revealed truths), but at the same time one must also come into real contact with the "active force" or personal "dynamism" of God, since revelation is "the mystery of a personal *meeting* between the living God and man."²⁸ If so, then surely the communication of divine revelation requires not only doctrinal teaching but also something more, something

24. Ibid., 29.
25. Ibid.
26. Ibid.
27. Ibid., 30.
28. Ibid., 31.

that conveys the existential dynamism of personal encounter with God.

Latourelle's understanding of prophecy is important here. The prophets often discern and interpret God's actions in history. Their inspired interpretation renders God's actions intelligible as revelation. As Latourelle observes, "The God of the Old Testament is a God who intervenes, and the prophet is the man who meditates upon these interventions, who grasps and proclaims their meaning for salvation.... If the realization of salvation in history is already the word of God, the precise content of this word becomes intelligible only through the word of the prophet."[29] God's actions in history are already in themselves "the word of God," but the prophetic interpretation is needed for the communication of the word of God.

Similarly, Jesus Christ's revelation of God by his deeds cannot be separated from his words, which carry divine authority. Latourelle comments that Jesus "speaks, preaches, teaches, testifies to what He has seen and heard in the bosom of the Father," and therefore he is "the summit and fullness of revelation."[30] With regard to the apostolic mediation of Christ's revelatory words and deeds, Latourelle emphasizes their witness and testimony. The apostles' direct experience of revelation, and their response of faith, made them true witnesses to the Word. Latourelle states: "Witness is thus the activity proper to those who have seen and heard Christ, who have lived in intimacy with Him and, as a result, possess a direct and living experience of His person, His doctrine, and His work."[31] The deposit of revelation in New Testament Scripture and apostolic Tradition comes from this witness of the apostles, which includes both the communication of cognitive content and the fruit of existentially having lived in such close contact with the Word. The unique apostolic status belongs also to Paul, since Paul encountered the risen Christ directly and was taught by Christ.

In Christ, God reveals his glorious plan for humans, a plan that Paul calls a "mystery" and whose cognitive content is the truths of the gospel. To understand this content at a deep level requires the Holy Spirit, not least because one needs charity in order to be able to appreciate Christ's

---

29. Ibid., 35.
30. Ibid., 45.
31. Ibid., 53.

charity. As Latourelle remarks, "The mystery reveals an abyss of wisdom and love," and it calls for the response of faith and love.[32] Since Christ is the incarnate Word, Latourelle emphasizes that Christ "is ontologically qualified as the only perfect Revealer."[33] Indeed, the Gospel of John makes clear that the Word incarnate, in revealing the Father, reveals that of which the Word himself is a witness. Only the Word can be such a witness, since only the Word knows the Father intimately. Even in being rejected by the world, Christ testifies to the supreme love of the Father. In turn, the apostles bear testimony to Christ, because they knew Christ intimately and because Christ and the Spirit enable them to perform works of power. The Father testifies to Christ by giving him mighty works to perform and by uniting humans to Christ in faith by the Holy Spirit. Latourelle concludes that for the Gospel of John, "testimony, whether it is interior or exterior, is aimed at faith; it is essentially an invitation to believe.... [T]his testimony is an activity which involves the entire Trinity."[34]

Latourelle engages briefly with Réginald Garrigou-Lagrange's *De Revelatione*.[35] Garrigou-Lagrange defines revelation as the word of God that is freely taught by God. God the teacher reveals what was hidden to our knowledge, and we receive it as taught by God, since God gives us a supernatural light that enables us to assent with certitude to his word as divine teaching. In response to Garrigou-Lagrange's position, Latourelle argues that testimony, rather than teaching, would be a more scriptural and personal way of conceiving the communication of the word of God, because it allows more clearly for interpersonal event and historical development of doctrine.[36]

---

32. Ibid., 66.
33. Ibid., 73.
34. Ibid., 76.
35. See Réginald Garrigou-Lagrange, OP, *De Revelatione per Ecclesiam catholicam proposita*, 2 vols. (Rome: F. Ferrari, 1950). For a much fuller, appreciative summation of this significant work, see Aidan Nichols, OP, *Reason with Piety: Garrigou-Lagrange in the Service of Catholic Thought* (Naples, Fla.: Sapientia Press, 2008), chapters 2–3.
36. See Latourelle, *Theology of Revelation*, 211. Latourelle states, "It is true that revelation teaches something that must be handed down as a body of doctrine. Still, what makes it specific as word is not knowledge but faith. In the genus of word, it belongs to the species of testimony rather than to the species of teaching" (ibid.). The context of *Dei Filius* and the particular problems to which it responds are central for Garrigou-Lagrange's emphasis on divine teaching.

Latourelle agrees with the then-current complaints about the neo-scholastic treatment of revelation. He notes that "de Lubac, Danielou, Fessard, Bouillard, Von Balthasar, take a stand against a certain intellectualism which tends to make Christian revelation a communication of a system of ideas rather than the manifestation of a Person who is Truth in Person."[37] He adds that according to de Lubac, "the majority of theologians are content to treat revelation with a quick, superficial view, frequently reducing it to a series of detached propositions."[38] Latourelle himself critically observes that neo-scholastic theologians "insist much more on the revealed truths than on God who both reveals and is revealed. They preserve an astonishing reserve on the interpersonal relationship which revelation establishes between God and men. These deficiencies, to all appearances, arise for the most part from an inadequate consideration of the data of Scripture."[39] God's personal presence, God's making himself known in an intimate and dialogic way, is the central element of divine revelation, and this interpersonal dimension is easily obscured by focusing on the set of revealed truths that God teaches.

With the interpersonal dimension firmly in view, Latourelle organizes his own constructive proposal for the theology of revelation under three headings: word, testimony, and encounter. First, with regard to "word," he remarks that the neo-Thomists (and the scholastics more generally) focus on word or speech as "the *unveiling* of the thought which is effected through the word and on the *sharing* of knowledge which is thus realized."[40] He finds that this way of thinking about the word is "a rather static conception" because it lacks an appreciation for "the interpersonal, existential, dynamic, and out-going character of the word."[41] The result is an overly intellectual account of revelation, lacking a fully historical and personal context. Distinguishing revelation from the simple communication of true propositions about divine realities, Latourelle observes that "word is not only simple information or instruction: it becomes *expres-*

---

37. Latourelle, *Theology of Revelation*, 213.
38. Ibid. See Henri de Lubac, SJ, "Le problème du développement du dogme," *Recherches de science religieuse* 35 (1948): 130–60, at 153–55. De Lubac's position here seems exaggerated.
39. Latourelle, *Theology of Revelation*, 212.   40. Ibid., 316.
41. Ibid.

sion (in the sense that we say an act can express ourselves), revelation of person, testimony regarding self."[42] We put ourselves into our words, so that our words communicate not only truths, but the "personal mystery" of our very selves. Our words are likewise addressed to the personal mystery of those whom we are engaging.

This interpersonal element is especially important when, as in biblical revelation, the revealer is revealing not simply propositional truths, but his very self. God's act of revelation cannot be separated from propositional truths. As the free revelation of the divine Persons to human persons, however, it is more than a set of truths about God and human beings. Latourelle comments that the volitional and affective dimensions necessarily join the intellectual dimension here: "When word attains this level, it is the sign of friendship and love; it is the welling up and expression of a freedom which opens to another person and thus *gives itself*."[43] In giving knowledge about himself, Christ "gives himself in a communion of love."[44] Furthermore, Christ offers gestures or deeds that expand the notion of teaching beyond the limits of propositional truth. In Christ's Cross, for example, "the *articulated* word becomes the *immolated* word"; the love of God is so great that it can be fully communicated, ultimately, only in the silence of "the outstretched arms and the body drained of its blood," although Christ's preaching prepared the disciples to understand his gift of self on the Cross.[45]

Having treated "word," Latourelle secondly addresses "testimony," namely the testimony of the prophets and the testimony of Christ, "the Witness par excellence."[46] Latourelle explains that "[w]hat the apostles hand down to the Church is a *testimony*, a *deposition* of witnesses."[47] Conceiving of revelation in terms of testimony gives us a better appreciation of its historical embeddedness. Far from being solely a communication of propositions, revelation depends upon witnesses who not only know the truths intellectually but have experienced the truths personally. In receiving this testimony, we place our trust in persons whose authority

---

42. Ibid., 317.
43. Ibid.
44. Ibid.
45. Ibid., 319–20.
46. Ibid., 320. In turn, the Father testifies to the Son, as does the Spirit.
47. Ibid.

we accept, since we have reason to believe that they testify about things that they are in a position to know. Latourelle explains that "[w]hereas demonstration makes its primary appeal to the intelligence, testimony, since it calls for an intensity of trust which is measured by the values that are risked on its behalf, enlists not only the intelligence, but also, in different degrees, the will and love."[48] He points out that there is always a risk involved in trusting human testimony, given the variability of human knowledge and truthfulness.

When Christ teaches about "the mystery of the life of the Divine Persons" as well as "the mystery of our new status as sons," this teaching is testimony; we are called to believe it on Christ's (divine) authority. When we believe, we do not merely know new propositional information, but rather we are joined in a relationship of friendship with the one who testifies, in "a confidence of love."[49] The miraculous signs that accompany Christ's testimony serve to assure us that the one who testifies is the living God, whose word is truth. When God moves us interiorly in faith, however, we assent to Christ's testimony based solely upon the authority of the God who testifies.

Third, Latourelle discusses revelation as "encounter." He observes that an encounter "can attain different degrees of depth."[50] When God speaks his word, we must respond in faith in order to encounter God. Latourelle explains, "When man opens his heart to God who speaks, shares in his thinking, lets himself be filled and directed by it, God and man meet each other, and this encounter develops into a communion of life."[51] Revelation, then, is an I-Thou encounter only when God's word implants faith in the one who responds. Put another way, one's embrace of the cognitive-propositional content of the divine communication is completed "by the encounter with the living and personal God."[52] The point, here again, is that the propositional and personal dimensions of divine revelation are inseparable. We are drawn to assent to Christ's teaching because of the love that he shows us (preeminently on the Cross), and thus a relationship is begun, a relationship that involves knowing but also

---

48. Ibid., 322.
49. Ibid., 323.
50. Ibid., 325.
51. Ibid.
52. Ibid.

involves self-sacrificial loving: "The very love with which the Father loves the Son and the Son loves the Father has now taken root in the heart of man."[53]

To understand divine revelation, then, we must always see its true propositions in the covenantal and historical context of the divine Lover reaching out to the Beloved through the testimony of Christ and of the prophets and apostles. We cannot simply set forth the truths of divine revelation without reference to the interpersonal communion of faith and love that enables us to be united personally to the tri-personal Presence of God. In sum, fully embracing the propositional content of divine revelation requires that we consistently view these propositions within their interpersonal context, as befits the words of self-revealing Persons.

A Survey of *Dei Verbum*: Persons and Propositions

Let me now investigate how *Dei Verbum*'s twenty-six paragraphs present divine revelation, and how the personal and cognitive-propositional dimensions of revelation relate according to *Dei Verbum*. Does *Dei Verbum* retain the balance achieved by Latourelle, or does *Dei Verbum* emphasize the personal encounter at the expense of the cognitive-propositional content, or vice versa? I should note that *Dei Verbum* begins with a one-paragraph Prologue, which is followed by chapter 1 on divine revelation itself (paragraphs 2–6), chapter 2 on the transmission of divine revelation (paragraphs 7–10), chapter 3 on the inspiration and interpretation of Scripture (paragraphs 11–13), chapter 4 on the Old Testament (paragraphs 14–16), chapter 5 on the New Testament (paragraphs 17–20), and chapter 6 on Scripture in the life of the Church (paragraphs 21–26).

The Prologue of *Dei Verbum* (paragraph 1) places the entire document under the rubric of a deeply personal and historical understanding of revelation, though without negating the place of propositional truth. The Council Fathers describe themselves as "hearing the word of God with reverence, and proclaiming it with faith" (§1).[54] To hear and

---

53. Ibid., 327.
54. Quotations are from *Dei Verbum*, in *Vatican Council II*, vol. 1, *The Conciliar and Post Conciliar Documents*, rev. ed., ed. Austin Flannery, OP (Northport, N.Y.: Costello Publishing, 1996),

proclaim something in faith requires the expression of revealed truths to which the mind assents. Yet the Council Fathers' stance vis-à-vis the word of God is also resonant of personal relationship, of ongoing encounter and event. The biblical quotation that immediately follows cements this sense of revelation as an experiential encounter with Christ and thereby also as a fellowship with the Trinity who unites the community of believers. The biblical text comes from 1 John 1:2–3: "We proclaim to you the eternal life which was with the Father and was made manifest to us—that which we have seen and heard we proclaim also to you, so that you may have fellowship with us; and our fellowship is with the Father and with his Son Jesus Christ" (§1). This sense of personal encounter with the self-revealing Word is intensified by the first verse of 1 John 1, implied in the verses quoted: "That which was from the beginning, which we have heard, which we have seen with our eyes, which we have looked upon and touched with our hands, concerning the word of life" (1 Jn 1:1). Revelation as word, testimony, and encounter—in Latourelle's formula—could not be more evident here. The personal dimension of revelation stands at the center, given the Council Fathers' identification with St. John as fellow witnesses to the revealed word.

Immediately after the quotation from 1 John, the Council Fathers go on to present themselves as "[f]ollowing in the steps of the Councils of Trent and Vatican I" (§1). These two earlier Councils are known for defining particular truths of faith that belong to the deposit of revelation; for example, doctrines regarding the Eucharist, justification, faith and reason, and papal infallibility. Thus the dual recognition that revelation is a personal encounter that involves fellowship or communion, and that revelation contains cognitive-propositional content, shapes the Prologue of *Dei Verbum*. Indeed, as the Prologue says, "this Synod wishes to set forth the true doctrine [genuinam ... doctrinam] of divine revelation and its transmission." Such true doctrine could be set forth only if revelation itself, within the community established by the self-revealing God, communicated doctrinal truths.

750–65. I have occasionally modified capitalization to configure it to the Latin text (as I have done here by lowercasing "Word").

The next five paragraphs of *Dei Verbum*, §§2–6 (chapter 1), exhibit the ways in which personal encounter/communion and the communication of cognitive-propositional content are integrally united. Drawing upon Ephesians 1:9, *Dei Verbum* §2 states, "It pleased God, in his goodness and wisdom, to reveal himself and to make known the mystery of his will." In revealing himself, he reveals truths about himself; just as in making "known the mystery of his will," God makes known truths about God's plan for humanity. At the same time, the phrase "the mystery of his will" comes from Ephesians 1:9, and includes the volitional, transformative dimension of revelation. As *Dei Verbum* §2 observes, "His will was that men should have access to the Father, through Christ, the Word made flesh, in the Holy Spirit, and thus become sharers in the divine nature." Revelation transforms us and draws us into the divine communion. This emphasis on revelation as establishing a friendship with God appears in the next sentence of *Dei Verbum* §2: "By this revelation, then, the invisible God (cf. Col. 1:15; 1 Tim. 1:17), from the fullness of his love, addresses men as his friends (cf. Ex. 33:11; Jn. 15:14–15), and moves among them (cf. Bar. 3:38), in order to invite and receive them into his own company."

Dei Verbum §2 continues by noting that in the "economy of revelation," both words and deeds are important, and neither is separable from the other. The communication of revelation involves the communication of truth about the mysteries or realities of faith, but this communication is always bound up with deeds. In this vein, *Dei Verbum* §2 remarks that "the works performed by God in the history of salvation show forth and bear out the doctrine and realities signified by the words; the words, for their part, proclaim the works, and bring to light the mystery they contain." This way of phrasing it avoids focusing solely on either the deeds or the words, and it underscores that revealed doctrine has to do with mysteries, with transcendent realities. Without exhaustively apprehending these mysteries, the words—preeminently those of Jesus Christ—reveal the saving truth about the realities that Christians confess in faith.

In accord with its appreciation for the mystery of the realities confessed in faith, paragraph 2 concludes by emphasizing that Jesus Christ himself is the fullness of saving truth in Person. *Dei Verbum* §2 states, "The most intimate truth which this revelation gives us about God and the salvation of man shines forth in Christ, who is himself both the mediator and the sum total of revelation." Those who suppose that they can engage revelation solely by unfolding propositional truths have thus made an error. Jesus Christ communicates saving truth, and this truth is himself: in receiving divine revelation, we are receiving a Person, Jesus, and so revelation establishes a relationship with this Person. The truths that God reveals for our salvation are summed up in Jesus Christ, who reveals God to us and who invites us to share in his life of wisdom and self-giving love. Of course, this does not mean that we can know the Person, Jesus, in a nonpropositional way, since the human act of knowing cannot bypass propositional judgments. Furthermore, Jesus' own propositional teachings and the apostles' teachings about him inform and instruct our personal encounter with Jesus.

If Christ is the fullness of revelation, however, why did God not give this friendship earlier or in a more universally decisive fashion? What about all the people who have never heard of Christ or who, despite hearing about him, have not come to know him? *Dei Verbum* §3 indicates that God's self-revealing presence has never been lacking among humans. Since all things are created through the Word, it makes sense that creatures point toward God: God "provides men with constant evidence of himself in created realities" (§3). The revelation of God's friendship with us in Christ builds upon the fact that the Creator has always willed to make his presence known. The gift of grace was never absent in human history. *Dei Verbum* §3 insists that "wishing to open up the way to heavenly salvation, he [God] manifested himself to our first parents from the very beginning. After the fall, he buoyed them up with the hope of salvation, by promising redemption (cf. Gen. 3:15); and he has never ceased to take care of the human race." While unfolding in the particular history of God's people, Israel, and culminating in the work of their Messiah, the invitation to friendship with the triune God is a work that always had all peoples in view and that never excludes them. God acts in and through specific people and not by universal divine fiat. But the revelation of God is not exclusionary: on the contrary, *Dei Verbum* §3 points out that God "wishes to give eternal life to all those who seek salvation by patience in well-doing (cf. Rom. 2:6–7)."

Dei Verbum §4 sets forth the ways in which Jesus is the fullness of revelation. For one thing, Jesus reveals saving truth about God: he is "the eternal Word who enlightens all men" and he came "to dwell among men and to tell them about the inner life of God" (§4). In addition to his words, Jesus reveals God by his deeds. Since Jesus reveals God and God's will for us by everything he does—"by the total fact of his presence and self-manifestation," especially by his Cross and Resurrection and his sending of the Spirit—*Dei Verbum* §4 notes that Jesus confirms revelation "with divine guarantees." If someone asks what or where is divine revelation, we can point them to Jesus, whose words and deeds reveal the personal presence of the Son, "to see whom is to see the Father (cf. Jn. 14:9)." According to *Dei Verbum* §4, Jesus not only teaches us "about the inner life of God" but also reveals that "God is with us, to deliver us from the darkness of sin and death, and to raise us up to eternal life." Jesus reveals these saving truths by his words and deeds, and fundamentally by his ongoing and salvific presence "with us."

Dei Verbum §5 underscores the necessity of responding to the self-revealing God with the "obedience of faith" (Rom 16:26). This obedient assent requires that there be propositionally knowable revelation to which to assent. Otherwise, one could not assent obediently to Jesus, since one would have literally no idea what Jesus' presence means. At the same time, this cognitive assent requires a personal relationship with God. Along these lines, *Dei Verbum* §5 develops the importance of the Holy Spirit's work. Because the content of revelation is a divine mystery, above reason's capabilities to judge, the assent of faith comes about only when the grace of the Holy Spirit moves the will interiorly. Revelation involves conversion and transformation, not merely an intellectual assent. Relationship with God stands at the center of both revelation's content and the way in which we make revelation our own. Through the gifts of the Holy Spirit, moreover, we receive "an ever deeper understanding of revelation" (§5).

The next paragraph, *Dei Verbum* §6, also combines the personal and cognitive-propositional dimensions of revelation. Consider this sentence: "By divine revelation God wished to manifest and communicate both himself and the eternal decrees of his will concerning the salvation of mankind" (§6). In manifesting and communicating himself—which God does both through the prophets' teaching and through the Incarnation of the Son and the sending of the Spirit—God displays the deep personal intimacy characteristic of revelation, a personal intimacy that necessarily involves cognitive communication. When God communicates his "eternal decrees," the emphasis necessarily falls upon the cognitive content of revelation, since decrees are propositionally knowable; yet God does this by communicating "himself" in the Person of Jesus. In light of this personal dimension, *Dei Verbum* §6 quotes two central texts from chapter 2 of Vatican I's *Dei Filius*, in which *Dei Filius* insists upon human reason's natural ability to know God as first principle and final end of all things, while also affirming that in our present fallen condition even such natural knowledge of God must be revealed (as it has been). The propositional emphasis of *Dei Filius* is thereby folded into *Dei Verbum*'s emphasis on the personal mode of revelation.

Beginning with paragraph 7, *Dei Verbum* shifts its attention to the transmission of divine revelation (chapter 2). Here too we find the same appreciation for revealed truths, on the one hand, and personal presence, on the other. For example, *Dei Verbum* §7 states that the gospel entrusted to the apostles is "the source of all saving truth." At the same time, the apostles communicate the gospel not only by teaching truths of faith—though they certainly do teach such truths—but also by the example of their lives and "the institutions they established" (§7). Their communication of saving truth (a communion) draws upon both what Jesus taught them when they shared in his life and ministry, and what the Holy Spirit teaches them. Their personal relationship with Christ and the Spirit enables them to communicate in writing and in oral teaching what they received "from the lips of Christ, from his way of life and his works" (§7), and from the Spirit. With regard to the personal relationship or fellowship with God that fuels the transmission of revealed truth, *Dei Verbum* §7 remarks, "This sacred Tradition, then, and the sacred Scripture of both Testaments, are like a mirror, in which the Church, during its pilgrim journey here on earth, contemplates God, from whom she receives everything, until such time as she is brought to see him face to face as he really is (cf. Jn. 3:2)." Personal encounter and cognitive-propositional intelligibility are inseparable.

The next paragraph, §8, similarly includes a description of the Church's communion and of believers' "intimate sense of spiritual realities which they experience," alongside the affirmation that "[w]hat was handed on by the apostles comprises everything that serves to make the People of God live their lives in holiness and increase their faith." Clearly "what was handed on" includes doctrinal and moral teachings, revealed truth. *Dei Verbum* §8 speaks of the ongoing development in the Church's understanding of the truths that comprise revelation: "the Church is always advancing towards the plenitude of divine truth." This advance in the understanding of revealed truths, however, never leaves out the element of transformation and personal relationship with God. Rather than a mere growth in the number of apprehended truths, *Dei Verbum* §8 holds that the growth occurs as "God ... continues to converse with the spouse of his beloved Son," through the activity of the Spirit. It is not solely a matter of the Church getting the truths right, although the Church does this through the Spirit's guidance; rather it is a matter of the Church becoming increasingly conformed to revelation, "until eventually the words of God are fulfilled in her" (§8).

In *Dei Verbum* §9, we find an understanding of Scripture that unites cognitive-propositional expression of revelation with the personal Presence and activity of God. The paragraph states, "Sacred Scripture is the speech of God as it is put down in writing under the breath of the Holy Spirit." The inspired human words of Scripture are associated with the Spirit's breath and with God speaking. This is a highly personal way of formulating God's relationship to the written words of the Bible, in which God gives commandments and prophetic promises, along with doctrinal and moral teaching. By the Spirit's breath, God speaks personally in human words; thus personal divine communication and the cognitive form that it takes are shown to be a unity, against any possibility of downplaying mere words. The process of Tradition, by which the entirety of the word of God is handed on, also involves the enlightenment of the apostles and their successors by the Holy Spirit, who is the "Spirit of truth." Again, there is no opposition between cognitive-propositional communication and the personal dimension of revelation.

In paragraph 10, Tradition and Scripture are described as "a single sacred deposit of the word of God, which is entrusted to the Church." The very notion of a "sacred deposit" indicates a determinative cognitive-propositional content, which may be more than, but certainly not less than, a body of truths. In this paragraph, which looks back to Acts 2:42 and thus implicitly also to Acts 20:18–35 (in which Paul passes on his ministry to the elders of the Church in Ephesus), the Magisterium of the Church is accorded the role of definitive interpreter of the "sacred deposit" of divine revelation. Here it might seem that we encounter revelation understood as solely a body of truths, unfolded by the Church's Magisterium through its dogmatic formulations over the centuries. However, *Dei Verbum* §10 takes pains to describe "the living teaching office [magisterium] of the Church" as profoundly relational in its reception and handing on of revelation. The Magisterium appears as the "servant" of the word of God, and the Magisterium's acts of listening to, guarding, and expounding the revealed deposit take place "[a]t the divine command and with the help of the Holy Spirit" (§10). From within the personal matrix of revelation, the Church's Magisterium performs its service in the handing on of revealed truth.

Paragraph 11 starts a new chapter, on the inspiration and interpretation of Scripture. *Dei Verbum* §11 places the focus squarely on personal realities, even while insisting upon the truthful cognitive-propositional communication of these realities in Scripture "under the inspiration of the Holy Spirit." It presents the Church as a personal reality rather than a mere institution: "Holy Mother Church." As paragraph 11 says, the whole of Scripture, including all of its parts, is "sacred" and has God as its "author," since the Spirit inspires the whole of Scripture. Recognizing Scripture's rootedness in "the faith of the apostolic age," which is the faith of the Church, the Church receives and accepts Scripture as it has been handed on to the Church, namely as divinely inspired and canonical. Paragraph 11 goes on to note that the human authors of Scripture, who were chosen by God, wrote in a fully human way and were "true authors," even though God "acted in them and by them." God's agency inspiring and guiding the development of the biblical canon does not mean that the human authors were not men of their times, "true authors." It does mean, however, that everything in Scripture belongs there as God's word, since God ensured that the human authors (without ceasing to be such) "consigned to writing whatever he wanted written, and no more" (§11). Here the personal intimacy of God inspiring the human authors, and the emphasis on the realities of faith communicated by the biblical writings, is tightly linked with cognitive-propositional expression.

Regarding the truth of Scripture, paragraph 11 states that "all that the inspired authors, or sacred writers, affirm should be regarded as affirmed by the Holy Spirit." This focuses attention on the (propositional) judgments of the human authors, but it also emphasizes the immediacy of our scriptural encounter with the Spirit. The same balance between personal-transformative and cognitive-propositional revelation appears in paragraph 11's affirmation that "the books of Scripture, firmly, faithfully and without error, teach the truth which God, for the sake of our salvation, wished to see confided to the sacred Scriptures." God meets us in Scripture "for the sake of our salvation"; the purpose of scriptural truth is transformation and salvation. Paragraph 11 supports this point by quoting 2 Timothy 3:16–17, "All scripture is inspired by God and profitable for teaching, for reproof, for correction, and for training in righteousness, that the man of God may be complete, equipped for every good work."

After reiterating the point that "God speaks through men in human fashion" in the books of Scripture, *Dei Verbum* §12 urges scholars to investigate the intention of the human authors, as part of the process of rightly understanding "what the sacred author wanted to affirm in his work" and thereby understanding "what God has wished to communicate to us." The sacred author's affirmations are propositional judgments of truth, even if they are not *abstract* truths but rather concern historical and experiential realities. In order to apprehend the intention of the human author, we should take care to appreciate the particular genre of writing and the cultural circumstances that shaped the author's approach. Rather than approaching Scripture in an ahistorical way, looking simply for ahistorical judgments of truth, we should be deeply aware of both "the customary and characteristic patterns of perception, speech and narrative which prevailed at the age of the sacred writer, and … the conventions which the people of his time followed in their dealings with one another" (§12).

Paragraph 12 adds that, in addition to investigating the human authorship and cultural circumstances of the scriptural text, we must equally pay attention to the divine authorship. This requires appreciating and investigating "the content and unity of the whole of Scripture, taking into account the Tradition of the entire Church and the analogy of faith" (§12). Scripture must be interpreted by Scripture, so that each scriptural passage is interpreted in the light of the whole of Scripture; and the Church's Tradition provides the living context and guide for this faithful interpretation. Biblical scholars, whose task is to "help the Church to form a firmer judgment" about the meaning of particular scriptural texts, should not fall into the mistake of treating Scripture as merely a compilation of ancient near-Eastern texts. In this way, *Dei Verbum* §12 reminds us that the interpretation of Scripture requires the interpreter to listen to the witness of the receptive community, a community commissioned by Christ. Ultimately, not academic scholars, but rather the Church has the "divinely conferred commission and ministry of watching over and interpreting the Word of God" (§12). God communicates to his people through Scripture, and so its interpretation is the task of the people of God and cannot be left to experts as though the scriptural texts did not belong to the personal communion between God and his people.

Paragraph 13 underscores God's "condescension" (an idea drawn from John Chrysostom) in communicating exalted divine mysteries through human and historically contextualized words, "without prejudice to God's truth and holiness." The point again is that Scripture itself, in its historical conditioning, bears witness to the personal relationship with God that God wills to be the context and fruit of revelation. Paragraph 13 compares God's use of human words to the divine Word's incarnation in the humanity of Jesus Christ.

Dei Verbum §§14–16 (chapter 4) pertain to the economy of the Old Testament, especially from God's choosing of Abraham onward. The personal action of God stands at center stage in these paragraphs. At the same time, of course, consideration for revealed (propositional) truth is hardly absent. *Dei Verbum* §15 insists that the books of the Old Testament, "even though they contain matters imperfect and provisional, nevertheless show us authentic divine teaching." An example of such authentic teaching is the Old Testament's overall understanding of "how a just and merciful God deals with mankind" (§15). Indeed, *Dei Verbum* §15 presents the whole Old Testament as "a storehouse of sublime teaching on God." Paragraph 16 underscores that no book of the Old Testament is isolated from the gospel, since God's revelation always has Jesus Christ in view. The Old and New Testaments mutually illuminate each other, as we would expect from texts that testify to the same self-revealing God.

In paragraphs 17–20 (chapter 5), the focus shifts from the Old Testament to the New Testament. Emphasis on God's personal action in revelation—the Incarnation of the Son, the inauguration of the Kingdom of God, the revelation of the Father, the sending of the Holy Spirit, and the commissioning of the apostles—is combined with a strong insistence on cognitive-propositional content. For instance, we find the assurance that "the apostles handed on to their hearers what he [Jesus] had said and done, but with that fuller understanding which they, instructed by the glorious events of Christ and enlightened by the Spirit of truth, now enjoyed" (§19). Similarly, *Dei Verbum* §19 affirms that the four Gospels teach "us the honest truth about Jesus" and have as their purpose the communication of this truth. Paragraph 20 emphasizes that the Epistles of Paul and the other New Testament writings convey revealed truth, not least insofar as they "firmly establish those matters which concern Christ the Lord" and "formulate more and more precisely his authentic teaching." Paragraph 20 concludes the chapter on the New Testament by reiterating the personal dimension of revelation: "For the Lord Jesus was with his apostles as he had promised (cf. Mt. 28:20) and he had sent to them the Spirit, the Counsellor, who would guide them into all the truth (cf. Jn. 16:13)."

The final six paragraphs of *Dei Verbum*, §§21–26 (chapter 6), address the role of Scripture in the life of the Church. These paragraphs emphasize the authority of Scripture for the Church. Scripture is "God's own word in an unalterable form" and "the preaching of the Church, as indeed the entire Christian religion, should be nourished and ruled by sacred Scripture" (§21). This way of putting it focuses on the written text and the (propositional) truths that it authoritatively conveys, but the very next sentence sounds a deeply intimate and personal note: "In the sacred books the Father who is in heaven comes lovingly to meet his children, and talks with them" (§21). This conversation with the Father, through

Christ and the Spirit, transforms believers and builds up the Church. Thus the emphasis in paragraph 21 is on revelation as transformative personal dialogue, but not in a manner that relativizes the authority of Scripture in its expression of saving truth. Likewise, after paragraph 22 focuses on the importance of translations of Scripture, paragraph 23 presents the Church as "the spouse of the incarnate Word" and as "taught by the Holy Spirit." This paragraph contains instruction for biblical scholars, who *Dei Verbum* hopes will be instruments of a biblical renewal among believers. Paragraph 24 describes the preeminence of Scripture for theological inquiry, whose task is to seek "the full truth stored up in the mystery of Christ" and to do so by allowing Scripture to be "the very soul of sacred theology." Paragraph 25 exhorts all priests and catechists, and indeed all the faithful, especially those in religious life, to read Scripture frequently and to do so in prayer, so as to allow for spiritual transformation via "a dialogue ... between God and man."

Paragraph 24 states that Scripture both "contain[s] the word of God" and is "the word of God"; it mediates divine revelation and is divine revelation. Here the twofold emphasis that we found throughout *Dei Verbum* is encapsulated: Scripture contains descriptions of God's personal presence and action in revealing himself to persons in history, and, since it is inspired by the Holy Spirit, Scripture itself is this revelation. The truths conveyed in Scripture receive equal footing with the saving events and encounters that form the basis for the written record of Scripture as well as for the written doctrinal and moral teachings of the Church in its communication of revelation. The personal is propositional, and the propositional is personal. The final paragraph, §26, closes with an emphasis on transformation through encounter with the God who reveals himself personally and propositionally: "So may it come that, by the reading and study of the sacred books 'the word of God may speed on and triumph' (2 Th. 3:1) and the treasure of revelation entrusted to the Church may more and more fill the hearts of men."

Conclusion: *Dei Verbum* as an Ongoing Theological Event

In an appended chapter included in the 1966 English edition of his book, René Latourelle comments on *Dei Verbum* §2's statement that "[i]t pleased God, in his goodness and wisdom, to reveal himself and to make known the mystery of his will." Observing that Vatican I too taught that God reveals himself, Latourelle specifies what *Dei Verbum* §2 adds to the perspective of Vatican I: by "saying that the object of revelation is God himself, the text thus personalizes revelation: before making known something, that is, his plan for salvation, God reveals someone, himself."[55] Latourelle also finds that in using the biblical term "mystery [*sacramentum*]," *Dei Verbum* succeeds in showing that God's plan of salvation is fundamentally a Person: "Concretely, this mystery is Christ."[56] Put another way—in light of *Dei Verbum* §1—it is proper to say that "God has stepped out of his Mystery," in this sense that the very divine life, otherwise hidden, has been personally revealed and offered to human beings.[57]

Latourelle goes on to compare the unity of God's deeds and words to the unity of body and soul, while at the same time noting that in the history of salvation, sometimes deeds are primary (as in Christ's Pasch) and sometimes words are primary (as in Christ's Sermon on the Mount). The deeds require words in order to be properly understood, and vice versa. For example, Latourelle notes regarding Jesus' death on the Cross: "It is the word of Christ, living on in the word of his apostles, which reveals the unheard-of dimensions of this death and, at one and the same time, proposes both the event itself and its salvific bearing on our belief."[58] Are there divine deeds that only later receive an interpretative divine word so as to become revelatory? Latourelle suggests that the answer is yes, so long as we do not fall into the mistake of supposing the word and the deed ever to be extrinsic to each other. He states, "The union in question here is a union of *nature*, not always a union in *time*.... Sometimes the event precedes the words, e.g. the creation of the world, the establishment of the royal line in Israel."[59] There

---

55. Latourelle, *Theology of Revelation*, 458.
56. Ibid.
57. Ibid., 456.
58. Ibid., 461.
59. Ibid., 462.

are also cases where the word precedes the deed, as for example in "the description of the Messiah as a Suffering Servant (cf. *Is.* 48:3–8; *Amos* 3:7)."[60] Since the deed or event is never completely unintelligible, Latourelle rightly insists upon "the interpenetration and mutual support that exists between word and work. God performs the act of salvation and at the same time develops its meaning."[61]

Latourelle is struck by *Dei Verbum*'s presentation of Jesus as the one "who reveals the mystery and is the mystery himself in person."[62] This personalist approach to revelation ensures the transformative power of revelation, rather than allowing us to conceive of revelation simply in terms of a set of propositions. Yet Latourelle makes clear that the personal and the propositional are not in opposition, but rather must be held together. He observes with regard to *Dei Verbum* §5: "The Council thus avoids two incomplete conceptions of faith: that of faith-homage, personal but without content; and that of faith-assent, doctrinal but depersonalized."[63] This integrated balance between the personal and the propositional is crucial.

In contemporary Catholic theology, this balance has been tested. In response to postconciliar critiques by Catholic theologians of the enduring truth-content of Catholic doctrine, theologians have given more attention to the role of propositions. Mats Wahlberg, for example, has pointed out that it is impossible for our minds to know anything if we utterly lack propositional knowledge.[64] The structure of our cognition means that we must formulate an insight (however limited and partial) about something for that thing to be intelligible to us. We cannot have a personal encounter with God if the encounter lacks at least the basic propositional knowledge that it is *God* whom we are encountering. Addressing the case of "manifestational" revelation, in which something is revealed without words, Wahlberg observes that even in this case propo-

---

60. Ibid.
61. Ibid.
62. Ibid., 463.
63. Ibid., 470.
64. See Mats Wahlberg, *Revelation as Testimony: A Philosophical-Theological Study* (Grand Rapids, Mich.: Eerdmans, 2014). On the integral connection of thought and language, see also such works as David Braine, *Language and Human Understanding: The Roots of Creativity in Speech and Thought* (Washington, D.C.: The Catholic University of America Press, 2014); Charles Taylor, *The Language Animal: The Full Shape of the Human Linguistic Capacity* (Cambridge, Mass.: Harvard University Press, 2016).

sitions are necessarily involved. For example, "if God *manifestationally* reveals that he loves a certain person—for instance, by making her feel his love in a mystical experience—then it is the receiver of that revelation who must conceptualize the relevant proposition (*that God loves her*) herself."[65] This proposition must be infused or revealed personally by God in order for the person to be justified in knowing that the experience of love is an experience of God. If an experience is utterly nonconceptual, then the experience cannot justify any particular belief about its source or meaning.

At the same time, theologians such as Wahlberg recognize that revealed mysteries can never be expressed exhaustively in finite propositions, as is underscored by *Dei Verbum*'s crucial emphasis on mystery. Criticizing the propositionalist model, according to which revelation is solely or primarily "information," Richard Gaillardetz argues correctly that *Dei Verbum* teaches that "revelation, in its primary mode, is not the transmission of information, as with the propositional model, but the sharing of divine life."[66] Gaillardetz also grants that "revelation is not just a subjective experience; revelation does possess some genuine objective content, as the propositional approach rightly affirms."[67] As we saw, *Dei Verbum* holds that the Church over the centuries, under the guidance of the Holy Spirit, has articulated certain truths that pertain to the apostolic deposit of faith and that require the obedience of faith.

Indebted to John Thiel, however, Gaillardetz goes on to identify a "sense of tradition as a reversal of past beliefs and practices."[68] He defines this "sense of tradition" as the Church's "communal recognition of dramatic *discontinuity* with its past," discontinuity that is dramatic or radical precisely in the sense that it does not rest upon "a consistent affirmation evident underneath the appearance of change and repudiation."[69] He argues for example that it is "a kind of historical dishonesty" to "see in the

---

65. Wahlberg, *Revelation as Testimony*, 32.
66. Richard R. Gaillardetz, *By What Authority? A Primer on Scripture, the Magisterium, and the Sense of the Faithful* (Collegeville, Minn.: Liturgical Press, 2003), 7.
67. Ibid.
68. Ibid., 49. See John E. Thiel, *Senses of Tradition: Continuity and Development in Catholic Faith* (Oxford: Oxford University Press, 2000).
69. Gaillardetz, *By What Authority?*, 49.

Second Vatican Council's teaching on religious liberty and the universal reach of God's saving offer nothing more than new formulations of past insights," which, however imperfectly or inadequately developed in the past, "can be found in the tradition."[70] In a section entitled "Disputed Questions" at the end of his chapter, Gaillardetz recognizes that *Dei Verbum* and other Vatican II documents (as well as Pope John XXIII's opening address to the Council) seek to avoid positing such radical discontinuity by making "a distinction between form and content. One can affirm that the content or substance of a particular dogma remains unchanged even as its concrete articulation is subject to revision and reformulation."[71] While granting that this distinction has been "helpful" in the past, he concludes his chapter by observing—not in his own voice, but giving this viewpoint the final word on the topic—that "many theologians today question whether this kind of distinction [between form and content] is really adequate. They note the important ways in which the meaning of the dogma cannot be so easily separated or detached from the cultural, philosophical and theological forms that are used to express that meaning."[72]

What is at stake here is whether it is possible, in any era, to formulate a doctrinal proposition whose content or meaning is enduringly true.

---

70. Ibid. I agree that the Council's teaching on religious liberty (for example) should not be described as "nothing more than new formulations of past insights," but I do not think that this means that the Council's teaching cannot "be found in the tradition," properly understood (in accord with the principles of doctrinal development as distinct from doctrinal corruption or rupture of definitive Church teaching). See for example David L. Schindler and Nicholas J. Healy Jr., *Freedom, Truth, and Human Dignity: The Second Vatican Council's Declaration on Religious Freedom. A New Translation, Redaction History, and Interpretation of* Dignitatis Humanae *(Grand Rapids, MI: Eerdmans, 2015)*. In his "For Further Reading," Gaillardetz cites works by Yves Congar as well as two works on which his own position largely rests: Thiel's *Senses of Tradition* and Terrence W. Tilley, *Inventing Catholic Tradition* (Maryknoll, N.Y.: Orbis Books, 2000). I engage more fully with the views of Thiel and Tilley in my *Engaging the Doctrine of Revelation: The Mediation of the Gospel through Church and Scripture* (Grand Rapids, Mich.: Baker Academic, 2014), chapters 5–6.

71. Gaillardetz, *By What Authority?*, 52.

72. Ibid., 53. See also Terrence J. Tilley, *The Disciples' Jesus: Christology as Reconciling Practice* (Maryknoll, N.Y.: Orbis Books, 2008), 263; and Ormond Rush, *Still Interpreting Vatican II: Some Hermeneutical Principles* (New York: Paulist Press, 2004), 79–84, although Rush focuses on issues of power and therefore continues to support "continuity with the great tradition" (*Still Interpreting Vatican II*, 84) rather than (so far as I can tell) discontinuity or rupture in what the Church has definitively taught in the realm of faith and morals.

The loosening of propositional bonds, however, does not lead to a deeper personal engagement with the self-revealing God. On the contrary, the effort to relativize and downplay the cognitive-propositional element in divine revelation succeeds mainly in undermining our ability to encounter the Person of Jesus. The personal dimension of revelation—the personal encounter today with the living Christ through the mediation of Scripture and Tradition—depends upon the ability of historically conditioned propositions (including biblical propositions, with their distinctive historical contexts) to get the self-revealing Persons right. For example, if Nicea's teaching that the Son is consubstantial with the Father is not true, then Jesus could only be a mere human whom we could not now encounter in a saving way. When one denies the fidelity of the propositional communication of divine revelation through Scripture and Tradition, one is left not with the Person of Jesus, but solely with the human community and its ever-changing praxis.

Fortunately, *Dei Verbum* offers a better approach, one that should guide the ongoing theological event inspired by the document. For *Dei Verbum*, divine revelation is found in the words and deeds of Jesus Christ, in fulfillment of God's revelation to his covenantal people, Israel. The personal and propositional dimensions of revelation are inseparably joined in Jesus, and the same holds for the mediation of divine revelation in Scripture and Tradition. Divine revelation is a personal and transformative encounter with Jesus Christ precisely because divine revelation communicates true knowledge of Christ. Insisting upon both the personal-encounter and cognitive-propositional dimensions of divine revelation, therefore, let us heed Paul's prayer "that Christ may dwell in your hearts through faith; that you, being rooted and grounded in love, may have power to comprehend with all the saints what is the breadth and length and height and depth, and to know the love of Christ which surpasses knowledge, that you may be filled with all the fulness of God" (Eph 3:17–19).

CHAPTER 2

ACTIVE PARTICIPATION

Sacrosanctum Concilium in Context

Sacrosanctum Concilium "did not suddenly appear out of nowhere, but was the culmination of over a hundred years of research, reflection, writing, and pastoral work of the Liturgical Movement."[1] In 1903, Pope Pius X

---

1. Pamela Jackson, *An Abundance of Graces: Reflections on* Sacrosanctum Concilium (Chicago: Hillenbrand Books, 2004), 3. See also the Orthodox theologian Nicholas E. Denysenko's *Liturgical Reform after Vatican II: The Impact on Eastern Orthodoxy* (Minneapolis, Minn.: Fortress Press, 2015). Denysenko argues that in the preconciliar Liturgical Movement, "Catholic and Orthodox theologians unearthed and refined the theological foundations for liturgy that had been obscured through centuries of neglect and decay, and that these foundations, particularly the multilayered priesthood of the assembly grounded in Christ the High Priest and their active and conscious participation in the liturgy inspired several concurrent models for liturgical reform" (Denysenko, *Liturgical Reform after Vatican II*, 32). Denysenko makes clear that the Liturgical Movement should be ongoing today: "While assessments of these [largely postconciliar] reforms vary, the key for the Churches to move forward is to continue the process of studying liturgical history to recover and update the foundations for liturgical reform.... One of the lessons from history is that Catholics

praised "active participation" in the liturgy as the source of the Christian spirit that should flourish among believers.[2] In 1928, Pope Pius XI's *Divini Cultus* urged the laity to take care not to be "strangers and silent spectators" in the liturgy.[3] Eminent contributors to the Liturgical Movement include the Benedictine Lambert Beauduin, whose *La piété de l'Église* appeared in 1914, Romano Guardini, Virgil Michel, Odo Casel, Josef Jungmann, and Louis Bouyer. Pamela Jackson remarks that "Lambert Beauduin's strong pastoral concern that laity and clergy alike understand the meaning of what is happening in the celebration of the liturgy so that they could truly experience it as source of their life as Christians finds a resonance throughout [*Sacrosanctum Concilium*]."[4] Jackson adds that when *Sacrosanctum Concilium* appeared, Pierre-Marie Gy and others identified strong links between it and Pius XII's 1947 encyclical *Mediator Dei*.[5]

Aidan Nichols likewise identifies significant connections between *Mediator Dei* and *Sacrosanctum Concilium*, although he sees differences as well. Notable among the connections is the two documents' shared understanding of "the Liturgy as the continuing expression of the Father's offer to us of new holiness through the sacrificial death of Christ."[6] Indeed, Nichols thinks that by comparison to *Mediator Dei*, *Sacrosanctum Concilium* tightens "the doctrinal link between the Liturgy and salvation."[7] He emphasizes that *Sacrosanctum Concilium*, like *Mediator Dei*, gives "a ratio-

---

and Orthodox have mutually benefitted from engaging in theological exchange while deliberating liturgical reform" (Denysenko, *Liturgical Reform after Vatican II*, 32–33).

2. Pope Pius X, *Tra Le Sollecitudini*, Motu Proprio, November 22, 1903, at www.vatican.va.

3. Pope Pius XI, *Divini Cultus*, Apostolic Constitution, December 20, 1928, §9, at www.vatican.va.

4. Jackson, *An Abundance of Graces*, 4.

5. Jackson cites Gy's "The Constitution in the Making," in *Vatican II: The Liturgy Constitution*, ed. Austin Flannery, OP (Dublin: Scepter Books, 1964). See also Pierre-Marie Gy, OP, *The Reception of Vatican II Liturgical Reforms in the Life of the Church* (Milwaukee, Wisc.: Marquette University Press, 2003). Gy concludes his book on a positive note: "If we look back to the last half century of the Church's liturgical life in our various countries, could we not say that, in spite of a few divergences and the lack of sufficient time needed to understand the liturgical reform deeply enough, the main effect of Vatican II on our spiritual life has been our experience of a deeper participation in the liturgy?" (Gy, *Reception of Vatican II Liturgical Reforms*, 53).

6. Aidan Nichols, OP, "A Tale of Two Documents: *Sacrosanctum Concilium* and *Mediator Dei*," in *A Pope and a Council on the Sacred Liturgy*, ed. Alcuin Reid, OSB (Farnborough, U.K.: Saint Michael's Abbey Press, 2002), 9–27, at 14.

7. Ibid.

nale for liturgical celebration which is entirely salvational in character," so that both documents "are worlds away from any sub-theological ideology of the Liturgy for which the purpose of the Liturgy might be, for instance, to affirm the group identity of the assembly; to express gender, class, or ethnic belonging; or to recognise in symbolic play the presence or action of the divine in secular life and reality."[8] He praises the strong eschatological dimension of the liturgy articulated by *Sacrosanctum Concilium*, by comparison to *Mediator Dei*'s lack of that dimension.[9]

Leaders of the Liturgical Movement gave *Sacrosanctum Concilium* an enthusiastic reception. A notable instance of this perspective is found in Louis Bouyer's 1964 book *The Liturgy Revived: A Doctrinal Commentary of the Conciliar Constitution of the Liturgy*. Throughout the book, Bouyer exhibits great enthusiasm for *Sacrosanctum Concilium*, which he praises for articulating "the basic principles of the whole Christian spirituality, stated with a strength and lucidity no less remarkable than the exceptional solemnity of their utterance."[10] He rejoices that *Sacrosanctum Concilium*, because of its status as a conciliar Constitution, "will never be superseded as the Church's fundamental teaching concerning what she does in her worship."[11]

In order to introduce *Sacrosanctum Concilium* as an ongoing theological event, I begin this chapter by surveying a book published by Bouyer shortly *after* the Council: *Liturgy and Architecture* (1967). In this book, Bouyer provides a condensed version of the historical overview that he offers in such works as *Liturgical Piety* (1954) and *Eucharist: Theology and Spirituality of the Eucharistic Prayer* (1966).[12] He also sets forth his vision

---

8. Ibid., 14–15. Nichols also notes some points of difference, including "the way in which Pius XII saw liturgical participation as offering us the opportunity for *synergia*, co-working, with the protagonist of our salvation, the immaculate Lamb" (ibid., 15), a vision of liturgical participation that Nichols finds to be neglected in *Sacrosanctum Concilium*. Nichols criticizes *Sacrosanctum Concilium*'s understanding of liturgical pedagogy: see ibid., 26.

9. See Nichols, "A Tale of Two Documents," 10.

10. Louis Bouyer, *The Liturgy Revived: A Doctrinal Commentary of the Conciliar Constitution on the Liturgy* (Notre Dame, Ind.: University of Notre Dame Press, 1964), 5.

11. Ibid., 6.

12. See Louis Bouyer, *Liturgical Piety* (Notre Dame, Ind.: University of Notre Dame Press, 1955); Louis Bouyer, *Eucharist: Theological and Spirituality of the Eucharistic Prayer* (Notre Dame, Ind.: University of Notre Dame Press, 1989).

for the renewal of the laity's active participation in the liturgy. In addition, Bouyer here suggests that active participation requires that the priest and people face in the same direction during the Eucharistic prayer.[13] By interpreting active participation in this way, Bouyer's *Liturgy and Architecture* will help us to understand why the ongoing theological event of *Sacrosanctum Concilium* consists today largely in debates about its practical implementation.

As a pivotal figure in the Liturgical Movement prior to the Council, Bouyer taught both at various European institutions and, as a distinguished visiting professor, at the University of Notre Dame, the Catholic University of America, and Brown University. Although his reconstructions of the history of the liturgy no longer hold the sway they once did, he continues to be a central authority for anyone interested in the liturgy. He did not have a role in the drafting of *Sacrosanctum Concilium*, but he influenced the document through his writings and friendships.[14] For Bouyer, *Sacrosanctum Concilium* puts "the stamp of the supreme authority in the Church ... upon the main results of the whole liturgical movement" and "makes it so clear that the liturgy is at the heart of the whole life of the Church."[15]

---

13. Although active participation is at its very heart, *Sacrosanctum Concilium* did not discuss the direction of the priest and people during the Eucharistic prayer. *Inter Oecumenici*, the 1964 instruction on the implementation of *Sacrosanctum Concilium*, "directed the creation of freestanding altars, and established the lawfulness of the priest celebrating Mass facing the people" (Rita Ferrone, *Liturgy*: Sacrosanctum Concilium [New York: Paulist Press, 2007], 58). In his *The Liturgical Environment: What the Documents Say*, 2nd ed. (Collegeville, Minn.: Liturgical Press, 2004), 30, Mark G. Boyer directs us to the Christological and ecclesiological significance of the altar: "The preface of the Eucharist Prayer said during the Mass of Dedication is an integral part of the rite of dedication of an altar. The preface refers to Christ, who offered himself to God on the altar of the cross and commanded his followers to celebrate the same sacrifice of the Eucharist in mystery until he returns in glory. The preface also refers to the Lord's table from which God's children are nourished by the Body and Blood of Christ and are gathered together as one. Finally, it refers to the Spirit from whom the members of the Church drink and become, in fact, a living altar."

14. For the influence of Bouyer's writings during the conciliar period, see for example Henri de Lubac, SJ, *Vatican Council Notebooks*, vol. 1, trans. Andrew Stefanelli and Anne Englund Nash (San Francisco: Ignatius Press, 2015), 165, 206. On Bouyer's *Le rite et l'homme: Sacralité naturelle et liturgie* (Paris: Cerf, 1962), which de Lubac and many others read during the Council, see also David M. Power, OMI, *Unsearchable Riches: The Symbolic Nature of Liturgy* (New York: Pueblo, 1983), 78–79.

15. Bouyer, *The Liturgy Revived*, 5; Bouyer, *Liturgy and Architecture* (Notre Dame, Ind.: University of Notre Dame Press, 1967), 2.

Louis Bouyer's *Liturgy and Architecture*

In *Liturgy and Architecture,* Louis Bouyer sets forth his view of the proper renewal of the liturgy, as well as the causes of what he considers to be the liturgy's late-patristic, medieval, and Baroque decline. Bouyer is negative toward Eucharistic adoration, at least during the liturgy, and he criticizes devotional practices such as privately saying the Rosary during Mass. His understanding of how to renew the liturgy revolves around his account of the transition from the Jewish synagogue to the Christian church. Put succinctly, he seeks to balance word and sacrament, meal and sacrifice, participation in Jesus' Cross and participation in his Resurrection. He insists that believers' liturgical participation in the Paschal mystery should be an eschatologically ordered awaiting of Christ's return in glory. Throughout his book, Bouyer finds, in *Sacrosanctum Concilium,* a much needed undercutting of "the 'seige' mentality of the Church of the Counter-Reformation."[16] At the same time, he cautions that the current temptation is to rush to the opposite extreme and, instead of rigidly refusing to change any external aspect of the liturgy, throw tradition out entirely. He therefore argues in favor of creative appreciation for the living tradition as a middle ground between rigidity and vapidity, a middle ground that should enable us to "realize both the richness and the vast amount of freedom that the Catholic tradition puts at our disposal."[17] This richness and this freedom come from the discovery of the inner core and "plenitude" of the living tradition, which flows from "the creative power of the Spirit."[18] Bouyer's goal is to renew, beyond mere rigid and misunderstood external forms, the "intelligent, active and fruitful participation on the part of the faithful (as the Council says again and again)."[19] Such active participation consists in nothing less than "a common life in the Spirit, a common life of God with men, through the experience of which men become one together, while becoming one with God in Christ."[20]

In describing the liturgy, Bouyer uses imagery of feasting and reconciliation: the liturgy "is that marriage feast of the Lamb where all are

---

16. Bouyer, *Liturgy and Architecture,* 2.
17. Bouyer, *Liturgy and Architecture,* 4.
18. Ibid.
19. Ibid.
20. Ibid., 4–5.

called, to be reconciled in the Body of the only Son."[21] He also uses the imagery of "scattered children" congregating and of humanity "gathering together" in God's house.[22] He refers to hearing God's word, to praying, and to "the sacramental celebration of the mystery proclaimed by His word."[23] He thus balances a number of aspects of the liturgy that must not be isolated from one another, and he focuses on the unity of humanity attained through full participation in Christ.

To exemplify the liturgical balance that he seeks, Bouyer returns not simply to the earliest Church but to the Jewish synagogue out of which Jesus, the apostles, and many of the first Christians came. He states, "Contemporary exegesis has underlined how the Church, as the Body of Christ, had its preparation in the Qahal, the assembly of the People of God, brought together to hear the word, to surrender to it in common prayer, to be sealed in the unity of the Covenant, an alliance with God."[24] Was the synagogue simply a place of hearing the word, cut off from the Temple's sacrificial cult? Bouyer shows that the answer is no. In the synagogue, the congregation and the rabbi all faced toward the Ark, which represented the Ark of the Covenant that had been lost when the Temple was destroyed at the time of the Babylonian exile. Each year, on the Day of Atonement, the high priest had sprinkled the Ark of the Covenant—and specifically the cover or "mercy seat" (Lv 16:2) upon which God was believed to be invisibly present and enthroned—with the sacrificial blood of the sin offering. The Ark of the Covenant contained the tablets of the Decalogue and the manna, and the Ark was the central object in the Holy of Holies, a part of the Temple into which even the high priest could come only rarely, because God was enthroned there.

In facing toward the representation of the Ark, worshippers at a synagogue were symbolically linked to the sacrificial cult of the Temple, as well as to the word of God (Torah). In addition, the synagogue worship had an eschatological dimension, because synagogues always faced "toward the Holy of Holies of Jerusalem, to the place where the Messiah was to appear and the diaspora to be gathered."[25] The synagogue's liturgy thus

---

21. Ibid., 5.
22. Ibid.
23. Ibid.
24. Ibid., 8.
25. Ibid., 19.

possessed the elements of divine word and presence, sacrificial atonement, and eschatological consummation; but what about the element of meal? Bouyer explains that the element of a shared meal was present in the ritual meals, including the Passover meal. The shared meals of communities such as that at Qumran intentionally sought to prepare for the eschatological age. Bouyer states, "In the breaking of the bread, in the blessing of the cup of thanksgiving and their common participation, they saw an inauguration of the messianic feast."[26] The last prayer ("the last *berakah*") over the cup contained the final portion of the *Abodah* prayer, which was "the consecration prayer of the daily burnt offering in the Temple."[27] Meal and sacrifice were thus placed together. To the *Abodah* prayer as recited in the synagogue, furthermore, there was "added an invocation that the 'memorial' of the People, of the house of David, of the Messiah, arise, be heard accepted before God and come to pass."[28] In the synagogue worship, therefore, the word and prayers remained intimately connected with the Temple sacrifice and the eschatological consummation, and both were linked with the ritual meal and its prayers.

How did this inform early Christianity? In answering this question, Bouyer focuses upon the oldest extant Syrian churches, which he identifies as "[t]he most ancient type of a Christian Church."[29] He states, "There we have the remnants of a primitive Christianity which, even when it had ceased to be purely Jewish, remained for a time purely Semitic."[30] How do the Syrian churches differ from the synagogue? For one thing, they are not oriented toward Jerusalem, but rather they face east toward the rising sun, the most potent symbol of Christ's return. This change signifies that Christians await not the restoration of Israel and the rebuilding of the Temple, but rather the new or heavenly Jerusalem, which "will be made of the gathering of the elect in His risen body," and which will need no Temple (since the Lord himself will be the Temple).[31] By facing east, the liturgy—expressed by the Syrian church architecture—conveys a Christian eschatology.

A second difference is that the apse at the eastern end of the church

---

26. Ibid., 23.
27. Ibid., 22.
28. Ibid.
29. Ibid., 24.
30. Ibid., 25.
31. Ibid., 28.

now contains a table or altar. Instead of facing a replica of the Ark of the Covenant, where the divine presence dwelt enthroned on the mercy seat, all worshippers now face the altar, the equivalent or fulfillment of the Holy of Holies. Bouyer states, "The Christians in their churches, hearing the word, are led by it from the Ark to the altar. And beyond the altar itself, they look toward no other earthly place but only toward the rising sun as toward the symbol of the *Sol justitiae* they are expecting."[32] Eschatology, divine presence, meal, and sacrifice are thereby united, since the Church remembers Christ's saving death each time the Eucharist is celebrated on the table or altar, and since this remembrance not only re-presents Christ's Passion, but also is a foretaste of our eschatological heavenly banquet with the Christ.

Christian worshippers, then, no longer face either toward Jerusalem or toward the Temple with its sacrificial cult and Ark. Instead, Christian worshippers face toward the east and "the eucharistic meal has taken the place of the former sacrifices."[33] The seat of the bishop now replaces the seat of Moses (on which the rabbi sat); the book of the Gospels replaces the Torah scroll. The words of the Gospel draw us toward the sacramental action. As Bouyer puts it, "The Gospel itself, to prepare us for the eternal gathering of the elect in the heavenly Jerusalem, leads us toward the expected Orient, whence its coming is hoped for, by inviting us to the messianic feast, the banquet of the Lamb, now already inaugurated in the eucharistic celebration."[34] Bouyer is careful to link meal/banquet/feast with sacrifice, and sacrifice with eschatological communion in the risen Lord. He observes that the Temple ritual is fulfilled "in the bloodless sacrifices [Eucharists] of that Lamb who has been immolated once for all, and remains for ever interceding on our behalf in the immediate presence of the Father," and he notes that "here on earth we partake of His resurrected body. Already we drink the new life of His love by taking part of the cup of blessing, the chalice of His Blood."[35]

Bouyer points out that in some of these churches, the seat of Moses is replaced not by the bishop's seat, but by the enthronement of the book of

---

32. Ibid., 31.
33. Ibid., 32.
34. Ibid.
35. Ibid., 33.

the Gospels. He considers this development, even if a rare one, to be highly positive, since it makes "clear that the Christian bishop, or any preacher of the Gospel, is only the surrogate for Christ."[36] All Syrian churches are structured so that after the readings and prayers, the clergy process to the east (the altar), carrying the offerings, and "the congregation reassembles itself around the altar for the eucharistic meal."[37] Since the only seats in these Syrian churches are for the bishops and clergy, it is possible for the congregation to move to the eastern end of the church. Bouyer strongly praises this arrangement. He states that "the whole assembly, far from being a static mass of spectators, remains an organic gathering of worshippers, first centered on the Ark, for hearing and meditating upon the scriptures, and finally going toward the East all together, for the eucharistic prayer and the final communion."[38] For Bouyer, the particularly exciting and exemplary thing is that the whole community, clergy and laity, act together in word and sacrament, just as the rabbi and congregants do in the synagogue. True, "[t]he presiding bishop or priest acts always as the center," since the body of believers is "assembled around him" (both to hear the word and say the prayers, and to celebrate the Eucharist), but the key point is that the bishop or priest never acts "as a single performer before an audience having only to look at him!"[39] Furthermore, although the bishop or priest is at the center, he never directs the attention toward himself. Instead he consistently refers the whole gathering of believers "to a transcendent focus," upon which all gaze together: "the word of the Gospel, the table of the Word made flesh and our food, and finally the eternal advent of the Lord of whom he is only the minister."[40] Jesus Christ is at the center of this worship, and bishop or priest and believers worship as a (hierarchically organized) "body acting together in unity."[41]

Not only, then, are all the dimensions of Christian worship held properly together in the Syrian churches—word, sacrament, meal, sacrifice, eschaton, and so forth—but even more importantly, the worship is arranged so that everyone faces toward the altar and toward the (eschatological) east. There is hierarchy, as established by Christ, but there is

36. Ibid., 34.
37. Ibid.
38. Ibid., 35.
39. Ibid., 35–36.
40. Ibid., 36.
41. Ibid.

no clericalist arrangement that deprives the laity of their full, active participation in the liturgy. Even better, unlike the way they were treated in the synagogue, women receive a proper liturgical place in the church, and both women and men assemble around the altar for the celebration of the Eucharist.

When and how did this full, active participation of the laity, and this Christ-centeredness of worship, begin to decline? Bouyer notes that the structure of the early churches in Rome is not known, but the shape of the Constantinian-era churches of Italy may be discernible through study of the ruins of Christian churches in North Africa, where the Muslim conquest relatively quickly extinguished Christianity. A bad development is already visible: "the seat of the bishop has been brought into the center of the apse [on the eastern end] and ... it is now a throne: not just a teacher's *cathedra* but the seat of honor of a high dignitary."[42] This architectural change signals, Bouyer thinks, that the Constantinian bishop was becoming an imperial figure, rather than a teacher and priest. Bouyer considers this to be "the first beginnings of what is now commonly called 'triumphalism,' the origin of which lies in the fact that bishops had become authorities of the state."[43] He hammers home his point: Constantinian Christian leaders became fundamentally separated from the congregation, so that they were now more linked with the state than with the Church community. The clergy were now separated, rather than simply distinguished, from the laity. The priests no longer linked the bishop with the whole people, but rather served as "flunkeys" or a "court" that enhanced the bishop's "dignity while separating it from the *vulgum pecus*."[44]

With the bishop now sitting enthroned in the apse at the eastern end of the church, the altar was moved to the center of the Church, where the bishop had previously sat. Bouyer indicates that this situation could have been worse. With the altar in the center of the Church, at least "when the bishop finally went to the altar for the eucharistic meal, he had still all his people grouped around him, just as before."[45] According to Bouyer, however, during the pontificate of Gregory the Great the decline of the

42. Ibid., 43.
43. Ibid., 44.
44. Ibid., 45.
45. Ibid.

liturgy accelerated precipitously. The bishop and clergy no longer joined the congregation in order to celebrate the Eucharist. Instead, the altar was moved to the apse, where the bishop sat enthroned. This development—or in Bouyer's view, this liturgical corruption—occurred as a result of Pope Gregory the Great's desire to move the altar to the place in St. Peter's Basilica right above the tomb of St. Peter. This change, which influenced churches throughout Europe, altered "the whole character of the primitive celebration," and confined the clergy to a "lofty isolation even for the eucharist."[46]

The collective worship of the People of God, the sharing in the Eucharist and active participation of the laity, now diminished sharply, according to Bouyer. He grants that this change already was occurring in the fourth century, the result of an increased frequency in people's attending the liturgy without receiving the Eucharist. Indeed, says Bouyer, "In the middle ages the communion of the faithful would even disappear entirely from the papal mass. It would never be reintroduced as a normal practice until the last popes, John XXIII and Paul VI."[47] The celebration of the Eucharist and the partaking in the Eucharistic meal became something that priests and religious did, but that lay people mostly watched—with the exception of a spiritual elite here and there. In Bouyer's view, the beautifully elaborate liturgy of the medieval period was basically a spectacle, celebrated "not so much for the Christian people as instead of them."[48]

At St. Peter's, the positioning of the altar meant that Mass was celebrated facing the people. Bouyer considers that the notion of celebrating the Mass facing the people, far from being the most primitive tradition or being a stimulant to the active participation of the laity, historically embodied the very opposite: it emerged as part of the clericalization of the post-Constantinian Church, and represented not the active participation of the laity but (to a large degree) their fundamental exclusion. For

46. Ibid., 48.
47. Ibid., 49.
48. Ibid. For more recent studies that have demonstrated the pervasive involvement of the laity in the medieval liturgy, see for example Eamon Duffy, *The Stripping of the Altars: Traditional Religion in England, 1400–1580*, 2nd ed. (New Haven, Conn.: Yale University Press, 2005); Augustine Thompson, OP, *Cities of God: The Religion of the Italian Communes, 1125–1325*, 2nd ed. (University Park: Pennsylvania State University Press, 2006).

the earliest Christians, in fact, "The communal character of a meal was emphasized just by the opposite disposition: the fact that all the participants were on the same side of the table."[49] Bouyer adds that the intention of Pope Gregory (or his successors) was not to "face the people." This phrase was never mentioned in any pre-modern liturgical manual. Rather, the key point for the pre-modern liturgy, in St. Peter's as elsewhere, was to ensure that the bishop or priest said "the eucharistic prayer, as all the other prayers, facing East."[50] Indeed, not only the bishop or priest, but the whole congregation, had to be sure to turn toward the east when saying the prayers. Thus, as Bouyer notes, "in churches with what we now call an altar facing the people" there would have been a significant part of the congregation "turning their backs to the altar during the whole of the consecration prayer."[51] Bouyer surmises that this is why most churches did not adopt the Roman architectural model as found in St. Peter's.

Here Bouyer explores more deeply what active participation means. Does it mean, for example, being able to see what the priest is doing with the elements? Bouyer points out that in the patristic era, there would have been little to see: the bishop or priest would simply have been saying the prayers aloud, the same prayers that the people were supposed to be following so as to give their Amen. In the medieval and Baroque liturgies, the celebrant undertook numerous gestures, including "plenty of signs of the cross, of kissing the altar, handling and elevating the elements, and, especially after the consecration, numberless genuflexions."[52] For Bouyer, such additions to the liturgy may be fine and good, but they are hardly the point. If such gestures must be present, which they need not be (since they were absent in the patristic liturgy), it is certainly not necessary for the laity to see them. The key point is that active participation in the liturgical action does not mean looking at what the bishop or priest does. That would be to define active participation in a clericalist way. Instead, Bouyer thinks that active participation is stimulated when the bishop or priest and congregation all face together toward the eschatological East, toward Christ the Lord.

49. Bouyer, *Liturgy and Architecture*, 54.
50. Ibid., 55.
51. Ibid., 56.
52. Ibid., 57.

In rather strong terms, Bouyer observes that "we must not confuse participating in the celebration with looking at it. The practice of looking curiously at the eucharistic elements themselves, especially at the time of the consecration, is a practice completely unknown to Christian antiquity."[53] Even though such a practice was added in the thirteenth century (with the double elevation), the key point remains that active participation in the liturgy cannot mean watching somebody else do something. Bouyer's point, implicit but clear, is that the implementation of *Sacrosanctum Concilium*'s call for active participation of the laity in the liturgy would be significantly harmed by having the bishop or priest face the people during the Eucharistic prayer.

After a section devoted to the development of the Eastern liturgy and architectural forms, including iconography, Bouyer returns to the Western churches and again reflects upon what he considers to be the period of liturgical decline and corruption away from the patristic high-point. In the early medieval period, the choir was screened off from the main body of the church in Western churches, and the offertory procession disappeared. The result was that the congregation now had nothing to do but watch, or at best perform private devotions such as the Rosary. The choir performed the singing; the readings and prayers were in Latin; the bishop or priest, in consecrating the Eucharist, was separated from the people. After the thirteenth century, various visible gestures were introduced to help the people participate, but Bouyer considers that this was simply "the beginning of the modern tendency to substitute for actual participation a mere visualization."[54] He grants that there were some positive developments in the medieval period, including efforts to introduce "a reduplication in the vernacular" of the readings and prayers (the "prone").[55] Furthermore, in churches constructed during the Counter-Reformation, the screen between the altar, where the priest stood, and the people was suppressed so that "the people could fully see and follow the eucharistic celebration itself, if not yet regain their participation in it."[56] Sometimes,

---

53. Ibid., 58.
54. Ibid., 72. For a more historically informed perspective here, see the works by Duffy and Thompson cited above.
55. Ibid., 75.
56. Ibid., 76.

too, male laypeople were encouraged to use the ample space "between the stalls of the clerics and choristers."[57] However, Bouyer laments the nineteenth- and twentieth-century introduction of permanent pews and the reduction of the pulpit to a place solely for preaching, because he considers that these changes made "of our churches just the equivalent of showrooms or classrooms, where a passive congregation has only to see from afar a clerical performance and passively to hear a clerical instruction."[58]

In his 1954 book *Liturgical Piety*, after giving examples of Baroque liturgical failures (what he calls a "gallery of horrifying examples"), Bouyer comments that "some readers might infer that I am completely out of sympathy with the spirit of the Baroque period."[59] He denies having such an attitude, and responds that "[o]n the contrary, my opinion is that that rigid and unintelligent traditionalism, which is so prominent a feature of the true Baroque mentality, was the providential means whereby the Church managed to keep her liturgical treasures safe throughout a long period when scarcely anyone was capable of understanding their true worth."[60] Rather than only criticizing the Baroque period's "rigid and unintelligent traditionalism," therefore, Bouyer in 1954 is quite willing to strongly criticize his own contemporaries. Indeed, he accuses some of his contemporaries of falling even deeper into the Baroque period's formalism—paradoxically while supposing themselves to be overcoming this formalism—by trying "to disguise a rubrically correct low Mass by reading and singing in the vernacular, to make it resemble as closely as possible the style of public meeting now popular, endeavoring also to give to the performance of the sacred rite itself a setting resembling that of the stadium, of the factory, or of the movie-theatre."[61] Bouyer instead desires to see the congregation in a semicircle gathered closely around the priest and altar during the Eucharistic prayer.

To sum up: in *Liturgy and Architecture* and in many earlier works as well, Bouyer is concerned with what he calls "the clericalisation of the liturgy" in the West, the robbing of the laity of the full active participation

---

57. Ibid., 80.
58. Ibid., 81.
59. Bouyer, *Liturgical Piety*, 3, 8.
60. Ibid., 8.
61. Ibid., 9. For these criticisms, see also his "Où en est le Mouvement liturgique?," *La Maison-Dieu* 25 (1951): 34–46.

that, in his view, they enjoyed in the first centuries of Christianity.[62] He favors such reforms as congregational singing, the use of the vernacular, frequent communion, communion under both species, the prayer of the faithful, and the kiss of peace. Even if Bouyer is too strong in his criticisms of earlier periods (and of his own day), his concern to resist "clericalisation of the liturgy" is a good one. In addition, he rightly insists upon a balance between meal and sacrifice and between the "memorial" and "eschatological" dimensions of the liturgy. For Bouyer, the priest must not be envisioned at the center. Rather, the center is Jesus Christ, to whom the prayers of both priest and people should be directed. For Bouyer, active participation requires that, during the Eucharistic prayer, the priest and the people face east together, so as to signify the eschatological dimension of awaiting the return of Christ in glory and to accentuate the Eucharist's status as a foretaste of the eschatological banquet and a participation in Christ's Paschal mystery.

Sacrosanctum Concilium

The very first sentence of *Sacrosanctum Concilium* makes reference to the Liturgical Movement's goal of the active participation of the laity: "It is the intention of this holy council to improve the standard of daily christian living among Catholics" (§1).[63] The importance of active participation in the liturgy flows from the fact that, as we find in the second paragraph, "the liturgy is each day building up those who are within into a holy temple in the Lord, into a dwelling place for God in the Spirit, until they reach the stature of the age of Christ's fullness [cf. Eph 2:21–22; 4:13]." Paragraph 2 states that the liturgy, "especially ... the divine sacrifice of the Eucharist," is "the chief means through which believers are expressing in their lives and demonstrating to others the mystery which is Christ." The liturgy also expresses and teaches what the Church is, since the liturgy involves visible things mediating divine realities, "in such a

---

62. Bouyer, *Liturgy and Architecture*, 81.
63. Quotations are from *Sacrosanctum Concilium*, in *Decrees of the Ecumenical Councils*, vol. 2: *Trent to Vatican II*, ed. Norman P. Tanner, SJ (Washington, D.C.: Georgetown University Press, 1990), 820–43.

way that the human within it is ordered and subordinated to the divine, and likewise the visible to the invisible, activity to contemplation, and the present to the city of the future which we seek" (§2). The liturgy effectively displays "the church to those who are outside as an ensign raised for the nations [cf. Is 11:12], under which the scattered children of God can be brought together into one until there is one fold and one shepherd [cf. Jn 11:52 and 10:16]" (§2).

On the basis of this theological sketch of the liturgy's purposes, paragraphs 3 and 4 introduce the intention of *Sacrosanctum Concilium* to provide principles and practical norms for the liturgy's renewal, with each of the approved rites of the Catholic Church retaining equal dignity and canonical force. Paragraph 5 then inaugurates chapter 1, titled "General principles regarding the renewal and encouragement of the liturgy." Section 1 of this chapter is titled "The nature of the liturgy and its significance in the life of the church." Paragraph 5 emphasizes that God wills to make himself known and to unite the whole human race in Christ, who came not as judge but as healer. Christ brought to fulfillment God's interactions with Israel, and he did so "above all through the paschal mystery, that is, his passion, his resurrection from the dead and his glorious ascension."[64] Understood in this way, the Paschal mystery gave rise not simply to the sacraments, but to "the tremendous sacrament [mirabile sacramentum] which is the whole church" (§5).

Paragraph 6 connects Christ's mission from the Father with the mission that Christ gave the apostles. Like Christ, they were filled with the Spirit and they were commissioned to preach the good news. In addition to proclaiming Christ's conquest of sin and his uniting us with the Father in the inaugurated kingdom of God, the apostles were given a sacramental mission: Christ empowered them "to enact what they were announcing through sacrifice and sacraments" (§6). In this way their words were not simply words, but rather proclaimed realities in which we participate

---

64. Bouyer coined the phrase "paschal mystery" in a book originally published in French in 1945: see Bouyer, *The Paschal Mystery: Meditations on the Last Three Days of Holy Week*, trans. Mary Benoit (Chicago: Regnery, 1950). See also Dominic M. Langevin, OP, *From Passion to Paschal Mystery: A Recent Magisterial Development concerning the Christological Foundation of the Sacraments* (Fribourg: Academic Press Fribourg, 2015).

through the liturgy. As paragraph 6 explains, "people are implanted into the paschal mystery of Christ through baptism," so as to "become the true worshippers whom the Father seeks." The Eucharistic meal is a sacrament linked with Christ's sacrifice, since to celebrate the Eucharist is to proclaim "the death of the Lord until he comes" (§6; cf. 1 Cor 11:26). Paragraph 6 goes on to say that the Eucharistic liturgy includes the reading of God's word (the Scripture) and the celebration of the Eucharist as the sacramental representation of Christ's Pasch.

Paragraph 7 treats "the sacrifice which is the mass [missae sacrificio]," in which Christ acts in the person of the priest to offer the same sacrifice that he offered on the Cross. Paragraph 7 also describes the analogous modes in which Christ is present liturgically, such as through the sacrifice of the Eucharist and through his word (Scripture), as well as whenever the Church is gathered to pray or sing hymns. The purpose of word and sacrament is to heal, unite, and elevate God's people, "the church who calls upon her Lord, and worships the eternal Father through him [Christ]" (§7). Thus, the entirety of the liturgy exhibits the "great process by which God is being perfectly glorified and human beings becoming holy," and so the liturgy is "the enacting of the priestly role of Jesus Christ" (§7). Indeed, in the liturgy, the priestly action of Christ is the priestly action of the whole mystical Body, head and members, offering true worship. Paragraph 8 adds that the liturgy on earth participates "by anticipation in the heavenly one, celebrated in the holy city, Jerusalem, the goal towards which we strive as pilgrims, where Christ is, seated at God's right hand."

In paragraph 9, *Sacrosanctum Concilium* observes that the Church must do a number of things in preparation for the liturgy, including evangelization, sacramental preparation, catechesis, and works of mercy. These other actions show that believers truly are "the light of the world" (§9), as Christ promised. Yet, paragraph 10 adds that the Church's other activities are not on par with the liturgy. The liturgy is "the high point towards which the activity of the church is directed, and, simultaneously, the source from which all its power flows out" (§10). Those who are united to Christ through faith and baptism "assemble together in order to praise God in the midst of the church, to share in the sacrifice [sacrificium participent], and to eat the Lord's supper" (§10). In the Eucharistic sacrifice and meal, the Lord renews his covenant with us, and this covenant renewal sets us aflame with "the overwhelming love of Christ" (§10). Paragraph 10 concludes that the liturgy is like a fountain from which grace pours forth upon us, with the result that the sanctification of humanity in Christ and the glorification of God—which together constitute the goal of everything done by the Church—are "realised in a fully effective way."

Thus all the dimensions of Bouyer's balanced presentation of the liturgy are present in paragraphs 5–10: word and sacrament, sacrifice and meal, faith and eschatology, human sanctification and divine glorification. *Sacrosanctum Concilium* §11, then, deepens and develops the crucial theme of active participation in the liturgy: "If ... this fully effective presence is to be appropriated, believers must approach the liturgy with the dispositions of a suitable heart and mind." Such dispositions enable believers not only to observe the proper exterior forms, but to participate interiorly in the liturgical action. This interior participation is required if the liturgy is to efficaciously build up each believer, and the whole community, into "a holy temple in the Lord." Paragraph 11 therefore strongly calls for the encouragement of active participation of the laity in the liturgy: "those with responsibility for leadership in worship must take care ... that the people are able to take part in it in such a way that they are active, that they know what is going on, and that they will receive benefit [ut fideles scienter, actuose et fructuose eandem participent]."[65]

After a couple paragraphs encouraging private devotions outside of the liturgy, *Sacrosanctum Concilium* focuses its attention on the active participation of the laity. Section 2 of chapter 1, composed of paragraphs 14–20, bears the title "Fostering liturgical formation and active participation." The first sentence of paragraph 14 makes clear the centrality of the laity's active participation for the renewal envisioned by *Sacrosanctum Concilium*: "The church [mater ecclesiae] very much wants all believers to be led to take a full, conscious and active part in liturgical celebration."[66]

---

65. For appreciative discussion of this passage, see Bouyer, *The Liturgy Revived*, 89–91.

66. For the connection here with Pope Pius X's encouragement of active participation, see Bouyer, *The Liturgy Revived*, 91–92. For strong criticism of the preconciliar liturgy, Charles E. Miller, CM, *Liturgy for the People of God*, vol. 1, *Foundations of Vatican II Liturgy* (Staten Island, N.Y.: Alba House, 2000), 102–3.

As paragraph 14 observes, this is no secondary aim that the liturgy can do without. On the contrary, the very "nature of the liturgy" requires the laity's active participation to be fully what the liturgy is. Likewise, the laity can fulfill their mission only when they actively participate in the liturgy, since this duty pertains to the baptismal priesthood of all believers. Lest there be any doubt, paragraph 14 reiterates: "This full and active sharing [actuosa participatio] on the part of the whole people is of paramount concern in the process of renewing the liturgy and helping it to grow, because such sharing is the first, and necessary, source from which believers can imbibe the true christian spirit." The conclusion follows that "all pastoral activity" should have in view the formation of believers so that they may participate actively in the liturgy, which makes sense given the exalted vision of the liturgy articulated in the earlier paragraphs of *Sacrosanctum Concilium*.

Since the active participation of the laity in the liturgy requires much more than just performing external actions, the clergy need to train the laity in active participation, rather than simply inviting the laity to be active. For this reason, paragraphs 15–18 focus upon the formation of seminarians and priests in liturgical theology. Prior to the Council, sacramental theology was central in seminaries; now *Sacrosanctum Concilium* mandates that the liturgy also be a necessary field of seminary study, indeed one of the "principal areas of enquiry" (§16). The history of the liturgy should be studied as well as the theology of the liturgy, and "its spiritual, pastoral and juridical aspects" should receive attention, along with the connections between the liturgy and other theological domains (§16). The liturgy should not only be studied, but should also take a central role in the spiritual formation of seminarians. Seminarians should learn how "to understand the rites of worship and share [participare] in them wholeheartedly" (§17).[67] The "spirit of the liturgy" (§17) should pervade the atmosphere of the seminary. In this way, seminarians who become priests will not only understand what is required interiorly and exteriorly for the active participation of the laity, but will also be able to communicate these requirements, because they will have internalized them.

---

67. See also Vatican II's *Optatam Totius*.

Sacrosanctum Concilium, then, conceives of the laity's active participation in a manner that requires an arduous process of entering into the "spirit of the liturgy." This perspective accords with Bouyer's understanding of the active participation of the laity as a "doing" rather than a "watching." The "doing" is primarily the interior action of sharing with the priest in the sacramental offering of Jesus Christ to the Father. Just as Bouyer values external as well as interior participation—he mentions with approval external modes of participation such as the singing of hymns and the use of the vernacular—so too *Sacrosanctum Concilium* urges that the laity should attain to "an active part [participationem] in the liturgy, both inwardly and outwardly" (§19). The principal element, however, is inward, which is why *Sacrosanctum Concilium* emphasizes the difficulty of the liturgical training of the laity. Paragraph 19 describes priests as needing to "conscientiously and patiently work to impart a liturgical formation to the people," a formation suited to the mode of life and "level of religious culture" of each person. The paragraph reiterates that priests not only should instruct the people in active participation, but should model it by their "example."

After a paragraph devoted to the conditions in which the Mass should be broadcast on television or radio, the next paragraph, §21, begins the third section of chapter 1, titled "The renewal of the liturgy." This section sets forth particular reforms that aim to foster active participation in the liturgy. Paragraph 21 teaches that "the texts and rites must be organised so as to express more clearly the holy things which they represent, and so that thus the christian people, insofar as this is possible, will be able to understand these things easily." Equipped with a better understanding of the meaning of liturgical texts and rites, the laity will be able truly to participate in the "holy things" of the liturgy "through a celebration that is expressive of their full meaning, is effective, involving [actuosa], and the community's own" (§21). This project of reform accords with the desire that Bouyer repeatedly expresses for the reform of the liturgy of his own day. Paragraph 23 adds that liturgical "changes should not be made unless a real and proven need of the church requires them, and care should be taken to see that new forms grow in some way organically out of the forms already existing" (§23).[68]

---

68. For discussion see Bouyer, *The Liturgy Revived*, 51–56.

Paragraph 24 notes that liturgical renewal requires a simultaneous biblical renewal, since the liturgical prayers, collects, hymns, scriptural readings, actions, and signs are intelligible only to those who know Scripture; and paragraph 25 mandates the revision of the liturgical books in consultation with trained liturgical scholars.

Paragraph 26 introduces the way in which the unity and diversity of the Church is liturgically expressed. Paragraph 27 strongly encourages priests to celebrate Mass "with the faithful present and actively participating," even though private Masses are not invalid. Importantly for the limits on the meaning of the active participation of the laity, paragraph 28 affirms that "[d]uring liturgical celebration, everyone, whether minister or in the congregation, should, while carrying out their own role, do all that and only that which is their due—this being determined by the nature of the celebration and by liturgical norms." This statement makes clear that active participation of the laity does not mean their taking over the priest's role.

Against the possible reduction of active participation to interior acts alone, paragraph 29 states that the external acts of serving, reading, and singing constitute "genuine liturgical ministry." Moreover, exterior acts that befit interior devotion are encouraged for the laity. Paragraph 30 states, "In order to encourage their taking an active share [actuosam participationem], acclamations for the people, together with responses, psalmody, antiphons and hymns, should be developed, as well as actions, movements and bodily self-expression. When it is appropriate, a worshipping silence should also be kept."[69] These external acts aim to draw the laity into a deeper unity with the priest's actions, and thereby visibly to unify the liturgical action of priest and people, without confusing the laity's role with the priest's. Along the same lines, paragraph 31 mandates that "[w]hen the books used in the liturgy are being revised, great care is to be taken that the rubrics envisage parts for the people."

Paragraphs 33–36 have to do with the liturgy as a teaching tool, by which believers are instructed. Here *Sacrosanctum Concilium* observes that God speaks to his people in the liturgy, and that "the prayers addressed to

---

69. See ibid., 72–73.

God by the priest, who presides over the gathering in the role of Christ, are said in the name of the entire holy people, and of all who are present" (§33). *Sacrosanctum Concilium* does not use the phrase *active participation* here, but it does emphasize that in all aspects of the liturgy, "the faith of those taking part [participantium] is nourished and their minds raised to God, enabling them to give him free and conscious service [rationabile obsequium: see Romans 12:1] and to receive his grace more abundantly" (§33). This is a description of active participation and its fruits.

Paragraph 34's guidelines for renewal or reform propose that "[t]he rites should radiate a noble simplicity; they should be brief and lucid, avoiding pointless repetitions; they should be intelligible to the people, and should not in general require much explanation." Paragraph 35 then focuses on the connection between word and sacrament. It emphasizes the value of the sermon and mandates a fuller set of biblical readings for the liturgy, so as to set forth the whole of salvation history. Likewise, it mandates instruction during the rite itself, where the rite would otherwise be difficult for the faithful to understand. An expanded use of the vernacular receives approval in paragraph 36. Similarly, inculturation of the liturgy receives encouragement in paragraphs 37–40, with the understanding that "the fundamental unity of the Roman rite is preserved" (§38).

Turning to the role of the bishop and the local church, including parishes, *Sacrosanctum Concilium* articulates the patristic theme of the centrality of the bishop in the diocesan liturgy. It also calls for each diocese to establish a liturgical commission staffed by liturgical experts and supported by pastoral liturgical institutes, along with commissions for art and music (see §§44–46). In this way, the liturgical renewal will enter into the Church at the local level, so that the parish's liturgical life will shape Christian thought and action. This fits with Bouyer's confidence in the fruitfulness of liturgical studies, in light of the Liturgical Movement.

Paragraph 47 inaugurates chapter 2, on "The holy mystery which is the eucharist." After a paragraph commenting on the sacrament of the Eucharist, which serves "to make his sacrifice of the cross last throughout time until he should return," and which is a "sign of unity, a bond of divine love, a special easter meal [convivium paschale]" that recalls Christ's "death and resurrection" (§47), paragraph 48 reiterates the centrality of the need for active participation. It states that "the church devotes careful efforts to prevent christian believers from attending this mystery of faith as though they were outsiders or silent onlookers." Nothing could be closer to Bouyer's fundamental concern. Drawing upon Pope Pius XI's famous phrase, paragraph 48 observes that the laity, "having a good understanding of this mystery, through the ritual and the prayers,... should participate in the sacred action consciously, piously, and actively [sacram actionem conscie, pie et actuose participent]."[70] This active participation should most importantly take the form of an interior union with the Eucharistic prayer spoken by the priest. Thus, according to paragraph 48—here drawing upon paragraphs 98 and 99 of Pope Pius XII's 1947 encyclical *Mediator Dei*—the faithful at Mass should not only "give thanks to God" but also, and more specifically, "should learn to offer themselves as they offer the immaculate victim—not just through the hands of the priest, but also they themselves making the offering together with him."

Paragraphs 49–58 specify particular reforms that seek to encourage a deeper and more active participation of the laity in the Eucharistic liturgy. The rites are to be made simpler, a cycle of Scripture readings developed, the homily strengthened, the prayer of the faithful restored, the vernacular employed, communion under both kinds allowed, and frequent communion encouraged. These reforms have to do with encouraging the laity's external participation, and they are reforms that Bouyer firmly supports. Given the unity of the liturgy of the word and the liturgy of the Eucharist, paragraph 56 calls for priests to urge the faithful "to share in the whole mass," rather than arriving only after the biblical readings and homily have been completed.

Paragraphs 59–82 constitute chapter 3, titled "The other sacraments and sacramentals." Again *Sacrosanctum Concilium*'s focus is upon encouraging a deeper participation on the part of believers. Paragraph 61 explains that "for believers who are suitably open, the liturgy of sacraments and sacramentals brings it about that practically everything which happens in life is sanctified with the grace that flows from the easter mys-

---

70. I have modified Tanner's translation, which reads: "having a good understanding of this mystery, through the ritual and the prayers, they should share in the worshipping event, aware of what is happening and devoutly involved."

tery of Christ's passion, death, and resurrection: the source from which all sacraments and sacramentals draw their power." In the instructions for reform that follow, we find mandates concerning the catechumenate for adults, the rites of adult and infant baptism, the rites of confirmation and penance, the rite of anointing, the rites of ordination, and the rite of marriage. Paragraph 73 teaches that "extreme unction" or "final anointing" should be called "anointing of the sick [unctio infirmorum]" so as to emphasize that it "is not a sacrament exclusively for those who are involved in the final crisis of life and death." Among the paragraphs that address sacramentals, paragraph 80 mandates the review of the rite of consecration of virgins and the establishment of a rite for religious profession and renewal of vows. Paragraph 81 requires that "[t]he funeral rites should express more clearly the paschal character of Christian death."

Chapter 4 includes paragraphs 83–101, and is titled "The divine office." This chapter mainly contains reforms that affect the lives of priests and religious, but it also invites the laity to recite the "divine office," or liturgy of the hours, and it encourages the public celebration of vespers by the laity in local churches and the recitation of the liturgy of the hours in the vernacular. After affirming the value of the liturgy of the hours as rooted in Christ's uniting to himself the "whole human community" and making "it his partner in this divine singing together of a song of praise" (§83), *Sacrosanctum Concilium* mandates some revisions. It suppresses the hour of "prime" and adapts the hour of "matins," while emphasizing the importance of "lauds" and "vespers." It calls for a revision of the psalmody and for a fuller breadth of scriptural readings, along with a better selection of the excerpts from the Fathers and Doctors and more attention to the historical credibility of the excerpts from martyrdom accounts or lives of the saints. With regard to the hymns found in the divine office, they should be restored as much as possible to their original medieval form. The choral obligations of orders of canons, monks, and nuns are specified, and priests are urged to recite a portion of the daily liturgy of the hours as a group rather than solely reciting it individually.

Finally, chapters 5–7 (paragraphs 102–130) offer succinct proposals for reforming the liturgical year, liturgical music, and liturgical art in accord with the principles outlined above. Paragraphs 102–106 describe the liturgical year, whose purpose is to unfold "the whole mystery of Christ over the cycle of the year" (§102), to honor the Virgin Mary, to commemorate martyrs and saints, and in general to form and instruct believers so as to foster active participation. Paragraph 106 lifts up the primary importance of Sunday, "the fundamental feast day" and "a day of rejoicing and of rest from work." Paragraphs 107–111 mandate some revisions of the liturgical year, including the requirement that "the liturgy of the season should be given its proper place above the feasts of the saints" (§108), the requirement that Lent's baptismal elements be foregrounded and that "the consequences of sin in society" (§109) be recognized, a call for public and collective penance during Lent, the keeping of the Paschal fast on Good Friday (and if possible Holy Saturday as well), and the requirement that "[o]nly those feasts commemorating saints whose importance really is universal should be extended over the whole Church" (§111), so as not to overshadow the feasts of the salvific mysteries that should be at the heart of Christian spiritual life.

Regarding music, *Sacrosanctum Concilium* not surprisingly encourages singing by the whole congregation: "When singing is used to heighten the celebration of religious services, with ministers of worship taking part and the people actively joining in [actuose participet], the liturgical activity takes on a richer character" (§113). Paragraph 114 likewise emphasizes that Church leaders must ensure that "the whole gathering of believers are able to take the active part which is proper to them in any event of worship meant to be conducted through song." Paragraph 116 gives primacy to Gregorian chant but allows "[o]ther sorts of sacral music, especially of course polyphony," and stipulates that these forms of music must "fit in with the spirit of the liturgical event [actionis liturgicae]." In paragraph 118, the emphasis on the active participation of the whole congregation appears once more: "Religious singing by the people is to be resourcefully encouraged, so as to enable the voices of believers to ring out in their religious devotions and worship—and indeed in liturgical events [liturgicis actionibus]." Paragraph 119 proposes an inculturation of music, so as to give "suitable scope" to the use of particular cultures' own traditions of music. Paragraph 120 specifies that the pipe organ should have pride of place, but "other instruments may be brought into the worship of God

... insofar as they are suitable for purposes of worship or can be made so, insofar as they cohere with the dignity of the temple, and insofar as they really contribute to the building up of believers." In paragraph 121, lastly, musicians are urged to develop music that, while exhibiting "the characteristics of true worshipping music," serves to "encourage the whole gathering of believers actively to take part." Thus the emphasis on active participation characterizes *Sacrosanctum Concilium*'s instructions on music.

With respect to art, *Sacrosanctum Concilium* observes that while the Church carefully separates out "works of art that are religiously consistent with its traditions of faith, holiness and law, and that are to be regarded as suitable for use in worship" (§122), nonetheless the Church canonizes no form of art but instead uses art from every age. Therefore, paragraph 123 states, "The art of our time also, and the art of every race and part of the world, should be allowed to function freely in the church, provided it is of service to the buildings of worship and the rites of worship, exhibiting due reverence and honour." Paragraph 124 very briefly addresses church architecture, and does so explicitly with active participation as the goal: "when churches are being built, care should be taken to see that they are suitable for the conducting of liturgical events [liturgicas actiones], and for bringing it about that believers actively share in them." Paragraph 128 calls for revisions that address "how churches should be built in a way that is dignified and suitable; the design and construction of altars; the need for the eucharistic tabernacle to be dignified, well positioned and secure; the practicability of having a suitable place for baptism." This paragraph foreshadows changes in church architecture, but in a broad way, in accord with the following principle: "What seems to be less in keeping with the renewed liturgy should be corrected or abolished; what in fact suits it should be kept or introduced."

Conclusion: *Sacrosanctum Concilium* as an Ongoing Theological Event

It should be clear that Bouyer and *Sacrosanctum Concilium* share a strong concern to enhance the active participation of the laity in the Eucharistic liturgy, preeminently interior participation but also external participation.[71] Bouyer and *Sacrosanctum Concilium* also seek to hold together word and sacrament, sacrifice and meal, and eschatology and remembrance. Furthermore, just as Bouyer is highly critical of the predominant modes of celebrating the preconciliar Roman liturgy, *Sacrosanctum Concilium* likewise mandates a number of alterations and favors significant reform, not only with regard to the liturgy of the Eucharist but also with regard to the other sacramental rites, the sacramentals, the liturgy of the hours, Church music and architecture, and so forth. In almost every instance, the motivation of these reforms consists in enabling believers to share more deeply in the Church's liturgical participation in Christ's Paschal mystery. Unlike Bouyer, *Sacrosanctum Concilium* does not mention facing east together, though it does call for an interior union of the laity with the priest during the Eucharistic prayer. Here the goal is that "during the sacrifice of the mass, we pray the Lord, 'to receive the offering of the spiritual victim', and then raise 'our very selves' to their perfection in becoming 'an eternal gift' for himself" (§12).[72]

In connecting active participation with priest and people facing east together, Bouyer in 1967 was swimming against the current. Among liturgical specialists in 1967, the prevalent opinion about active participation was the one that Jack Wintz and John Feister, citing *Sacrosanctum Concilium* §14, describe approvingly (in 2005) as follows: "Before Vatican II, the priest celebrated Mass in Latin with his back to the people, making the action of the Mass seem far away. It was easy for the faithful to fall into the role of spectators. Now the assembly is more actively engaged, helping us to experience 'all of us' celebrating the Eucharist with the priest."[73] As an enthusiastic pro-

---

71. With regard to the relationship of external and internal liturgical participation, Pamela Jackson rightly observes, "The Council's liturgical reforms restored various forms of external participation to make it easier for worshippers to participate internally in the spiritual realities mediated by the liturgy" (Jackson, *An Abundance of Graces*, 58). At the same time, Jackson describes "the first goal of the Liturgical Movement" as the fostering of "intelligent internal participation in the Church's liturgical worship" (ibid., 60). For a similar perspective, see Clara Dina Hinojosa's "Full, Conscious and Active Participation," in *Full, Conscious and Active Participation: Celebrating Twenty-Five Years of Today's Liturgy*, ed. Michael R. Prendergast (Portland, Ore.: Pastoral Press, 2003), 5–11.

72. The interior quotations come from the Roman Missal, prayer over the gifts for Monday within the octave of Pentecost.

73. Jack Wintz, OFM, and John Feister, "Road Map for the Future: Teachings of Vatican II," in *Vatican II Today: Calling Catholics to Holiness and Service*, ed. Judy Ball and Joan McKamey

ponent of *Sacrosanctum Concilium*, Bouyer helps us to appreciate the document as an ongoing theological event, because he presses us to specify what we mean by liturgical "active participation" in Christ's Paschal mystery.

The Episcopalian scholar Richard Kieckhefer observes that when *Liturgy and Architecture* "appeared in 1967, Bouyer was seeking many of the same goals as other reformers. He was as insistent as anyone on overcoming the clericalist approach to liturgy, with its assumption that liturgy is something done by the clergy on behalf of the laity."[74] Kieckhefer notes that as a young scholar, Bouyer had advocated the celebration of the Eucharist facing the people. But while other anti-clericalist liturgical reformers continued to hold that to have the priest face the congregation would be the best way to enhance the active participation of the laity in the liturgy, by 1967 "Bouyer envisioned more venturesome ways to attain the reformers' goals."[75] Kieckhefer thinks that Bouyer's broad historical knowledge gave Bouyer an unusually wide perception of the various options available in pursuing the goals of liturgical reform.[76]

The Catholic liturgist and church-designer Richard Vosko bemoans the fact that, with regard to church art and architecture, "[d]ifferent camps have arisen since Vatican II, each with its arguments. The feelings are deep and it may take generations before a common ground is realized. Unfortunately the eucharistic liturgy has become the touchstone for these disagreements."[77] Vosko lists four basic principles set forth by the central conciliar and post-

---

(Cincinnati, Ohio: St. Anthony Messenger Press, 2005), 1–9, at 4. See also Charles Miller, *Liturgy for the People of God*, vol. 1, *Foundations of Vatican II Liturgy*, 103–4.

74. Richard Kieckhefer, *Theology in Stone: Church Architecture from Byzantium to Berkeley* (Oxford: Oxford University Press, 2004), 281. When Bouyer served on the Commission that reformed the liturgy in the year following the Council, he was deeply disappointed by what he found to be the "claim of recasting from top to bottom and in a few months an entire liturgy it had taken twenty centuries to develop," and he has scathing things to say about the leading figure in overseeing the reform, Archbishop Annibale Bugnini (Bouyer, *The Memoirs of Louis Bouyer: From Youth and Conversion to Vatican II, the Liturgical Reform, and After*, trans. John Pepino [Kettering, Ohio: Angelico Press, 2015], 219; cf. 224–25). His concerns about the "hasty reform" of the liturgy—a revision that he nonetheless grants has "excellent elements" and "scattered pearls"—do not touch upon *Sacrosanctum Concilium*, whose theological perspective and program of reform retained his support (Bouyer, *Memoirs*, 221, 224).

75. Kieckhefer, *Theology in Stone*, 281.

76. See ibid., 281, 292.

77. Richard S. Vosko, *God's House Is Our House: Re-imagining the Environment for Worship* (Collegeville, Minn.: Liturgical Press, 2006), xi.

conciliar documents: (1) the universal call to holiness, (2) the Church as the sacrament of unity, (3) the obligation of the baptized "to participate in worship as partners and not spectators," and (4) the necessity that architecture reflect the above three points.[78] Writing in 2005, Vosko warns that "[o]n the liturgical front some church authorities and laity clearly wish to return to a pre-Conciliar mode," which Vosko associates with clericalist emphasis on the role of the priest in the liturgy.[79] In accord with the need to encourage the active participation of the laity in the liturgy, Vosko emphasizes, much like Bouyer, that "a worthy worship place does not begin with an architectural or artistic idea but a liturgical one. Thus the building must first serve the worship of the assembly and foster its engagement."[80] Vosko's liturgical ideas allow for the distinction between priest and people but seek to minimize it where possible, as does Bouyer through his emphasis on the priest and people being in close proximity during the Eucharistic prayer. Much like Bouyer, Vosko holds that "care should be taken not to create a sense of division between clergy and laity especially at the eucharistic table."[81] Like Bouyer, too, Vosko is critical of the way in which the liturgy developed in the medieval and Baroque eras. He states in this regard that "as the laity participated less and less during the liturgy they became preoccupied with their private prayers or with the pageantry carried out by the clergy and choir."[82]

In underscoring the need for "active, conscious participation," however, Vosko argues that churches should be designed so that the altar is in the middle, surrounded on all sides (in a circular way) by the pews of the congregation.[83] In his view, this design "can and most often does create the kind of worship setting where the participation of the whole congregation is expected."[84] By contrast, he considers that noncircular churches in which rows of pews all face the altar from the same direction have adopted a design that "discourages and often makes impossible the participation expected of every member of the assembly."[85] Moreover, he argues that such designs "convey quite a different notion of the church from those favored by the Council," because they favor a clericalist notion of the Church.[86]

78. Ibid.
80. Ibid., xv.
82. Ibid., 91.
84. Ibid.
86. Ibid.

79. Ibid., xiv.
81. Ibid., 95.
83. Ibid., 58.
85. Ibid., 59.

The differences between Bouyer and Vosko in this respect are not as wide as might first seem to be the case. Bouyer certainly thought that rows of pews all facing the altar from the same direction was far from ideal and could foster a clericalist understanding of the liturgy.[87] Vosko seeks to overcome clericalist understandings of the liturgy by encircling the priest with the people, whereas Bouyer advocates arranging the people in a semicircle close by the priest. But for Bouyer this arrangement does not fully address the problem of active participation in the Eucharistic liturgy, because he considers that facing the altar together and facing east together are a significant part of participating actively in the eschatological action that is the Eucharistic liturgy.[88] By facing east together in close proximity to one another, priest and people face toward the Christ who will come in glory. According to Bouyer, the congregation thereby signifies that even now it is sharing in the eschatological heavenly banquet of the Lord. Altar and table are joined together, and in participating in the sacrificial offering, we participate in the meal.

Joseph Ratzinger insightfully remarks in his 1999 book *The Spirit of the Liturgy* that "if we want to discover the kind of doing that active participation involves, we need, first of all, to determine what this central *actio* is in which all the members of the community are supposed to participate."[89] Ratzinger observes that the liturgy enables us to participate in Christ's sacrificial self-offering, so that in the liturgy "the difference between the *actio Christi* and our own action is done away with. There is only *one* action, which is at the same time his and ours—ours because we have become 'one body and one spirit' with him."[90] Caught up in the Trinitarian life, believers

---

87. In my view, such an outcome is unlikely.

88. Vosko's theological reflections are often cliché-ridden and vague in their reference. Thus in his afterword he remarks that "the Church has grown into a powerful institution. Now it is going through a challenging time of transition. The old paradigms are changing. The future of the Church will depend not only on respecting tradition but also using the imagination. The objective is to build upon foundations in order to rise to new heights. This is why all matters pertaining to worship are important. We have learned that the liturgical life of the Church is both a source and a summit. The roots are well known but the destination is not. The quest just might be found in the journey" (ibid., 231).

89. Joseph Ratzinger, *The Spirit of the Liturgy*, trans. John Saward (San Francisco: Ignatius Press, 2000), 171.

90. Ibid., 174. Thus, Ratzinger concludes that "if the liturgy degenerates into general activity, then we have radically misunderstood the 'theo-drama' of the liturgy and lapsed almost into parody. True liturgical education cannot consist in learning and experimenting with external activities. Instead one

give thanks to the Father, through-with-in Christ our Head, in the Holy Spirit. Believers do so in communion with the heavenly liturgy (which we yearn to join), with all the earthly communities of the whole Church (we name the bishop of our diocese and the pope as the head of the universal college of bishops), and with those believers now undergoing purgation. Centrally, our thanksgiving is motivated by and shares in the Paschal sacrifice of Christ, which is made present in the Mass. Thus active participation primarily means devout interior participation in the Eucharistic prayer, though it includes exterior acts as well.

The differences among the above scholars—and many others could be named—make clear that the theological event of *Sacrosanctum Concilium* is still ongoing. All parties in the discussion agree with the insistence of *Sacrosanctum Concilium* that the whole assembly is called to active liturgical participation in Christ's Paschal mystery, and that this is the central goal of liturgical reform. Most agree, too, that the active participation of the laity in the liturgy does not imply a contest between priest and laity over who has more "active agency."[91] *Sacrosanctum Concilium* demonstrates that we are *all* called in the liturgy to participate actively in Christ's Paschal mystery, though in different modes, in accord with the differentiation between the baptismal and ministerial priesthood. Disagreements remain about how best to strengthen the active liturgical participation of the laity in Christ's Paschal mystery, and in my view there are advantages to the priest and people facing east together during the Eucharistic prayer. But no matter how this matter is settled, the ongoing theological event of *Sacrosanctum Concilium* grounds us in the central liturgical desideratum: that all Christians, united liturgically in Christ's Pasch, interiorly offer our "bodies as a living sacrifice, holy and acceptable to God, which is [our] spiritual worship" (Rom 12:1).

---

must be led toward the essential *actio* that makes the liturgy what it is, toward the transforming power of God, who wants, through what happens in the liturgy, to transform us and the world" (ibid., 175).

91. For the tug-of-war over "active agency," see Vincent J. Miller, *Consuming Religion: Christian Faith and Practice in a Consumer Culture* (New York: Continuum, 2004), 215. Miller is focusing on "how the liturgy can serve as a setting for lay practice and a formation for lay agency outside the liturgy" and, in this context, his account of active agency emphasizes that "a fundamental asymmetry remains between the passive scripted style of liturgical agency and the active, creative application of the wisdom of the tradition to daily life envisioned for the laity outside of the eucharistic gathering" (ibid., 214, 217).

CHAPTER 3

TRUE AND FALSE REFORM

Lumen Gentium in Context

In her *Mystery of the Church, People of God: Yves Congar's Total Ecclesiology as a Path to Vatican II*, Rose Beal shows that Congar's unpublished treatise *De Ecclesia* profoundly shaped the key chapters of *Lumen Gentium*.[1] For Congar as for *Lumen Gentium*, the mission of the Church is to enable the whole world to enter into the people of God, which is the body of Christ and the temple of the Spirit. Beal considers that "[i]n its main lines, the Second Vatican Council achieved the ecclesiology that Congar had sought for decades."[2] She adds that Congar, after the Council, found himself defending elements of the Church that he had taken more for granted prior to the Council, notably "the incorporation of the

---

1. Rose M. Beal, *Mystery of the Church, People of God: Yves Congar's Total Ecclesiology as a Path to Vatican II* (Washington, D.C.: The Catholic University of America Press, 2014).
2. Ibid., 214.

hierarchy as a necessary part of an ecclesiological synthesis"—an element that receives full appreciation in *Lumen Gentium*.[3]

In Yves Congar's *True and False Reform in the Church* (1950, revised edition 1968), which influenced Pope John XXIII's decision to call the Second Vatican Council and which has been called Congar's "most original book and the most important,"[4] Congar states that the widespread desire for reform of the Church is "the fruit of a deep Christian consciousness coming to grips with human reality and with the apostolic needs of the present. It is not about intellectual or aesthetic exercises, nor is it concerned about some false notion that the church might have mistaken the faith and that it might be necessary to lead it dogmatically back to the gospel."[5] The same confidence that the Church has not misunderstood the content of faith, and the same desire to engage present-day apostolic needs, is found in *Lumen Gentium*. This Constitution should be read in light of the reforming impulses to which Congar alludes, since *Lumen Gentium* seeks to restore the bishops to their full apostolic position vis-à-vis the pope and seeks also a renewal of the place of the laity in the Church, not least through an insistence upon the universal call to

---

3. Ibid., 215.

4. Jean-Pierre Jossua, OP, personal letter to Gabriel Flynn, cited in Flynn, "Yves Congar and Catholic Church Reform: A Renewal of the Spirit," in *Yves Congar: Theologian of the Church*, ed. Gabriel Flynn (Leuven: Peeters, 2005), 99–133, at 133n113.

5. Yves Congar, OP, *True and False Reform in the Church*, trans. Paul Philibert, OP (Collegeville, Minn.: Liturgical Press, 2011), 337. For discussion of Congar's ecclesiology in *True and False Reform in the Church*, see also Aidan Nichols, OP, *Yves Congar* (London: Geoffrey Chapman, 1989), chapter 10; as well as Joseph Famerée, *L'ecclésiologie d'Yves Congar avant Vatican II. Analyse et reprise critique* (Louvain: Louvain University Press, 1992). Paul Philibert observes: "It is clear that Archbishop Angelo Roncalli (later to become Pope John XXIII) discovered and read *True and False Reform* during his years as papal nuncio in France. He asked in response to reading it, 'A reform of the church: is such a thing really possible?' A decade later, he presided over the opening of the Second Vatican Council which he had convened. In his opening address at the council, he described its goals in terms highly evocative of Congar's description of authentic reform" (Philibert, "Translator's Introduction," in Congar, *True and False Reform in the Church*, xi–xvi, at xii). For crucial background, see also Jared Wicks, SJ, "Tridentine Motivations of Angello Roncalli/Pope John XXIII before and during Vatican II," *Theological Studies* 75 (2014): 847–62; Wicks, "Vatican II Taking Hold of Its (and Pope John's) Council Goals, September 1962–May 1963," *Josephinum Journal of Theology* 19 (2012): 172–86. See also, for creative ways of connecting Trent (and the Tridentine period) and Vatican II, while differentiating them in accord with the new challenges that Vatican II seeks to address, George Weigel, *Evangelical Catholicism: Deep Reform in the 21st-Century Church* (New York: Basic Books, 2013); Thomas Joseph White, OP, "The Tridentine Genius of Vatican II," *First Things*, no. 227 (November 2012): 25–30.

holiness. *Lumen Gentium* should also be read in light of Congar's rejection of the "notion that the church might have mistaken the faith and that it might be necessary to lead it dogmatically back to the gospel." The Constitution exhibits serene confidence in the divine foundation of the Church, the holiness of its divine gifts, and the truthfulness of its proclamation of faith.

In the preconciliar period and the first year of the Council, Congar was sometimes thought to have overemphasized the element of reform. In his posthumously published *My Journal of the Council*, he records on 9 December 1962 that Cardinal "Ottaviani reproaches me for saying sometimes good things, sometimes bad things in my *Vraie et fausse Réforme*."[6] Although Congar does not say what the "good things" are, they likely have to do with Congar's insistence upon the unchanging divine elements of the Church,[7] whereas the "bad things" are likely his reform proposals. For Ottaviani, Congar complains, "Everything [that the Curia says or does] is praiseworthy, everything must be praised. They know only ONE line: the one that is homogeneous and favourable to the assertion of their authority."[8]

Joyfully, Congar perceived in early February 1963 that Pope "John XIII's idea" was "to make the Church move into a largely collegial and episcopal way of operating.... It really seems that the internal result of the Council will be this: to put in place WORLD-WIDE organisms and no longer simply Romano-Catholic ones."[9] From an early stage, Congar was involved

---

6. Yves Congar, OP, *My Journal of the Council*, trans. Mary John Ronayne, OP, and Mary Cecily Boulding, OP, ed. Denis Minns, OP (Collegeville, Minn.: Liturgical Press, 2012), 249.

7. Indebted to Congar, Avery Dulles observes: "From the Catholic perspective, the Church is intrinsically holy in its formal or constituent elements—the word of God, the sacraments, the ecclesiastical office, and the gifts and graces bestowed by the Holy Spirit, who has been poured forth upon the Church as its life-giving principle" (Avery Dulles, SJ, "Church, Ministry, and Sacraments in Catholic-Evangelical Dialogue," in *Catholics and Evangelicals: Do They Share a Common Future?*, ed. Thomas P. Rausch, SJ [New York: Paulist Press, 2000], 108).

8. Congar, *My Journal of the Council*, 249.

9. Ibid., 255. For Congar's understanding of Councils, see his "The Council as an Assembly and the Church as Essentially Conciliar," trans. Alain Woodrow, in *One, Holy, Catholic and Apostolic: Studies on the Nature and Role of the Church in the Modern World*, ed. Herbert Vorgrimler (London: Sheed and Ward, 1968), 44–88. In reflecting upon Karl Rahner, SJ's contention that Vatican II inaugurated the "world church," John W. O'Malley, SJ, observes: "What is striking about Vatican II is not any prominent role played by 'the new churches' of former colonies but how dominated it was by Europeans. The leading figures were almost exclusively from the Continent, and those few that were not,

in consultations regarding the schema *De Ecclesia* that would become *Lumen Gentium*. Late in 1962, Congar urged in the pages of his journal that the Council "ought to limit itself to ONE question only, namely a treatise on the Church, in itself and in relation to the world."[10] Meeting in early January 1963 with the influential Belgians Émile de Smedt and Gérard Philips, along with Cardinal Léon-Joseph Suenens, Congar helped to work out a four-chapter structure for *De Ecclesia*, focusing on the mystery of the Church, the bishops, the laity, and Mary. At another January 1963 meeting, this time with Philips, Edward Schillebeeckx, Piet Smulders, Joseph Ratzinger, Karl Rahner, Alois Grillmeier, Otto Semmelroth, and Rudolph Schnackenburg, Congar discussed and critiqued the German proposal for *De Ecclesia*. In his entry for 4 March 1963, similarly, he reports spending three enjoyable hours with Philips, Charles Moeller, and Rahner working on "a new version of Chapter II of *De Ecclesia*."[11]

At the very end of the Council, in his entry for 7 December 1965, Congar looks back at the Council and sums up his work. In addition to his contributions to consultations and his work in helping to draft numerous chapters, including a number of chapters of *Lumen Gentium*, he observes that "objectively, I did a great deal to prepare for the Council, elaborating and diffusing the ideas that the Council consecrated."[12] This assessment is accurate. As John O'Malley points out, Congar "was brought to Rome by John XXIII for the preparatory work for the council. Once the council got under way, he became an almost ubiquitously influential *peritus*. He

---

like the American Jesuit John Courtney Murray and Archbishop Paul-Émile Léger of Montreal, were European in the broad sense. The council was even more deeply Eurocentric in that the issues it dealt with originated in the history of Western Europe. Europe, its concerns, and the legacy of its history provided the framework within which Vatican II operated" (O'Malley, "What Happened and Did Not Happen at Vatican II," in O'Malley, *Catholic History for Today's Church: How Our Past Illuminates Our Present* [Lanham, Md.: Rowman and Littlefield, 2015], 115–32, at 116; cf. Rahner, "Towards a Fundamental Theological Interpretation of Vatican II," *Theological Studies* 40 [1979]: 716–27, especially 718, 724). With Catholic Christianity now reduced in Europe to relatively few active believers, and with an Argentinian—Pope Francis—as Bishop of Rome, it is providential that (as O'Malley goes on to say) "a wider vista was trying to break through" at the Council (O'Malley, "What Happened and Did Not Happen at Vatican II," 117). For a recent example of this vibrant "wider vista," rooted in the scriptural testimony to divine revelation, see Cardinal Robert Sarah et al., *Christ's New Homeland—Africa: Contribution to the Synod on the Family by African Pastors*, trans. Michael J. Miller (San Francisco: Ignatius Press, 2015).

10. Congar, *My Journal of the Council*, 235.   11. Ibid., 265.
12. Ibid., 870.

was sought for his opinion on almost every major issue before the assembly."[13] The result was that, in the words of Gabriel Flynn, "his thought is enshrined in its [the Council's] pivotal documents."[14]

Throughout his life, Congar consistently opposed a vision of the Church in which the pope alone is the center, to the diminishment of other elements of the Church such as the bishops and the laity.[15] In so doing, he may have left himself vulnerable, at least when his writings came to be employed by thinkers less committed to Scripture and Tradition than himself, to the weaknesses of what he termed the "anti-Roman attitude."[16] But in opposing an overemphasis on the papacy, Congar rightly understood himself to be insisting upon two unchanging divine elements of the Church, namely the bishops' full stature as successors of the apostles and the priesthood of all believers.

In an article in the first issue of *Concilium*, published in 1964, Congar offers a richly biblical and theological portrait of the "people of God," fully including the hierarchy and understood Christologically through the

---

13. John W. O'Malley, SJ, *What Happened at Vatican II* (Cambridge, Mass.: Harvard University Press, 2008), 119–20.

14. Flynn, "Yves Congar and Catholic Church Reform," 101. See also Gabriel Flynn, "*Mon Journal du Concile*: Yves Congar and the Battle for a Renewed Ecclesiology at the Second Vatican Council," *Louvain Studies* 28 (2003): 48–70; J. J. Scarisbrick, "An Historian's Reflections on Yves Congar's *Mon Journal du Concile*," in *Yves Congar*, ed. Gabriel Flynn, 249–75.

15. See, for example, Congar, *My Journal of the Council*, 874.

16. See Hans Urs von Balthasar, *The Office of Peter and the Structure of the Church*, trans. Andrée Emery (San Francisco: Ignatius Press, 1986 [original German ed. 1974]), 182, quoting the first edition of Congar's *Vraie et fausse réforme dans l'Église* (Paris: Cerf, 1950), 69–70. With regard to the deep strife and general collapse of faith after the Council, especially in Europe (a phenomenon already emerging in 1965, and still plaguing the Church today), J. J. Scarisbrick suggests that Congar, like many reformers, was naïve about the impact that his ideas, however valid, would have upon rank-and-file believers (and about the way some of his ideas would be misused by "radical liberals" in the Church): "No one could have predicted the size of the disasters which befell the Church in the wake of the Council. But we can legitimately ask whether Congar was as sensitive as he should have been to the seriously unsettling effect on many good, devout souls of the rapid changes which he had vigorously promoted. In a very revealing passage early in the *Diary* he reports that Italian bishops were said to be 'bewildered' because the Council has thrown into doubt so much that they had taken as 'classiques et sacrées.' What they were saying was truly ominous. One cannot help wondering whether it was exactly such feelings, more intense perhaps, which later caused so many priests and religious, male and female, to quit. So much that they had been taught to regard as important, distinctive, precious and, if not *de fide*, then non-negotiable, had been discarded or demoted, that it was easy to wonder whether much else would soon be jettisoned.... Faced with the Italians' dilemma, Congar showed neither comprehension nor sympathy" (Scarisbrick, "An Historian's Reflections on Yves Congar's *Mon Journal du Concile*," 269–70).

image of the Body of Christ.[17] Congar conceived of his own position as reformist, but rooted always in a desire for "the church's complete return to the Gospel."[18] On this view, true reform means a "return to the Gospel," which ceaselessly renews the Church in history. Thus, in the 1968 edition of *True and False Reform in the Church*, Congar praises *Lumen Gentium* for presenting "the church coming forth from God, but committed to human history as it moves laboriously to its culmination,"[19] since *Lumen Gentium* thereby exhibits the ecclesiology that true reform requires: the Church exists as "at once holy and always in need of purification" and as following "the path of penance and renewal" (§8).

In order to introduce *Lumen Gentium* as an ongoing theological event, therefore, this chapter begins by examining the first two parts of Congar's *True and False Reform in the Church*. As a second step, I survey the paragraphs of *Lumen Gentium* in light of Congar's work on true and false reform, since the doctrinal teaching of *Lumen Gentium* reforms earlier understandings of constitutive elements of the Church and does so in a "true" manner, namely one that illumines rather than undermines the Church's enduring divine gifts of dogma, sacraments, and hierarchical offices.[20] As Avery Dulles rightly observes, "Vatican II could almost be called Congar's Council."[21]

17. See Yves Congar, OP, "The Church: The People of God," in *The Church and Mankind: Dogma*, ed. Hans Küng and Edward Schillebeeckx, OP, Concilium, vol. 1 (Glen Rock, N.J.: Paulist Press, 1964), 11–37. See also Congar's *Le Concile de Vatican II. Son église: Peuple de Dieu et corps du Christ* (Paris: Beauchesne, 1984).

18. Congar, *True and False Reform in the Church*, 5. For Congar's postconciliar assessments on how to interpret the Council, see Andrew Meszaros, "Vatican II as Theological Event and Text according to Yves Congar," forthcoming in the *Josephinum Journal of Theology*. Note that Congar eschews a *historicist* view, according to which no "return" to the "Gospel" would be possible—since rather than allowing for a unified "Gospel," historicism perceives an irreducible diversity of texts and perspectives emerging out of specific cultural contexts that can no longer be returned to in any meaningful way.

19. Congar, *True and False Reform in the Church*, 80.

20. My purpose is not to suggest that *Lumen Gentium* is an *action-plan* for reforming the Church, since in fact the conciliar Decrees (not *Lumen Gentium*) are where we find specific mandates for renewed practice. For the relationship of *Lumen Gentium* to the specific practical mandates for reform found in the Decrees of Vatican II, see Jared Wicks, SJ, "Vatican II in 1964: Major Doctrinal Advances, but Also Fissures on Addressing the Modern World," *Josephinum Journal of Theology* 20 (2013): 4–19, at 10–12.

21. Avery Dulles, SJ, "Yves Congar: In Appreciation," *America* 173 (15 July 1995): 6–7. For a succinct introduction to the contributions of Congar and other figures of the *nouvelle théologie*, see

Yves Congar's *True and False Reform in the Church*

In *True and False Reform in the Church* (I employ the 1968 second edition, whose main lines are unchanged from the original 1950 edition), Yves Congar cites a number of articles from the decades prior to 1950 that beg for Church reform, articles written by theologians from Germany and Austria who asked at least for freedom of discussion. Congar does not doubt that the Church is in need of such criticism and reform. He thinks that since the sixteenth century, the Church has been overly sensitive to public criticism, which the Church has perceived as a threat to its very foundations rather than as constructive criticism by loyal and obedient Catholics. Congar also thinks that apologists have often deified the Church as though the Church were perfect, when in fact it is obviously imperfect. At the same time, he holds that "love of the church" is required for good criticism, as is—most importantly—"a return to the sources of theological and pastoral thinking within the living rivers of a Catholic tradition rediscovered in its deepest expressions."[22] These "living rivers" have divine revelation as their ever-present fount, and thus the Church's teaching is no merely human work. Although he hopes for reform of certain structures and habits into which the Church (especially since Trent) has fallen, therefore, Congar has no doubt that secular "ideas of the 'outdated' or of 'change' do not bear upon Christianity in itself or upon its dogmas and its hierarchical structure."[23] These unchangeable elements are divine both in origin and in the realities they make manifest.

What true reform should do, then, is to enable the Church to mediate the divine realities more fully, and thereby enable the Church to be human not in a fallen way but in a sanctified way. In 1950, Congar gives the example of the liturgy: "People want a Mass that is genuinely the praise and the self-offering of a community united in faith, not just a ritual that goes its own way page after page as people, who may or may not follow

---

Gerald O'Collins, SJ, "*Ressourcement* and Vatican II," in *Ressourcement: A Movement for Renewal in Twentieth-Century Catholic Theology*, ed. Gabriel Flynn and Paul D. Murray (Oxford: Oxford University Press, 2012), 372–91. As a friend accurately told Congar on November 13, 1965, "You are winning all along the line" (reported in Yves Congar, OP, *My Journal of the Council*, 841).

22. Congar, *True and False Reform in the Church*, 35, 40.

23. Ibid., 45.

the Mass, watch."[24] The goal is for people to enter fully into the divine mysteries mediated by the Church, rather than merely to watch, uncomprehending, as such mysteries pass by. The same holds, Congar points out, for dogma: it must become real for believers, not merely abstract. Congar suggests that the problem often has to do with accretions that the Church has received over the centuries and that can now be mistaken for necessary elements of the Church. These accretions obscure the authentic manifestation of the gospel, and thereby play into the hands of cultural critics of Christianity who see hypocrisy and artifice everywhere. As Congar puts the problem, "it is truly difficult to think in an evangelical way when one carries the weight of triumphalism, prestige, certainty, and power."[25]

From this perspective, chapter 1 of *True and False Reform in the Church* examines "The Church's Holiness and Our Failures." He begins by contrasting the patristic vision of the Church (which lasted through the first millennium) with our modern perspective. For the Fathers, the Church was "a descent to earth of heavenly realities," "a mystery of holiness," a Spirit-filled body constituted visibly by the sacraments, and thus "a divine reality."[26] The divine reality of the Church was not merely limited to the interior dimension of the Church, since the Church was viewed as a unified whole whose public, exterior dimension could not be easily distinguished from an interior, mystical dimension. Reconciliation itself was public and social, not a private, individual affair. The Church was seen as truly excellent, and it was so, by comparison with the pagan world. Tradition was valued over novelty in every domain. Since the Church was viewed in this way, the personal failings and hypocrisies of individual believers did not threaten people's view of the Church in the way that such personal failings do in the subjectivity-focused culture of modernity.

Congar observes that the modern focus on personal authenticity has produced criticism not only of individual hypocrites but also of the whole Church. In 1950, he points to the scandal caused by the Church's rejection of modern historical progress, which appears inauthentic to modern people because it denies the obvious "truth that reality has this dimension of becoming."[27] The Church seems repressive and fortress-like against the

24. Ibid., 46.
26. Ibid., 55.
25. Ibid., 49.
27. Ibid., 59.

new-found freedoms and privileges of humanity. And at the same time, the Church now understands itself differently from the way that the patristic Church did: the Church now seems to be focused on its juridical ecclesiastical structures, rather than on participatory expression of the heavenly mysteries. Ecumenically, Congar finds that Catholics today, in their quest for authenticity, "have become more sensitive to the weaknesses of their church," more willing to admit its historical and present-day faults.[28]

Congar then embarks upon a more detailed tour of the ecclesiology of not only the Fathers, but also the Bible and the Magisterium. Biblically speaking, Israel understood itself as a sinful people; whereas Christ inaugurated the kingdom of saints, but a kingdom that is not yet consummated and that therefore still contains both wheat and weeds. Paul is painfully aware of the extent of sinfulness among his communities—both personal sin and ecclesial divisions caused by false doctrine—despite his equal assurance of the power of the Spirit. The same thing is found in the letters of John and in the Book of Revelation. Congar argues that the Church is more, though not less, than the Israelite people of God: the Church is now "the Body of Christ, the Spouse of Christ."[29] For Congar, the phrase "people of God" conveys the (fallen human) fallibleness to which the people of Israel admitted, whereas the phrase "Body of Christ" conveys the Church's Spirit-filled faithful mediation of truth.

For their part, the Fathers think of the Church in terms of the moon, enlightened and made holy not by its own resources (which are dark) but by the divine Sun; and they also think of the Church in terms of the Bride of Christ, sinful in itself but purified and made virginal by Christ. The key is that, whatever the sins of the members, "the Spirit remains forever in the church, which remains forever holy because of this."[30] Although the Church is holy, its holiness does not come from its members (who are sinners), but from its Head, who works by the grace of the Spirit, through the holy sacraments and holy teachings, to incorporate his members ful-

---

28. Ibid., 61.
29. Ibid., 69.
30. Ibid., 73. See also Congar's later study, *I Believe in the Holy Spirit*, 3 vols., trans. David Smith (New York: Crossroad, 1997).

ly into himself, a process that will not be completed until the eschaton. Congar sums up by saying that the Fathers "showed that there is an incorruptible sanctity which comes to the church from its faith, from the sacraments, and from the hierarchical powers of the priesthood," despite the evident sinfulness of the Church's members, for which the Church continually repents.[31]

This way of understanding the divine and (fallen) human dimensions of the Church enabled the leaders of the Council of Trent, as Congar shows, to insist upon the culpability of the bishops for causing the scandalous situation to which the Protestant Reformation responded, without thereby speaking of a sinful Church. In more recent papal statements, says Congar, there is a general admission of the guilt of the Church's leaders, but the divine mission and holiness of the Church per se are not questioned. Here, in the 1968 text, Congar takes the opportunity also to cite *Lumen Gentium* at some length. The point is that since the Church is not only divine but also (fallen) human, it constantly needs reform.

Congar next reflects speculatively upon the holiness of the Church. He observes that since God is infinitely holy, the Church can be holy only insofar as it participates in God. As he says, "If the church is holy and infallible in itself, that is only insofar as it is *from God*; it is so according to the aspect that it comes *from God*, and to the degree that it is *of God*."[32] Insofar as the Word incarnate and the Spirit teach and sanctify in the Church, the Church is holy. But insofar as the Church "is from us, it is subject to our limitations and our failures."[33] As Congar points out, the difficulty consists in distinguishing the divine and human elements without, as it were, dividing the Church in two. Given that the Church is obviously human, how can we say that the Church itself does not sin, without positing a hidden Church-within-the-Church?

In response, Congar makes some important distinctions. First, the Church can be seen as the congregation of believers. This emphasizes the human element. But the Church also communicates the faith to believers, and here we see the divine element as mediated and possessed by humans.

---

31. Congar, *True and False Reform in the Church*, 76.
32. Ibid., 83.
33. Ibid., 84.

Similarly, the Church is made up of the baptized, and yet the Church bestows baptism. We easily see the congregation of baptized believers, and we know that they are sinners (albeit being sanctified). It is more difficult to perceive the Church that is in some way prior to believers, that is to say the Church that gives faith and that gives baptism. Congar emphasizes that there is "a reality of the church *as mystery*, anterior to its reality as *congregatio (collectio) fidelium*."[34] The Church is already present in Christ, both in God's eternal plan and at the moment of the Incarnation, when Christ becomes Head of the entirety of humanity. Furthermore, the means by which Christ builds up his Church are prior to the congregation of believers. Congar identifies these holy means as "the deposit of faith (and principally the revelation of the Holy Trinity); the sacraments of the faith, instituted by Jesus Christ, as the means for being united to the mystery of his passage to the Father; and, finally, the ministries or apostolic powers."[35]

In this context, Congar addresses the question whether the Church existed already in Israel. He thinks it did, but Jesus lifted up the people of God in the new covenant, by revealing the fullness of faith (the Trinity) and by giving both the sacraments, whose power comes from his Passion, and the apostolic powers with their prophetic, priestly, and royal office—as well as by sending his Spirit upon the Church at Pentecost. The Church, then, is holy in its divine "faith and its sacramental life," as well as in its offices.[36] But this holiness must then be truly communicated to the believers who are the members of the Church, and thus who are the Church. These believers are sinners being sanctified. When believers are fully sanctified, in the eschaton, then finally "the church will be the *true* temple, the *true* spouse, and the integral Body of Christ—the *whole* Christ."[37]

According to Congar, if one insists upon speaking of the Church only in its aspect of mystery, its divine aspect, then one practices a "*theology of glory*" that falsifies the Church.[38] When the Church is looked at from the

---

34. Ibid., 85.
35. Ibid., 85–86.
36. Ibid., 86.
37. Ibid., 87.
38. Ibid. A "theology of glory" is a disparaging phrase coined by Martin Luther as a contrast to an appropriate "theology of the cross."

side of its members (who are indeed the Church), the Church is caught up in sin and in need of constant reform. It is only when the Church is looked at from the side of the means of salvation, which the Church possesses in Christ, that the Church is holy. Both perspectives on the Church are correct; both speak about the real, visible Church. As Congar states, "It is the same church that is the people of God destined to a historical existence and that is also a divine institution as the universal sacrament of salvation."[39] The Church cannot be divided into a visible and an invisible Church.

Congar identifies four valid ways of speaking about the "Church": (1) the Church as "constituted through faith and the sacraments of faith" and thus as "considered in its formal and constitutive principles which come from God"; (2) the Church as made of up humans, the community of believers; (3) the Church as seen in its representative bearers of divine powers received from God, that is to say the hierarchy (as when we say that "the Church teaches"); and (4) the Church as the conjunction of "the divine formal principle with the human material principle."[40] In his view, the fourth way of speaking of the Church stands out for its ability to encompass the total reality of the Church, divine and human. He therefore defines the Church as "the result of the synergy of a gratuitous divine gift that is pure in itself and a human activity that is characterized by human freedom, limitations, and natural fallibility."[41] The objective holiness of the Church, in its divine aspect as mediating divine mysteries, serves to make holy the sinful and limited members of the Church, who are in the process of being sanctified. The saints on earth are in constant need of sanctification, the only exception being the Virgin Mary, who thereby stands as an icon of holy Church.

Congar also specifies that the Church in its divine aspect—the Church as a mystery constituted by holy divine gifts—is in fact the work of the Holy Spirit. This is why we can say in the Creed that we believe in the holy Catholic Church: we mean that we believe in the Holy Spirit's uniting the Church in holiness. The holiness of the Church, therefore, "can only be

---

39. Ibid.   40. Ibid., 88–89.
41. Ibid., 90.

affirmed by faith in the Holy Spirit," since it is the Spirit's activity that bestows the Church's objective holiness.[42]

Congar proceeds to apply these principles. With regard to its divine aspect—its faith (the content of revealed truth), its sacraments, its offices, its charisms, and its place in the divine plan—the Church is holy and participates "in divine infallibility," even when these gifts have been mediated through humans (such as the prophets and apostles).[43] This is the domain that allows us to say rightly that "the church is impeccable, infallible, and virginal," because the Church is constituted by divine gifts that are truly given (without, it should go without saying, thereby making these gifts autonomous from the divine giver).[44] Congar affirms that "with respect to these things in themselves, there is no question of limitation, aging, or being out of touch," and he adds that "with respect to its essential principles, the church is incapable of failure and has no need to reform itself."[45] In its real possession of these gifts through the work of the Spirit, the Church is Christ's holy Bride and Body. But the human aspect remains fully present and active, of course, since the members of the Church can misuse the principles or can be too weak to exercise them rightly. The Church's members do not have the power to fundamentally distort the divine gifts, and so the Church's holiness and truth cannot be lost; the sovereign God gives and sustains the gifts, prior to and independent of merely human activity. But quite another matter is "the use that human beings make of these gifts—humans with all their freedom, their weakness, their instability, and their essential fallibility."[46] Here we find the Church in constant need of reform.

With regard to the human aspect of the Church, or the aspect of the Church that is not yet fully configured to Christ, Congar distinguishes two kinds of failures that require reform so that the divine gifts of the Church might have their full efficacy. The first kind of failure is the sins of the people who make up the Church. These sins inevitably wound the Church and hamper its mission of worship and evangelization. The second kind of failures consists not in sins, but in "historical faults brought

42. Ibid., 92.
44. Ibid.
46. Ibid., 95.

43. Ibid., 93.
45. Ibid.

about through narrow-mindedness and slowness to respond."[47] Again, the fact that during their earthly lives all the faithful (except the Virgin Mary) are sinners cannot mar the holiness of the Church; nor can the sins of the members undermine God's eternal plan of election or predestination. But sinners, insofar as they are sinners, are not yet fully inserted into the holy Church.

When sinners abuse the gifts that God bestows upon the Church or turn away interiorly from God, does this mean that the Church sins? Congar prefers to say that in and through its sinful members, "the church knows temptation and sin" and "is spotted by diverse stains."[48] So long as the Church lives in this world rather than fully in the kingdom of God, such sins and stains will constantly emerge, requiring penitence on the part of the members, including penitence for sins committed in the name of the Church by its leaders. In this sense, the Church itself must continually ask forgiveness from its Lord, asking him to heal its self-inflicted wounds, wounds that do much damage in the world. There was no perfect period of the Church's history when such sins did not mar the Church's members and require the penitence of the Church. Even the earliest Church, as seen in the New Testament, is marred by sins. Furthermore, not all the visible members of the Church are in fact united by charity to Christ or are necessarily among the elect; all the members are sinners, but some have interiorly parted from Christ more decisively. Here Congar uses Christ's metaphor of a field containing weeds and wheat.

Is the presence of sinners in the Church, who weaken the Church's witness and cause scandal, indicative that something has gone wrong with God's plan? On the contrary, the Church is precisely the place for sinners to be, since "[t]he church's proper work is ... to ceaselessly purify sinners from their sin" as "the place and the instrument for the application of Christ's redemption."[49] Even though Christ has definitively accomplished redemption and given the Church infallible means of grace (through the working of the Spirit), nonetheless each generation of members of the Church manifests sin's presence in a new and inevitably damaging way. In the Church as the mystical Body, the process of the redemption and

47. Ibid.
48. Ibid., 97.
49. Ibid., 99.

conquest of such sin is underway, as the power of Christ's Passion and Resurrection are applied to and appropriated by sinners. The important point here is the need for public confession of sin and active repentance. Thus the liturgy for the dedication of a church building includes Luke 19:1–10, the story of Zaccheus: "when Jesus comes under his roof, he acknowledges that he is a sinner, and he rectifies the injustices that he has committed."[50]

The purpose of the Church is to serve people in their moving from mere worldliness to being truly the repentant people of God who are undergoing sanctification. Thus, as Congar puts it, "The church according to its first meaning (as institution of salvation [the divine and holy aspect]) incessantly brings holiness into the church in the second sense of the word (as the community of the faithful and the people of God)."[51] Drawing heavily on distinctions developed by the Benedictine theologian Anscar Vonier, Congar emphasizes that the Church, as the mystery of salvation constituted by the divine means of grace, is not sinful, even though the Church's members (other than Mary) are all sinners during their earthly lives. It follows that one can properly speak of the sins of the "people of God" but not of the sins of the Church.

What then should we say of the Church as the people of God? Here we can speak not only of sins, but, as Congar has already mentioned, also of sociological and historical mistakes. Christendom, for example, often tended to obscure the true features of the Church, whether behind narrow social attitudes (such as—although Congar does not explicitly say so here—attitudes toward monarchy, toward women, and toward Jews) or behind the acquisition and administration of worldly power. In Congar's view, "the church reappears and shines forth more clearly when the conventional (but inauthentic) facades of the Christian world fall apart."[52]

Taking up the third way of understanding the world "Church"—namely as the hierarchy (the organ through which the Church speaks and acts)—Congar grants that not only do popes and bishops commit personal sins that harm the Church's witness, but also they commit sins and exhibit blind spots precisely in their hierarchical roles. When a pope,

50. Ibid.
51. Ibid.
52. Ibid., 101.

because of a personal blind spot or a personal vice, blunders in handling a particular prudential matter, this harms the Church's witness. Certainly, when it is a matter of definitive teaching or the administration of the sacraments, the Church's hierarchy will not be able to undermine the holiness and truth that Christ gives his Church, in the Spirit, as the means of salvation. But clergy certainly can obscure the greatness of the sacraments by their careless celebration of the liturgy, for example; and the Church's liturgical forms also can contain elements, added at particular time periods, that no longer illumine the beauty of the sacramental reality. Congar points to examples of sociological blunders such as the liturgical use of Latin even when few understand it, and to the failure to inculturate the liturgy in non-Western (missionary) countries.

Likewise, although definitive magisterial teaching has an infallibility guaranteed by the Spirit, who preserves the truth of the faith, it is nonetheless the case with regard to conciliar (and papal) definitions that "[t]he work of the persons involved remains influenced by their own limitations, even in the final product, the definition of dogma. God's guarantee to spare the church of error is nonetheless marked by circumstances, and the resulting human statement is not beyond improvement."[53] Indeed, in his private views, as distinct from his formal articulation of dogma, a pope can be heretical, as medieval theologians already recognized. In the lengthy process of the development of doctrine, too, there can be all sorts of impediments caused by either sin or sociological and historical factors. Congar adds that especially "in the area of social doctrine"—perhaps he has slavery or religious freedom in view—"the development of theological truth is conditioned by the state of the world."[54] At a lesser, but still deeply influential, level, catechetical instruction and preaching by the clergy can fall to a very low standard.

Does this mean that the Church, possessed of infallibility with regard to doctrine and sacraments, is no more than a merely human institution with regard to practical or prudential matters? Citing Charles Journet, Congar accepts that the Church has a certain "practical infallibility" analogous to its doctrinal infallibility, but he adds that in both cases the Church's infal-

---

53. Ibid., 103.
54. Ibid.

libility must be understood in a limited sense. In other words, in prudential matters (matters of government) the Church is preserved from going astray definitively; but Congar emphasizes the limitations of this preservation. Thus he reminds us that the "men who exercise the most sacred authority can be lacking in information or intelligence. They can spoil occasions, alienate people, provoke irreparable damage by their narrowness or their lack of understanding."[55] As examples, he points to the high-ranking clergy whose mutual acts of offence deeply exacerbated the eleventh-century East-West split; as well as the high-ranking clergy whose corrupt actions paved the way for the sixteenth-century Reformation. Even popes make serious prudential errors: examples are Pope Liberius (d. 366), who signed the formula of Sirmium; Pope Honorius (d. 638), who misunderstood and indulged Monotheletism; Pope Paschal II (d. 1118), who gave way to the pressure exercised upon him by Emperor Henry V; and Pope Pius VII (d. 1823), who signed the Concordat of Fontainebleau. As Congar observes, "There is no point in going into detail about the faults of so many popes, bishops, priests, and religious. This history is rather well known and the church has suffered abuse because of it."[56]

Drawing on John Henry Newman's Preface to the third edition of his *Via Media*, Congar nonetheless mentions a few examples to help us see what he means. He observes that in Christendom, in the post-Constantinian feudal context, "prelates and popes have exercised powers deriving from another competence than that of their strictly spiritual jurisdiction: rights of overlords, arbiters, moderators of Christendom, judges of the Christian princes," and so forth.[57] Obviously such prelates and popes were not immune from misusing these prudential powers, and they did misuse them, thereby causing scandal and leading to bitter reaction—as can be seen in the anti-Catholicism of secular polities from the Enlightenment onward. There were "acts of simony, nepotism, abuse of power, violent constraint, [and] use of spiritual arms for temporal ends," due to the fact that "in a world subjected to the church, the spiritual power naturally took on a spirit of jurisdiction."[58] Popes and bishops have no infallibility in this domain, and they made errors that damaged the Church, even if God does not allow

---

55. Ibid., 105.
57. Ibid., 107.
56. Ibid., 106.
58. Ibid., 108.

his Church to go prudentially astray in the way that a merely human institution (none of which lasts for very long) does. As Congar comments, "The scandal comes ... from the contrast between these concrete experiences of the church, on the one hand, and the church's claims to a supernatural sanctity, on the other, without distinguishing between the two contexts so as to see the facts about its holiness and its failures."[59] The laity, too, are deeply implicated in such failures, and also in the damaging intransigence that can resist the needed penitence and renewal.

Is the history of the Church, then, a mere juxtaposition of pure sacraments and dogma with deeply impure political and sociological processes? If so, then how could the two aspects truly be a unity, so as to be really one Church? In fact, says Congar, there is only one Church, in which the divine and human aspects are fused. As "the communion of men and women in whom the Spirit and the energies of Jesus Christ are active and at work," the Church in history exhibits the means of grace, the fallenness of sinners, and the work of redemption.[60] The sins of the members—even of the hierarchy—are not sins of the Church in a strict sense, but they can still rightly be called "the faults of the body, since 'we are all members of one another.'"[61] For Congar, the best way to think of the Church, then, is as a "holy church of sinners," keeping in view that the sinfulness of the members is not an isolated domain, but rather is undergoing sanctification, due to the work of the Holy Spirit, through "the constitutive principles of the church as the instrument of our salvation."[62]

Chapter 2 of *True and False Reform in the Church* treats "Why and in What Way Do the People of God Need to Be Reformed?" Here Congar begins with the principle of historical development: as the Old and New Testaments show, God's plan unfolds in such a way that each period, in the light of its own pressing problems, contributes fruitfully to the understanding and embodiment of the revelation that the people of God has received. God values our agency, our response to grace, and so God works through history despite the limitations and sinfulness of each historical period and of each historical agent. No period of salvation history,

---

59. Ibid., 109.
60. Ibid., 112.
61. Ibid.
62. Ibid., 116.

including our own, represents the final and definitive form; instead what we have is true development (and thus not rupture) over successive stages.

But how can this apply to the Church, since after all the new covenant in Jesus Christ is the last stage, and no further stage is to be expected? Congar responds that, indeed, the inauguration of the Church and the gift of its "deposit of apostolic faith, of the sacraments, of the apostolic powers" are "definitive" and "unchangeable."[63] But there can still be plentiful development, since we continue to await the eschatological consummation. For one thing, what the Church does ministerially is not an end in itself; everything is a means, and will not be present in the consummated kingdom. For another, the work of evangelization necessarily unfolds historically and in a wide variety of cultures, and all these people must be brought to Christ. Furthermore, these people for whom Christ died are, in fact, a changing humanity: "Humanity lives, grows, and becomes diverse, evolving even across time, filling up the changes of time as it fills the space of its progressive developments."[64] It follows that, in order to evangelize the world, to which the members of the Church belong, it is fitting and indeed necessary that "the church (even though it is changeless with respect to what it receives from on high) has to follow humanity in expanding and evolving and thus experience a parallel development within itself."[65]

How is it, though, that a developing Church remains changeless with regard to the deposit of faith? Congar argues that in the dialogue with the world—a dialogue in which the Church can sometimes, because of a desire to preserve past forms and also sometimes because of a laudable caution, be too slow to perceive the contributions that the world makes—the Church is able "to develop or to adapt her forms to new realities," without changing the Church's "essential structures."[66] The development simply enables essential structures of the Church (the deposit of faith, sacraments, and offices) to be understood more deeply in light of, and in the context of, the "new realities" of history. Congar notes that "reform" constitutes only one aspect of "the whole process of the gradual self-realization of the

---

63. Ibid., 127.
64. Ibid., 130.
65. Ibid.
66. Ibid., 134.

church's life," which, it should be emphasized, "is guided by an interior law of development and by a transcendent impulse of the Holy Spirit" rather than merely drifting on the tides of history.[67]

Turning to the specific content of reform, Congar begins with the reform made necessary by the perennial temptation to substitute means for ends. In Congar's view, scholastic theology has fallen into this temptation at least since the sixteenth century, by promoting a school-theology generally adverse to new modes of thought and to addressing new problems.[68] Erasmus stands as a hero in this section, both for his sensitivity to the need for pastoral and biblical reform, and for his moderation (by contrast to Luther). Congar is concerned with Christendom's temptation to substitute temporal flourishing, temporal achievements, for spiritual ends. But his central goal consists in persuading clergy not to stand in the way of any and all change by "an excessive attachment to historical forms that give the church its cultural expression, and are by that very fact dated and partial."[69] In particular, he urges the older generation of clergy—he wrote this book while in his forties—to avoid squelching the "fresh energies and ideas" of the younger generation.[70]

Throughout the book, he seeks to maintain a moderate tone, both through his repeated insistence on the unchangeableness of the deposit of faith, and through his recognizing that "it is wise and indeed more true if we do not let ourselves too quickly give credit to a judgment that ecclesial institutions may be out-of-date or obsolete. Often we are happy, fi-

---

67. Ibid.

68. This position overlooks the achievements of Salamancan Thomism, among other oversights. For a succinct exposition see Romanus Cessario, OP, *A Short History of Thomism* (Washington, D.C.: The Catholic University of America Press, 2005).

69. Congar, *True and False Reform in the Church*, 149.

70. Ibid. Tragically, in fact, Congar's ideas in *True and False Reform in the Church* and in other writings from this period got him into trouble with the Vatican. In a move precipitated by an article on the worker-priest controversy but rooted in the Vatican's broader concern about his writings on ecumenism, the laity, and reform in the Church, Congar's Dominican Superior removed him from his teaching position in 1954. In the period between 1954 and 1956, he lived in Jerusalem and Cambridge, where he endured painful isolation and was forced to sharply curtail his scholarly writing. For discussion of this terrible period of Congar's life, see Étienne Fouilloux, "Friar Yves, Cardinal Congar, Dominican: Itinerary of a Theologian," trans. Christian Yves Dupont, *U.S. Catholic Historian* 17 (1999): 63–90, at 76–79. Between 1956 and 1960 he lived in a Dominican friary in Strasbourg, France, but he remained under suspicion and did not resume his teaching activity.

nally, that the church hung onto what once appeared as anachronisms."[71] He gives examples, nonetheless, of episodes in which Christians held on too long to real anachronisms rather than seeking to find (and to defend through new forms, which often turn out to reprise the earliest practice) the deeper meaning of the action under consideration. With his own time in view, Congar speaks warmly of "epochal moments of great transition."[72] From the vantage point of 1950, he argues that the key issues today are pastoral and catechetical, as they also were, he suggests, in 1500—and reform in 1500 might have staved off the rupture produced by the Reformation. The reform that he calls for will revitalize the "evangelical spirit" of the Church in a way that, by contrast to all defensiveness, "generously agrees to attune itself to the structures of the emerging world and of a renewed society—which it also needs to baptize."[73]

In chapter 3, Congar investigates "Prophets and Reformers." The key here is the need for reformers "to become familiar with the principle of life itself, going deeper than habits and customs."[74] Again the lead-up to the Reformation plays a significant role; Congar suggests that if the ecclesiastical reformers of the fifteenth century (and there were many) had been able to think outside the late-medieval system in which they were raised, the eventual rupture could have been avoided. True reformers have the capacity to focus afresh on the end (and thus on the deepest principles) rather than on the means. From the same perspective, "[p]rophets always push God's people to growth."[75] Significantly, Congar argues that true prophets and reformers must acutely, through personal experience, perceive and appreciate the divine aspects of the Church, so as to be able to renew the people's perception of them.

The second part of *True and False Reform in the Church* is devoted almost entirely to presenting four conditions for authentic reform without schism. The first is "the primacy of charity and of pastoral concerns."[76]

---

71. Congar, *True and False Reform in the Church*, 151.
72. Ibid., 158.
73. Ibid., 167. Here one should think of the reform decrees of the Council of Trent, which became incarnate in pastoral bishops such as Charles Borromeo, in whose image the episcopate of most of Europe was transformed in the seventeenth century.
74. Ibid., 170.   75. Ibid., 174.
76. Ibid., 215.

Charity enables the reformist impulse to avoid falling into sectarianism or a one-sided clinging to a particular point-of-view. The key is that, for the true reformer, "the church has to remain a *given*, not only intellectually but also existentially"; the reformer seeks to renew a holiness that the Church in fact possesses, not to criticize the Church so as to make it holy or to make its truth conform with one's own thinking.[77]

The second condition is to "remain in communion with the whole Church."[78] This enables the reformer not to become a narrow partisan for a partial truth, which is an inevitable temptation for a religious genius (Congar has Luther especially in view). As Congar puts it, "Only through communion with the whole body, which itself is subject to the guidance of the magisterium, can someone grasp a truth in its totality."[79] The "whole body" here includes not only the whole Church as it presently exists on earth, but the Church from the apostles onward. The true reformer is not an innovator or a revolutionary, since to be such would be to misunderstand the nature of the Church and thus be unable to reform the Church. Indeed, true reform will be tested, and ultimately approved and adopted, by the whole Church. The Spirit who moves the true reformer also moves the whole Church, and reform therefore cannot be opposed to obedience to the hierarchical Magisterium or reject the Magisterium's role in the service of unity. True reform seeks more unity, not less. It is for this reason that the Magisterium must constantly be alert and open to listening to true reform movements. Here Congar calls for a specific reform, namely for there to be, "alongside the central power, in the midst of the top administration of the church, a substantial representation of all the elements of the *Orbis*, of all the tendencies of the periphery"—a "supreme advisory council" representing the various nations and, more importantly, the various problems that the Church faces around the world.[80] In a 1968 addendum to this passage, Congar recognizes with delight that Vatican II explicitly moves in this direction.

The third condition consists in "having patience with delays."[81] Impatience produces schism; patience allows for the proposed reforms to

---

77. Ibid., 217.
78. Ibid., 229.
79. Ibid., 230.
80. Ibid., 262.
81. Ibid., 265.

be gradually sifted and, if approved, adopted. Impatience signals that one merely wants the Church to confirm one's own zealous intellectual views. It indicates that one is overly sure of oneself, not sufficiently open to the possibility one might be wrong. By contrast, patience signals an appreciation for lived development, which is the only way that true reform can happen. As Congar says, "Everything that involves life experience, at least here below, presupposes delays which cannot be sidetracked or avoided. Only what's done in cooperation with the nature of time itself can conquer time."[82] Congar is again critical especially of Luther, who set himself up "*against* the church and *against the integrity of its tradition*," as for instance in his rejection of the sacramental priesthood.[83] Congar warns against confronting the Church with an ultimatum. Instead, true reform should act "in and for ecclesial life by opening up creative or adaptive possibilities that the authorities do not disavow," by way of an experimental initiative from which the whole Church can ultimately benefit.[84] In this way, the periphery (the local church) can contribute creatively, rather than having everything flow from the central authority (Rome). Yet, while calling for patience on the part of reformers, Congar encourages the Church's leaders not to be too slow to accept change; there are times when the Church must act before a rupture occurs.

Finally, the fourth condition is "genuine renewal through a return to the principle of tradition (not through the forced introduction of some 'novelty')."[85] Congar explores the way in which new elements—for example, new ideas from human culture, or new ideas that come to the fore as responses to current needs and problems, or new ideas that belong to inculturation—can be brought into the Church. Focusing on the new idea in itself would be a mistake. Instead, one must focus on the particular aspect of the Church that is at stake. By focusing on the Church, and thus on the reality of faith, one can accomplish "a genuine 'renewal' (a true 'development') that is a reform *in* and *of* the church."[86] In this way, the introduction of a new aspect from the human dimension of the Church will not harm the divine dimension of the Church, but will instead serve the Church's divine deposit.

82. Ibid., 267.
83. Ibid., 270.
84. Ibid., 280.
85. Ibid., 291.
86. Ibid., 292.

Congar emphasizes that "we must study Catholic Tradition and not turn to masters foreign to the Tradition."[87] On this view, Modernism misunderstood true development, because the Modernists focused not on reforming Christianity from within its deepest principles, but on introducing principles exterior to Christianity that they thought would make Christianity palatable. Congar applies this insight to contemporary ecumenism, arguing that we need an ecumenism that recognizes "that the church of Christ and of the apostles *exists*," rather than beginning in a manner that ignores the existing catholicity and unity of the Church.[88] In a nutshell, says Congar, anyone who seeks reform of the Catholic Church "will be obliged to begin with a return to the fundamental principles of Catholicism. It will be necessary first of all to consult the tradition and to become immersed in it."[89]

What, in Congar's view, is Tradition? It has to do with the Church's continuity-in-development over the centuries since the gift of the unchanging apostolic deposit. Congar states, "Tradition is the presence of the *principle* in all the stages of its development. It is therefore sources (Scripture, the events of the primitive church), the thought of the Fathers, the faith and the prayer of the whole church (liturgy), the authentic investigations of the church's doctors and spiritual masters, the development of piety and doctrine."[90] But once this is understood, Tradition cannot be seen merely as something from the past. It also involves the contemporary operation of the deposit, the "principle," in the Church. Today as much as ever, Tradition is active in the life of the Church. This does not mean that the student of Tradition can focus on today's Church rather than returning to the deepest sources, but it does mean that today's Church is the living subject of Tradition. Among the "strictly normative" aspects that the Church hands on in its Tradition are "the Sacred Scriptures, dogmatic definitions, doctrine unanimously embraced"; then at a second level, as

---

87. Ibid.

88. Ibid., 293.

89. Ibid. In hindsight, one observes with amazement how quickly this crucial principle of *ressourcement* was forgotten by many theologians in the postconciliar period.

90. Ibid., 294. See also Congar's *Tradition and Traditions: An Historical and Theological Essay*, trans. Michael Naseby and Thomas Rainborough (New York: Macmillan, 1967), originally published in French in two volumes appearing in 1960 and 1963, respectively.

an "exceptionally authoritative norm," the liturgy; and lastly "a great number of doctrinal expressions, historical experiences, and particular contributions of different moments or different aspects of the tradition."[91]

What then does a *ressourcement* of the Tradition involve? It is not a mere antiquarian study of ancient sources, since it necessarily involves "absolute respect for ecclesial expressions that are permanent and always viable."[92] At a second level, the practitioner of *ressourcement* should exhibit "a critical and intelligent respect for transitional forms, in a spirit of loyal respect and affection for all the forms."[93] But how can one distinguish between permanent ecclesial expressions and "transitional forms" that can be discarded if new circumstances warrant the implementation of reform? Congar suggests that obtaining the ability to distinguish between permanent and transitional expressions requires "earnestly studying the very sources of Catholicism" and "being penetrated by the spirit of the church."[94] We cannot assume that we have this "spirit of the church"; rather, it is something that may come to us through earnest study of the deepest sources. If we are indeed "penetrated by the spirit of the church," then we will be able to go "beyond what the church said with respect to a particular problem in the past," because we will see the motivations—the inner dynamic—that resulted in the formulation of the Church's response. Having grasped the inner dynamic, we can engage present problems in the same spirit and with appreciation for the deepest dynamic of the Church's Tradition.

As Congar goes on to say, the above understanding of *ressourcement* emerged from the liturgical movement, which predated the biblical and patristic renewals. He observes, "Already the first efforts of this return to the sources have shown much promise. In this threefold return to liturgical, biblical, and patristic sources, the movement of *ressourcement* has found its true character."[95] Although Congar values historical research tremendously, he thinks that *ressourcement* has a different focus. Namely, "*Ressourcement* consists in a recentering on Christ and on the paschal mystery."[96] It goes right to the very heart of Christianity. The study of the

---

91. Congar, *True and False Reform in the Church*, 294.
92. Ibid., 295.
93. Ibid.
94. Ibid.
95. Ibid.
96. Ibid.

history of theology is an important mode, but historical research must be rooted in a primary focus on the Paschal Mystery of Christ. Congar adds that this focus requires the commitment of one's whole life to Christ. He observes, "Without the commitment of a corresponding life, a reform effort, even profiting from an intellectual return to the sources and a recentering, will not arrive at the necessary spirit of evangelization or at the fullness of authenticity and efficacy."[97]

Thus, a true reformer must enter deeply into the Church's sources, but not as a mere scholar. Congar portrays the Liturgical Movement as especially exemplary in this respect, given its pastoral and Christological focus and its commitment to "the dogmatic, sacramental, and hierarchical structure of the church."[98] On this basis and only on this basis—return to the sources, recentering on the Paschal Mystery, and conversion of life—can true reform proceed in the Church. As Congar puts it more technically with regard to the discernment and assimilation of a new element (an innovation that constitutes a development rather than a rupture), "in order for an adaptation not to be mechanical or purely exterior, but rather to represent a development of Christian principle, the Christian principle must both guide and assimilate the new element," namely "by discerning the aspects or parts of the new element which are appropriate for expressing the principle's growth."[99] It is the Church's essential structures that govern true development, because development expresses ever more fully, and in new contexts, the apostolic deposit.

Congar concludes (writing in 1950) that "all the big problems facing contemporary Catholicism are such that solving them with quick and mechanical adaptations would lead to catastrophe."[100] While advocating reform, Congar well recognizes "the seriousness of what is involved. Before all else, the church has to safeguard its very being as well as the integrity of its principles. *Depositum custodire*—'Guard what has been entrusted to you' (1 Tim 6:20)."[101]

---

97. Ibid. Here one should see H. Outram Evennett, *The Spirit of the Counter-Reformation*, ed. John Bossy (Cambridge: Cambridge University Press, 2008), which nicely describes the spirituality underlying true reform, and which praises the work of the Fathers of the Council of Trent.
98. Congar, *True and False Reform in the Church*, 296.
99. Ibid.   100. Ibid., 298.
101. Ibid., 310.

Lumen Gentium

According to Congar, the Church bears an unchanging divine apostolic deposit consisting of the gospel (found in inspired Scripture, and proclaimed dogmatically), the sacraments, and the hierarchical offices. Yet there is room for development and reform nonetheless, since the Church can gain a greater understanding of these divine aspects, and since the divine aspects can be obscured by elements that may have suited an earlier historical moment but do not suit our own. What do we find when we explore *Lumen Gentium* in this light?

The opening paragraph of *Lumen Gentium*, which inaugurates the first chapter of the Constitution, expresses the Church's participation in the holiness of Christ through the Holy Spirit. It states, "Since Christ is the light of the nations, this holy synod, called together in the holy Spirit, strongly desires to enlighten all people with his brightness, which gleams over the face of the church, by preaching the gospel to every creature."[102] The resplendence of Christ is manifested in the Church. Only thereby can the Church be, in Christ, "a sacrament or instrumental sign of intimate union with God and of the unity of all humanity" (§1). This sacramental signification of the Church indicates the importance of the Church's presence in history.

The second paragraph then offers a brief synopsis of salvation history. The history of the Church stems from the very outset of creation, since from the outset God had already "decided to raise human beings to share in the divine life" (§2). The Church, prepared for in Israel and prefigured from the first chapters of Genesis, is the community of those who "share in the divine life." This community is manifested at Pentecost and will be consummated at the eschaton.

Paragraph 3 identifies the Church as "the kingdom of Christ already present in mystery." Through the sacraments of this kingdom, Christ sanctifies us (see Jn 12:32; Jn 19:35; 1 Cor 5:7; and 1 Cor 10:17). The Eucharist is "the sacrifice of the Cross" as "celebrated on the altar," and in

---

102. Quotations are from *Lumen Gentium*, in *Decrees of the Ecumenical Councils*, vol. 2, *Trent to Vatican II*, ed. Norman P. Tanner, SJ (Washington, D.C.: Georgetown University Press, 1990), 849–900.

this way it effects the redemption of those who receive it in faith and love. The Eucharist is also a meal through the sharing in "the eucharistic bread," and in this way it represents and produces the Church's unity. Thus the Church mediates in the Eucharist the power of healing and deification, a power that only God has.

The Holy Spirit's role in making the Church holy is addressed in paragraph 4. If the Church were not holy—in its faith, sacraments, and offices—then believers would have far greater difficulty, to say the least, in receiving "through Christ access to the Father in one Spirit (see Eph 2, 18)" (§4). Pentecost does not simply sanctify the apostolic community alone, as distinct from the later Church. Rather, Pentecost indicates the ongoing holiness of the Church, since the "Spirit was sent to sanctify the church continually" (§4), for the purpose of uniting believers to the triune life. In light of paragraph 3's discussion of the Eucharist, paragraph 4 describes the Holy Spirit's work of sanctifying the Church with regard to the content of faith and to the Church's offices as follows: "He [the Spirit] leads the church into all truth (see John 16:13), and he makes it one in fellowship and ministry, instructing and directing it through a diversity of gifts both hierarchical and charismatic, and he adorns it with his fruits." Although the Church will enjoy the perfect fullness of truth only in the life to come, the Church's definitive teaching is true and salvific, just as the Church's unity is real though not yet perfected. Its ministry or offices, too, are holy because the Holy Spirit ensures that they are fitted to their purpose.

At the same time, the paragraph also makes clear the constant need for reform of the Church insofar as, in its human aspect, the Church can grow old and dull. Paragraph 4 comments, "Through the power of the gospel he [the Spirit] rejuvenates the church, continually renewing it and leading it to perfect union with its spouse." The Church would not need renewal and rejuvenation if its union with Christ were already perfect. The Church is sanctified by the Spirit who "dwells in the church and in the hearts of the faithful as in a temple" and who "bears witness to their adoption as children" of God, but the Church in its human aspect constantly needs renewal so as to attain "to perfect union with its spouse" (§4). Paragraph 4 concludes that the Spirit's work ensures that "the universal church appears as 'a people made one by the unity of the Father and the Son and the holy Spirit.'"

Paragraph 5 depicts the Church as founded by Jesus Christ and thus as the inaugurated, but not yet consummated, kingdom of God. Christ reveals the kingdom, and indeed the kingdom is the presence of Christ. When people are united to Christ by faith and the sacraments, people become members of the kingdom, but they have to grow into full maturity through sanctification. The kingdom thus will not be perfect until the eschaton. Yet, because of the gifts and mission that it receives from Christ, the Church "has formed the seed and the beginning of the kingdom on earth" (§5). This paragraph describes both the human aspect of the Church, composed of people in the process of sanctification, and the Church's divine aspect, since the Church could not be the inaugurated kingdom if the Church lacked the divine gifts that paragraphs 3 and 4 discussed.

Paragraph 6 surveys biblical images of the Church that complement the image of kingdom: a sheepfold whose door is Jesus Christ; a flock led by Jesus through human shepherds; a vineyard with Christ as the true vine and people as the branches; a household in which God's family dwells; a temple with the people as living stones; the holy Jerusalem; and the holy bride of Christ. These images emphasize the participation of humans in Christ and exhibit the union of divine and human elements in the Church. Paragraph 6 concludes by emphasizing that the Church yearns for a perfect communion in the divine things that Christ has revealed: the Church "is like an exile who seeks and savours the things that are above, where Christ is seated at the right hand of God, where the life of the church is hidden with Christ in God until it appears in glory with its spouse (see Col 3:1–4)." Just as Congar does, *Lumen Gentium* envisions the Church as divine in its foundation ("hidden with Christ in God") and journeying toward a full sharing in the divine mysteries in which it now imperfectly "seeks and savours."

Paragraph 7 begins with Christ's death and Resurrection, by which he redeemed humanity, made it a new creation, and, by sending his Spirit, constituted his Mystical Body. Regarding the Church's divine gifts, paragraph 7 states, "In this [mystical] body the life of Christ is communicated to believers, who by means of the sacraments in a mysterious but real way are united to Christ who suffered and has been glorified." After speaking of baptism and the Eucharist, which unite believers in one Body, the paragraph goes on to discuss the Spirit's distribution of diverse gifts, the way in which the members of the Body suffer with and rejoice in Christ, and the headship of Christ over his Body. The paragraph praises Christ's lordship: "through his supereminent perfection and activity he fills the whole body with the riches of his glory (see Eph 1:18–23)." As befits the divine aspect of the Church, Christ "perpetually distributes the gift of ministries in his body which is the church; and with these gifts, through his power, we provide each other with helps towards salvation, so that doing the truth in love, we grow up in all things into him who is our head (see Eph 4:11–16)" (§7). The Spirit of Christ, given to his Body, functions like the soul does to a material body, by giving life, movement, and unity to the Church for the purpose of continually renewing the Church. The paragraph concludes by connecting divine gifts and human journeying: "'For in him [Christ] the whole fullness of deity dwells bodily' (Col 2:9); and he fills with his divine gifts the church, which is his body and his fullness (see Eph 1:22–23), so that it may aspire towards and arrive at the whole fullness of God (see Eph 3:9)."

Paragraph 8 cautions that the earthly "society ... equipped with hierarchial structures, and the mystical body of Christ, a visible assembly and a spiritual community, an earthly church and a church enriched with heavenly gifts, must not be considered as two things, but as forming one complex reality comprising a human and a divine element." Reflecting upon the unity of the human and divine elements in the Church, the paragraph goes so far as to compare the Church to the mystery of the Incarnation. Just as the Word's humanity serves the Word in the work of salvation, so also the human elements of the Church serve the Spirit's building up of the Church by means of "heavenly gifts." Paragraph 8 notes that Christ established the Church upon the apostles led by Peter, and Christ gave his Church the mission of evangelization. The Church can accomplish this mission only because of its divine constitution as "the pillar and foundation of the truth" (1 Tm 3:15). The Church, in its fullness, "subsists in the catholic church, governed by the successor of Peter and the bishops in communion with him" (§8).¹⁰³ The hierarchical Church led by Peter and his successors is the one, holy, catholic, and apostolic Church. But paragraph 8 allows for the ways in which other Christian communions share in the divine gifts given to the Church (such as Scripture and baptism) and enjoy degrees of participation in the one Church. Paragraph 8 notes with regard to the Church that "outside its structure many elements of sanctification and of truth are to be found which, as proper gifts to the church of Christ, impel towards catholic unity."¹⁰⁴

Paragraph 8 also makes clear that the Church must follow the path of the crucified Christ. The Church exists to spread self-sacrifice, not self-aggrandizement of any kind. Just as Christ did, the Church must draw close to the poor and afflicted. But unlike the perfectly sinless Christ—and here the analogy of the Incarnation breaks down—the Church itself is made up of human sinners. Paragraph 8 explains that "the church, containing sinners in its own bosom, is at one and the same time holy and always in need of purification," for which reason the path of the Church—as Congar emphasizes—is one of "penance and renewal" (§8). The human weakness of the Church means that its afflictions come not only from outside, but from the Church's own members. Even so, the Church "reveals his [Christ's] mystery faithfully in the world—albeit amid shadows" (§8). The Church's strength for pursuing its mission does not come from itself, but rather from Christ.

Chapter 2 begins with paragraph 9 and focuses on "The people of God." Paragraph 9 first explains the scope of salvation history: in all times and places, God has always accepted those who fear him and do what is right (cf. Acts 10:35), but he chose Israel to be his particular people because he willed to save humanity not merely as individuals, but as a people united in worship and truth. Through his covenants with Israel and his sending of the prophets, he gradually instructed and sanctified Israel, in preparation for the coming of Christ. Christ more perfectly revealed God

---

103. The phrase "subsists in [subsistit in]" replaced "is" during the drafting of the document. How to interpret this replacement has been a matter of controversy. For discussion, see Benoît-Dominique de La Soujeole, OP, *Introduction to the Mystery of the Church*, trans. Michael J. Miller (Washington, D.C.: The Catholic University of America Press, 2014), 123–29.

104. See Vatican II's *Unitatis Redintegratio* and *Nostra Aetate*.

and established the new covenant "in his blood (see 1 Cor 11:25)" (§9). In this new covenant, he united Jews and Gentiles to himself through his Spirit, thereby forming his Church as "the new people of God" (§9; see 1 Peter 2:9–10). The head of this "messianic people" (§9) is Christ. Indwelt by the Spirit and having received the law of love, this people has the status of adopted children in the Son and has as its goal the perfect kingdom of God, of which it is the inauguration on earth as a "communion of life, love and truth" (§9).

Thus, rather than being merely another people among the nations of the earth, this people "constitutes for the whole human race a most firm seed of unity, hope and salvation" and serves "as the instrument of salvation for all," with an evangelizing mission to the whole earth (§9). In addition to the terms "people of God" and "messianic people," paragraph 9 describes the Church as "the new Israel," a "temple" of the Holy Spirit, and a "visible sacrament" of "saving unity" that is in history but is not limited to a particular geographic boundary. The people of God receives from Christ the "means suitable for visible and social unity," and the people of God holds fast to "perfect fidelity" as "the worthy spouse of its Lord" by the grace of the Spirit (§9). Paragraph 9 also grants the fallen human aspect of the Church, since it concludes by presenting the Church as constantly "renewing itself" under the Spirit's action.

Paragraph 10 focuses on the priesthood of all believers in relation to the ministerial priesthood. Regarding the former, the paragraph states that "by the regeneration and anointing of the Holy Spirit the baptised are consecrated as a spiritual dwelling and a holy priesthood," so that they can offer "spiritual sacrifices" and constitute a holy sacrifice to God (§10). All the baptized "exercise their priesthood in receiving the sacraments, in prayer and thanksgiving, through the witness of a holy life, by self-denial and by active charity" (§10). The ministerial priesthood exists to serve the priesthood of all believers, by forming and governing the people of God. The paragraph specifies that all believers "join in the offering of the Eucharist," but it is the ministerial priests who act "in the person of Christ" in offering the sacrifice of the Eucharist to God on behalf of the whole people of God (§10). Paragraph 11 addresses baptism, confirmation, and the Eucharist, with an emphasis on the latter's unitive power and signification. The other sacraments are then discussed: penance (which reconciles us with God and with the Church); anointing of the sick; holy order; and matrimony, which symbolizes and participates in the charitable unity of Christ and the Church. Marriage is the basis of the family—"the domestic church," in which the parents are the first "preachers" of the faith to their children (§11)—and children are born as members of human society and by baptism become adoptive children of God. The key point here is that all humans are "called by the Lord, each in their own way, to that perfect holiness whereby the Father is perfect" (§11).

In paragraph 12, *Lumen Gentium* turns to the *sensus fidei*, the "supernatural sense of the faith" granted to the people of God, a sense that is infallible when the whole people, clergy and laity (and religious), together affirm doctrine. The *sensus fidei* is not a reflection of the autonomy of the laity, let alone of their ability to construct their own versions of Christianity—not least because the clergy also belong to the people of God that possesses the *sensus fidei*. The *sensus fidei* testifies to the fact that the people of God receive the word of God, penetrate more deeply into it, and apply it, all of which takes place through the movement of the Spirit and "under the guidance of the sacred magisterium to which it [the whole people of God] is faithfully obedient" (§12). Paragraph 12 goes on to emphasize the gifts of the Holy Spirit to the people of God for the purpose of "the renewal and the building up of the church."

Paragraph 13 addresses the unity of the Church in relation to the diversity of the members. The Church does not impose a uniformity but rather allows for a diverse catholicity, which enables believers from various cultures and regions to contribute to the Church and thereby "to recapitulate the whole of humanity, with all its riches, under Christ the head in the unity of his Spirit" (§13). This point explains how there are churches and other ecclesial bodies within the Catholic Church that retain their own rites and traditions.[105] There are plenty of differences that are not Church-dividing, and that therefore can be protected and guided in some way by the papacy in its task of ensuring the unity of the Church in truth and love. Paragraph 13 also praises the ways in which churches in

---

105. See also Vatican II's *Orientalium Ecclesiarum*.

particular areas of the world help needy churches in other areas.[106] The paragraph ends by affirming that "to this catholic unity of the people of God, which prefigures and promotes universal peace, all are called, and they belong to it or are ordered to it in various ways, whether they be Catholic faithful or others who believe in Christ or finally all people everywhere who by the grace of God are called to salvation."

In paragraph 14, attention is given to the necessity of the Church for salvation: "those cannot be saved who refuse to enter the Church or to remain in it, if they are aware that the catholic church was founded by God through Jesus Christ as a necessity for salvation." To be fully a member of the Church, one must be filled with the Spirit and charitably embrace the Church's faith, sacraments, and hierarchical structure as given by Christ. Thus the key to the people of God is its constitution by God, and to be fully a member of the people of God one must recognize the binding character of the God-given means of salvation and depend entirely upon them rather than upon one's own resources. The paragraph adds that those who publicly and sincerely profess their desire to be Catholic are fully joined to the Church, even while they are only catechumens.

What about non-Catholic Christians? Paragraph 15 reaches out to baptized believers who merit the name Christian even though they "do not profess the faith in its entirety [Protestants] or do not preserve the unity of communion under the successor of Peter [Orthodox]." With regard to the former, it praises all who honor Scripture as the authoritative "norm for believing and living" and who "lovingly believe in God the almighty Father and in Christ, the Son of God and savior." Protestant Christians practice the sacrament of baptism, along with "other sacraments that they recognise and accept in their own churches or ecclesial communities" (§15). Paragraph 15 sets apart the Orthodox churches, which "possess the episcopate, celebrate the sacred eucharist and foster devotion to the virgin mother of God." The paragraph goes on to lift up the "communion of prayers and other spiritual benefits" and the "true bond in the holy Spirit" (and in martyrdom) enjoyed by Catholics with other Christians. Since the Spirit is the Spirit of unity, we can be sure that "the Spirit arouses in all of

---

106. See also Vatican II's *Christus Dominus*.

Christ's disciples desire and action so that all may be peacefully united, in the way established by Christ, in one flock under one shepherd" (§15).[107] The Catholic Church prays for this more perfect unity and at the same time "exhorts its children to purification and renewal so that the sign of Christ may shine more clearly over the face of the church" (§15).

Paragraph 16 discusses the Jewish people, emphasizing the permanence of God's election; and it also discusses Islam, some of whose beliefs are consonant with Judaism and Christianity.[108] It refers as well to those who search for God "in shadows and images" (§16) and to those who are ignorant of Christ but who are sincerely seeking to find God and obey conscience. All such persons, by God's grace, "can obtain eternal salvation," and in fact even those who deny God's existence but yet strive to act uprightly may be saved through God's grace (§16). The point is that although Christ and the Church are the path of salvation, others may participate in that path by sincerely following the promptings of grace, which God does not withhold from anyone. This optimistic tone is dampened by a note of caution: "More often, however, deceived by the evil one, people have gone astray in their thinking and exchanged the truth about God for a lie and served the creature rather than the creator (see Rm 1:21, 25)" (§16).

Not least because idolatry is alive and well, Christ's command to evangelize must be obeyed today. Christ commanded his apostles to go forth preaching, baptizing, and celebrating the Eucharist, and this work must continue, since God "constituted Christ as the principle of salvation for the whole world" (§17). Lest it seem that only a few are called to evangelize, paragraph 17 emphasizes that every Christian has a duty to spread the faith.[109] Although everyone can proclaim the faith and even baptize new believers, priests have the special responsibility of "building up the body through the eucharistic sacrifice" (§17), which stands at the heart of evangelization. Thus the people of God reaches out in various ways to embrace the entire human race, in hopes that "the fullness of the whole world may move into the people of God, the body of the Lord and the

---

107. See also Vatican II's *Unitatis Redintegratio*. See Jared Wicks, SJ's "Lutheran-Catholic Dialogue: On Foundations Laid in 1963–64," *Concordia Theological Journal* 39 (2013): 296–309.
108. See also Vatican II's *Nostra Aetate*.
109. See also Vatican II's *Ad Gentes*.

temple of the holy Spirit" (§17), so that in Christ the whole human race may truly give glory to the Father.

Chapter 3 takes up the topic of "The hierarchical constitution of the Church and in particular the episcopate." The hierarchy of the Church serves the mutual cooperation of the people of God on the path to salvation. After grounding the offices of the Church in a permanent divine gift—"Christ the Lord instituted a variety of ministries which are directed towards the good of the whole body"—paragraph 18 describes Christ's commissioning of the apostles, led by Peter. Chapter 3 affirms the primacy of Peter and "his infallible magisterium" (§18), in accord with the First Vatican Council. It presents the apostles and their successors (the bishops) as a "college" led by Peter and his successors, "while the chief corner-stone is Christ Jesus himself (see Rev 21:14; Mt 16:18; Eph 2:20)" (§19). The succession of today's bishops (and pope) goes back to the very beginning, as does their enduring divine office of teaching, sanctifying, and governing. Paragraph 20 emphasizes that the bishops are fully successors of the apostles: "by divine institution the bishops have succeeded to the place of the apostles as shepherds of the church: and the one who hears them hears Christ but whoever rejects them rejects Christ and him who sent Christ."

The main purpose of this section is to ensure that the bishops are not considered mere stepchildren of the pope.[110] Indeed, the bishops possess "the fullness of the sacrament of order," a fullness that "is conferred by episcopal consecration" (§21)—a clarification about episcopal consecration that is an instance of doctrinal development. At the right hand of the Father, Christ works through the bishops to bestow the divine gifts of the gospel and of the sacraments. Paragraph 21 states that the bishops are chosen by Christ to be "the ministers of Christ and the dispensers of the mysteries of God (see 1 Cor 4:1)."

Paragraph 22 praises the collegial character of the body of bishops, headed by the bishop of Rome and made especially manifest in Church Councils, where the bishops (precisely as united to the pope, and not otherwise) exercise "supreme and full power over the universal church." The

---

110. See also Vatican II's *Christus Dominus*.

college of bishops represents the diversity of the Church and also, united under the pope, the unity of the Church. So as not to be misunderstood, paragraph 22 also strongly affirms the pope's "full, supreme and universal power over the church, a power he is always able to exercise freely."

These points seek to clarify the constitution of the Church in its offices, which belong to the divine aspect of the Church (as Congar emphasizes). Paragraph 23 adds that the bishop, in his diocese, serves as a principle of unity, just as the pope does for the whole Church. Bishops should be concerned not only about their dioceses but also about the whole Church. Indeed, "All the bishops ... have a duty to promote and defend the unity of faith and discipline common to the whole church" (§23). The paragraph encourages the collaboration of bishops, not least through such things as missionary work and charitable aid. The paragraph also approves of certain groupings of local churches, "especially the ancient patriarchal churches" with their own rites and traditions.[111] Such diversity exhibits not discord but catholicity.

Paragraph 24 specifies that bishops receive their commission directly from Christ. The paragraph states, "The bishops, as successors of the apostles, receive from the Lord, to whom all power in heaven and on earth has been given, the mission to teach all nations and to preach the gospel to every creature, so that all may gain salvation through faith, baptism and the keeping of the commandments." To accomplish this mission of teaching and sanctifying, the bishops are empowered by the Holy Spirit. With regard to the "canonical mission of bishops," there are various ways in which someone can be appointed to the episcopacy, including direct appointment by the pope (§24). The pope can also reject an appointment or refuse apostolic communion to a candidate for the episcopacy, in which case "the bishop cannot be admitted to office" (§24).

Paragraph 25 emphasizes that teaching the gospel is the primary task of bishops. Bishops do not possess the charism of infallibility in their teaching, except when they concur with one another and with the pope in definitively teaching a doctrine, as for instance in Church Councils. Even so, a bishop's teaching should be greeted with reverence by the faith-

---

111. See also Vatican II's *Orientalium Ecclesiarum*.

ful in his diocese. Paragraph 25 states that "the faithful ought to concur with their bishop's judgment concerning faith and morals which he delivers in the name of Christ, and they are to adhere to this with a religious assent of the mind." Out of respect for the teaching office of the pope, given to him by Christ, the faithful should also respond with this "religious assent of the mind" to the teachings of the pope on faith and morals even when he is not defining doctrine *ex cathedra*.[112]

Paragraph 25 addresses the infallibility of the pope. Like the infallibility of bishops when defining doctrine with the pope, the infallibility of the pope is limited to the interpretation of "the deposit of divine revelation that is to be guarded as sacred and faithfully expounded" (§25). Given this significant limitation, the pope can teach infallibly "on faith or morals," by means of a "definitive act" that he undertakes "as the supreme teacher of the universal church" (§25). In this regard, paragraph 25 states that "his definitions are rightly said to be irreformable of themselves, and not from the consent of the church, for they are delivered with the assistance of the holy Spirit which was promised to him in blessed Peter; and therefore they have no need of approval from others nor do they admit any appeal to any other judgment." Both alone and in union with the whole college of bishops, the pope can teach infallibly only on matters of divine revelation. In such instances, the Holy Spirit ensures that the pope's (or the Council's) decisions are in accordance with divine revelation, "to which all must conform" (§25). Christ gives his Church the mission of proclaiming the gospel and sends the Spirit to ensure that in its definitive teaching of faith and morals, the Church does not distort the content of the gospel. What is at stake is the transmission of divine revelation so that it might be "sacredly preserved" and "faithfully expounded"; there is no "new public revelation" that can be added to the deposit of faith (§25). The Holy Spirit also brings about the interior assent of the faithful to the decision of the pope (or of the bishops in union with the pope), by inspiring the whole Church to receive the whole divine deposit that Christ has given his Church, including the gift of the teaching office.

---

112. See Augustin-Marie Aubry, *Obéir ou assenter? De la "soumission religieuse" au magistère simplement authentique* (Paris: Desclée, 2015).

Paragraph 26 explains that every local church, in preaching the gospel and celebrating the Eucharist under the direction of its bishop, makes "truly present" the Church of Christ, because in each local church, no matter how small or poor, "Christ is present by whose power the one, holy, catholic and apostolic church is gathered together" (§26). In each local church God calls together his people in the Holy Spirit "by the preaching of the gospel of Christ" and the celebrating of the Eucharist (§26), so as to make manifest the charity and unity that bond believers together in the Body of Christ. Paragraph 26 goes on to describe the sanctifying office of the bishops, who administer the divine gifts of the sacraments (united always to the ministry of the word). The bishop is in charge of all celebrations of the Eucharist in his diocese, and has charge of the other sacraments as well. In accord with their sanctifying office, bishops must lead by the example of a holy life.[113]

With regard to the governing office of the bishops, paragraph 27 emphasizes that the bishops are "vicars and legates of Christ" (rather than of the pope) and exercise a "proper, ordinary, and immediate" power in the name of Christ in their dioceses (§27). The pope's "supreme and universal power" (§27) does not overthrow the bishops' power, but affirms and strengthens it in accord with Christ's will that the apostles and their successors be led by Peter. The bishops exercise their power under that of the pope, but their power nonetheless "is proper to themselves" so that the bishops truly are "presidents of the peoples they govern" (§27). Paragraph 27 portrays the bishops' power through the images of a head of a household and of a good shepherd. True governance must be service, even to the point that the one governing is willing to die for those whom he serves. As one subject to weakness and failure, the bishop should have sympathy for those who go astray. The bishop should "listen to his subjects whom he looks after as truly his children" (§27) and should consider all persons in his diocese as part of his charge, caring for them by praying, preaching the gospel, and undertaking works of charity on behalf of all. The unity of the faithful with the bishop should be like the Church's union with Christ and Christ's with the Father.

---

113. For these paragraphs, see also Vatican II's *Christus Dominus*.

In discussing "the divinely instituted ecclesiastical ministry," paragraph 28 describes the office of priests, who "by virtue of the sacrament of order ... are consecrated in the image of Christ," in order "to preach the gospel and nourish the faithful and celebrate divine worship."[114] Without minimizing the dignity of the proclamation of "the divine word to all people," the priestly office is identified above all with the celebration of the Eucharist, in which priests act in the person of Christ and "in the sacrifice of the mass make present and apply ... the one sacrifice of the new covenant, that is, the sacrifice of Christ who once and for all offers himself as an unblemished victim to the Father (see Heb 9:11–28)" (§28). As they teach, sanctify, and govern their congregations under the bishop's authority, priests make the universal Church present in their local churches. Priests must cooperate with and obey the bishop as their father, and the bishop must treat them "as sons and friends" (§28). Priests must be an example to all people by their lives and must especially seek out those who have fallen away from the Church. Again unity is the central theme: indeed, paragraph 28 concludes with the hope that the Church will help to "wipe out every cause of division so that the whole human race may be brought into the unity of God's family" (§28). More briefly, paragraph 29 treats the office of deacons, and it restores the order of permanent deacons in the Church.

Chapter 4, beginning with paragraph 30, discusses the laity. The paragraph emphasizes the dignity of the laity's role: "The sacred pastors are well aware of how much the laity contribute to the well-being of the whole church" (§30). The people of God consists of clergy, religious, and laity; and all the baptized who are not clergy or religious are "laity."[115] Not only bishops and priests, but also the laity are "sharers in Christ's priestly, prophetic and royal office" and play a crucial part in the Church's mission of evangelization (§31). The laity work to sanctify the world from within the world. As paragraph 31 states, "It is the special vocation of the laity to seek the kingdom of God by engaging in temporal affairs and ordering these in accordance with the will of God," thereby fostering "the sanctification of

---

114. See also Vatican II's *Presbyterorum Ordinis* and *Optatam Totius*.
115. In postconciliar canon law, by contrast, all religious who are not clergy are counted as laity.

the world." Like clergy and religious, the laity "are called to holiness" (§32), as befits the fact that the rich diversity of the Church aims always at unity in Christ. Indeed, the laity should conceive of their pastors as their brothers in Christ; there is no elite in the Church, even though there is a hierarchical order given by Christ for the purpose of ministry and service. Although the laity's task is to evangelize the world and in this way to ensure "the growth of the church and its continual sanctification," the "apostolate of the laity" can and often does include "a more immediate cooperation in the apostolate of the hierarchy" (§33) in service to the Church.[116]

The laity share in Christ's priestly office through "offering spiritual worship" in the Eucharistic celebration and by the tasks of their daily life in the world, by which they consecrate the world to God (§34). They share in Christ's prophetic office by understanding the faith and infusing "family and society" with the teachings of faith,[117] so that the hope given in Christ will "be expressed through the structures of secular life," which must be transformed by personally and socially overcoming the domination of demonic powers (§35). In the witness borne to Christ by the laity, faith and life must form a unity; no aspect of life can remain untouched by faith. Married life is of particular importance, insofar as "[t]he christian family proclaims aloud both the virtues of the kingdom of God here and now and the hope of a blessed life to come" (§35). Even if laity are not directly involved in the Church's offices, they must work for the "growth of the kingdom of Christ on earth" and therefore must "try diligently to deepen their knowledge of revealed truth" in prayer and study (§35). Finally, the laity share in Christ's royal office by their "royal freedom" in overcoming "the reign of sin within themselves," and by leading others "to the King, to serve whom is to reign" and valuing "the whole of creation and its orientation to the praise of God" (§36). Transformation from sinfulness to holiness is the key theme here.

The result will be a world in which there will be "a more equitable distribution" of the goods of creation, "universal progress in human and Christian freedom" in the light of Christ, and reform of "those secular structures and conditions which constitute an inducement to sin" (§36). The laity

---

116. For these paragraphs, see also Vatican II's *Apostolicam Actuositatem*.
117. See also Vatican II's *Inter Mirifica*.

thereby prepare the world for the gospel and empower the Church to proclaim the gospel more widely. Paragraph 36 concludes by urging the laity to remember that temporal matters are all contained within God's dominion, so that although human society "is governed by its own principles" rather than by the Church, any view of society must be rejected "which claims to construct society without any reference to religion, and which attacks and undermines the religious freedom of the citizens."[118]

Paragraph 37 speaks of the laity's right to receive "the help provided by the word of God and the sacraments," since these enduring divine gifts are for the whole Church. It describes the right of the laity also to make known their opinions on matters pertaining to the Church, so long as this is done with "respect for the truth," with prudence, and in "a spirit of reverence and love" toward the hierarchical priesthood (§37). At the same time, the laity (like the clergy and religious) should be prompt to obey the decisions of those who exercise hierarchical authority in the name of Christ. Such obedience imitates the salvific obedience of Christ. The laity should also pray for their pastors. Reciprocally, the pastors of the Church should listen carefully to the laity and place them in positions of trust in the Church, and should not attempt to limit the laity's just freedom to act independently in the sphere of secular affairs. If laity are configured to Christ as they should be, they will "be a witness to the world of the resurrection and life of the Lord Jesus" and will "spread throughout the world that spirit which is the life of the poor, the meek and the peacemakers" (§38).

Chapter 5 is titled "The universal call to holiness in the church." The divine aspect of the Church is signaled strongly once again at the outset of this chapter: "The church ... is held to be indefectibly holy as a matter of faith," because of the work of Christ and the Spirit (§39). In accord with the beatitudes and with Christ's command that we must "be perfect" as the Father is perfect (Mt 5:48), paragraph 39 insists that God calls all people to holiness and that the Church's holiness is manifested in countless ways, as believers are sanctified more and more. It commends particularly the practice of the evangelical counsels. Those who have been justified in faith and baptism "are therefore really made holy," but this holiness needs

---

118. See also Vatican II's *Dignitatis Humanae*.

to be not only maintained but perfected (§40). There is recognition here of the need to grow in holiness, and therefore of the presence of imperfection and sin (the Church in its human aspect). The holiness of the members of the Church enriches not only the Church but also the societies in which believers live. The saints are the great exemplars of this impact. Despite the variety of vocations, there is only "one holiness cultivated by all who are led by the Spirit of God" (§41), and bishops, priests, religious, and laity must be holy, by loving God and neighbor, avoiding vice, proclaiming the gospel, and giving their lives for others. Paragraph 41 notes that married couples "offer to all an example of untiring and generous love" and "bear witness to and cooperate in the fruitfulness of mother Church," and the contributions of widows and single people are also commended. The paragraph encourages both laborers, who imitate Christ the carpenter, and those who, as a result of poverty or illness, "are united in a special way with Christ in his suffering for the world's salvation" (§41).

Concretely, paragraph 42 explains that charity for God and neighbor grows in us when we listen to God's word, participate in the sacramental life of the Church, and deliberately lead a life of "prayer, self-denial, active fraternal service and the practice of all the virtues." In its highest form, charity expresses itself through martyrdom, and all must be willing to suffer for Christ "along the ways of the cross amid the persecutions which the church never lacks" (§42). Virginity or celibacy also bears witness to Christ, through the person's total commitment to following Christ for the sake of the kingdom. Likewise, embracing voluntary poverty and obedience is a way of being configured to the Christ who "emptied himself, taking the form of a servant ... and became obedient unto death" (Phil 2:7–8) for the sake of the salvation of the world. Paragraph 42 warns that all Christians must avoid being "held back from the pursuit of perfect charity by using this world's goods and being attached to riches in a way that is against the spirit of evangelical poverty."

The sixth chapter focuses on religious, those who vow to live in chastity, poverty, and obedience for the sake of Christ.[119] Chastity, poverty, and obedience, the "evangelical counsels," are "a divine gift which the Church

---

119. See also Vatican II's *Perfectae Caritatis*.

has received from its Lord and maintains always with the help of his grace" (§43). Paragraph 44 emphasizes that "the religious state ... makes clear to all believers the heavenly goods that are already present in this world" and "foretells the resurrection that is to come and the glory of the heavenly kingdom." By imitating Christ's manner of life, religious show forth the exalted demands of the kingdom of God and make manifest the power of Christ and the Spirit. By formally recognizing (and regulating) vowed religious as a canonical state of life, the Church fosters the flourishing of the religious life and "shows through its liturgical action that it is a state consecrated to God" (§45). Paragraph 46 addresses the question of whether religious, by denying themselves certain earthly goods, are impeding their own personal fulfillment. The answer is certainly no, since the counsels "contribute not a little to the purification of the heart and to spiritual freedom" (§46). In their self-denial, religious are configured to Christ and freed to serve others in monasteries, schools, hospitals, and missions; and by their prayer they hold others "present in the bowels of Christ and cooperate spiritually with them, so that the building up of the earthly city may be always founded in the Lord and directed towards him" (§46). They are participating personally in the reform and renewal of the Church. The chapter concludes with an exhortation to religious to "persevere and make greater progress in the vocation to which God has called them, for the richer holiness of the church" and for the glory of the Trinity, the source of all holiness (§47).

Chapter 7 explores "The eschatological character of the pilgrim church and its union with the heavenly church." To contrast the earthly Church with the heavenly Church, as though the former were human and the latter divine, would miss the point entirely. It is one Church that "will reach its completion only in the glory of heaven, when the time for the restoration of all things will come" (§48). Paragraph 48 focuses on the work of Christ at the right hand of the Father in constituting his Body the Church "as the universal sacrament of salvation" and in leading all people to the Church, whose members are strengthened by the Eucharist. The full "restoration" and renewal of all things, promised by God, has begun in Christ and even now "by means of the Spirit continues in the church" (§48). History therefore is not a mere delay of the eschaton; rather, history is the place of Christ's transformative work through the Holy Spirit, bringing about the ecclesial unity of humans with God. The Church on earth is the pilgrim Church, with imperfect but real holiness and with a covenantal mission to evangelize the world in self-sacrificial love, which requires believers to "put on the armour of God, so that we can stand up against the snares of the devil and resist in the evil day" (§48). Indeed, paragraph 48 emphasizes that believers must be on guard to live always for Christ in love, so that "we may deserve to enter the nuptial celebration with him and be counted among the blessed (see Mt 25:31–46), and not be ordered, like the evil and lazy servants (see Mt 25:26), to go down to the eternal fire." The Church, which like Christ endures suffering in the present age, yearns for Christ's coming in glory, for "the arrival of the new heavens and new earth in which justice dwells," and for the resurrection of the dead to glorified life (§48).

Paragraph 49 refers to the various states in which Christians now live: on earth, in purgatory, and in heavenly union with Christ, enjoying the beatific vision of the triune God. Since all in Christ form one Church, those on earth enjoy a communion with the saints in heaven, who "intercede for us to the Father, displaying the merits they gained on earth through the one mediator between God and humanity, Christ Jesus" (§49). Paragraph 50 explains the Church's prayers for the dead and honoring of the saints, the holy angels, and the Blessed Virgin Mary. In the lives of the saints, configured as they are to Christ, "God makes vividly manifest to humanity his presence and his face" so that we can see what union with Christ looks like and so that we can be led by them to a deeper communion with Christ (§50). As paragraph 50 makes clear, what is at stake is the affirmation of the work of salvation: God "is wonderful in his saints and in them is glorified." The union of the Church in heaven and the Church on earth is manifested supremely in the liturgy, where those whom Christ has united to himself join together in one song of praise, so that it is true to say that "[w]hen we celebrate ... the eucharistic sacrifice we join very closely the worship of the heavenly church" (§50). Paragraph 51 cautions, however, against excesses in the cult of the saints, since what counts is the love that makes us "one family in Christ," communicating with one another "in mutual love and in the one praise of the most holy Trinity" in a foretaste of the supreme beatitude of the new Jerusalem.

Paragraph 52 begins the final chapter of *Lumen Gentium*, on "The blessed virgin Mary, mother of God, in the mystery of Christ and the church."[120] Mary possesses the "supreme office and dignity of being the mother of God the Son, and therefore she is the specially loved daughter of the Father and the shrine of the Holy Spirit; and by this gift of pre-eminent grace she surpasses by far all other creatures in heaven and on earth" (§53). But why should Mary, who after all is a member of the Church, be discussed in a document on the Church? The answer is that not only is Mary the preeminent member of the Church, but also Mary is the Church's "model [typus]" and "exemplar" in faith (§53; cf. §63), as well as the "image and the beginning of the church" (§68). Even more, she is the "mother in the order of grace" (§61) of all members of the Church, because of her unique cooperation with Christ—which continues today through her "motherly love" (§62) for all believers. Paragraph 55 presents her as the fulfillment of the people of Israel, "the exalted daughter of Sion." Since she was "predestined to be the mother" of God, she was "[e]nriched by the first instant of her conception by the splendour of a most singular holiness" (see Lk 1:28) so that she could embrace "the salvific will of God wholeheartedly and without being held back by any sin" (§56). Assenting by grace to God's word and receiving God's Word made flesh into her womb, she freely and faithfully cooperated with God as the new Eve, with the effects of her obedience reversing the effects of Eve's disobedience.

Surveying the biblical testimony, paragraph 57 remarks that the "union of the mother with the Son in the work of redemption is manifest from the instant of the virginal conception of Christ right on to his death." Paragraphs 58 and 59 provide biblical evidence of this cooperation, most importantly Mary's associating "herself with a mother's heart

---

120. The first and final chapters of *Lumen Gentium* mirror the structure of Henri de Lubac's 1953 *Méditation sur l'Église*, which appeared in English in 1956 as *The Splendor of the Church*, trans. Michael Mason (New York: Sheed and Ward, 1956). There was debate at the Council over whether to publish a separate document on the Blessed Virgin Mary, or to include this theme in the document on the Church. By a narrow margin, the Council Fathers voted to treat Mary within *Lumen Gentium* in order to underscore that Mary is a member of the Church. During the Council, Pope Paul VI added to the Litany of Loreto the title "Mother of the Church," a title that emphasized her unique relationship to all other members of the Church. See Cesare Antonelli, *Il dibattito su Maria nel Concilio Vaticano II. Percorso redazionale sulla base di nuovi documenti di archivio* (Padova: Edizioni Messaggero di Sant' Antonio, 2009).

with his sacrifice" and, at the foot of the Cross, "lovingly consenting to the immolation of the victim that had been born from her" (§58). She was in the upper room with the apostles in the days prior to Pentecost, and her cooperation with her Son in his redemptive suffering received its crown when, having completed her life on earth, she "was taken up body and soul to heavenly glory" in full configuration with her Savior (§59).

Does Mary's role undermine Christ's stature as the one Mediator (see 1 Tm 2:5–6)? Paragraph 60 insists that, on the contrary, "the maternal role of Mary towards humanity in no way obscures or diminishes this unique mediation of Christ; rather it shows forth its power." Her work is founded entirely upon the grace that flows from his mediation, and completely depends upon his mediation at every instant. From eternity, God willed for her to be the "mother of God" and willed for her to have not merely a biological role but to share, as a real mother, in the life of her Son (§61). Entirely by the grace of her Son, she cooperated with her Son in an extraordinary way. She shares uniquely in the "one mediation of the redeemer" through her "participated cooperation" with her Son (§62). Since she is Christ's mother, she is the mother of all who belong to his Body "in the order of grace" (§61), and even now she prays constantly for her children. Certainly "no creature can ever be counted along with the incarnate Word and redeemer," but Christ can and does enable believers to participate in him and in his work, and Mary is the supreme example of this (§62).

As mother and virgin, Mary is like the Church, since the Church "is also rightly called mother and virgin" (§63) in bringing forth children through the Holy Spirit by faith and obedience, and by virginally keeping "integral and pure the faith she has given to her spouse" (§64). Like Mary, the Church is holy. Indeed, paragraph 65 notes that "in the most blessed Virgin the church has already attained the perfection by which it is without stain or wrinkle (see Eph 5:27)." By contemplating Mary, the Church draws closer to Christ, because the Church thereby enters "with reverence more and more deeply into the inmost mystery of the incarnation" and becomes more like Christ (§65). We must bear Christ in our hearts as Mary did in her heart and womb.

Paragraph 66 specifies that the veneration of Mary "differs essentially from the cult of adoration which is given to the incarnate Word and equally to the Father and the holy Spirit." Devotion to Mary, if properly practiced, leads to her Son. With an eye to the fallen human aspect of the Church, however, paragraph 67 cautions that theologians and preachers should "carefully ... avoid all false exaggeration" about Mary's privileges and "should sedulously avoid ... anything that might lead our separated brothers and sisters or any other people into error concerning the true teaching of the church" (§67), although a narrow minimalism should also be avoided. The chapter, and *Lumen Gentium* as a whole, concludes by noting that Mary, as "the image and beginning of the church which will receive fulfilment in the age that is to come," "shines forth as a sign of sure hope and comfort for the pilgrim people of God" (§68)—and does so not only for Catholics but also for Orthodox. The Council asks Mary's intercession for unity among Christians and, indeed, for the gathering of all peoples "in peace and harmony into one people of God to the glory of the most holy and undivided Trinity" (§69).

Conclusion: *Lumen Gentium* as an Ongoing Theological Event

In his 1968 Afterword in *True and False Reform in the Church*, Yves Congar defends the Council's teaching and criticizes elements of preconciliar theology such as "the heretofore simplistic interpretation of the Scriptures, and other simplistic (but traditional) interpretations of supernatural realities."[121] At the same time, Congar expresses concerns about the postconciliar situation of the Church. He lists five ways in which protest in the Church could go too far: (1) by destroying Catholic unity or wounding the bond of mutual love; (2) by calling "into question the hierarchical structure of the church's pastoral life, given to us by the Lord's own institution"; (3) by denying or irresponsibly questioning "the articles of doctrine, for which one rather ought to be willing to give one's life"; (4) by excluding certain persons as useless; and (5) by protesting in the middle of the celebration of the liturgy. On this list, numbers two and three especially show Congar's commitment to what he describes in *True*

---

121. Congar, *True and False Reform in the Church*, 341.

and False Reform in the Church as the divine elements of the Church: the content of faith, the sacraments, and the offices of the Church. These elements are given by Jesus Christ and are unchangeably holy. Like Henri de Lubac, Congar rejects (as de Lubac put it in his 1969 commencement address at Saint Louis University) "a 'pluralism' which is not the pluralism of the theological schools but that of entirely different beliefs from those of the normative faith."[122]

Edward Schillebeeckx's influential *Church: The Human Story of God* (1989) represents a different perspective. Schillebeeckx holds that "the four marks [one, holy, catholic, and apostolic] do not describe our real churches in their historical forms."[123] For Schillebeeckx, the real Catholic Church in history, comprising particular local churches, therefore lacks central elements that Congar and *Lumen Gentium* say that it possesses. In light of "the liberating freedom of Jesus Christ," Schillebeeckx critiques the Church's "feudal and hierarchical structure of authority" and "the form of its authoritation and hierarchical mediation."[124] Indeed, he leaves little positive room for the "hierarchical structure of authority" and "hierarchical mediation" that Congar considers to be a divinely given and unchanging element of the Church. Although Schillebeeckx grants that the Church must inevitably have a leadership that exercises authority, he challenges the term "hierarchy" because "in all official documents of the Roman Catholic church 'hierarchy' is used specifically as an argument for rejecting any democratic exercise of authority and thus democratic participation in the government of the church by the people of God."[125] For Schillebeeckx, not only has the Church obscured the liberative freedom

---

122. Henri de Lubac, SJ, "The Church in Crisis," *Theology Digest* 17 (1969): 312–25, at 319. For discussion of this address, see Joseph A. Komonchak, "Vatican II as an 'Event,'" in *Vatican II: Did Anything Happen?*, ed. David G. Schultenover, SJ (New York: Continuum, 2007), 24–51, at 24–26. De Lubac published his essay also in French, and he expanded it into a short book: see de Lubac, "L'Église dans la crise actuelle," *Nouvelle revue théologique* 91 (1969): 580–96 and de Lubac, *L'Église dans la crise actuelle* (Paris: Cerf, 1969).

123. Edward Schillebeeckx, OP, *Church: The Human Story of God*, trans. John Bowden (New York: Crossroad, 1990), 197; this book originally appeared in Dutch in 1989.

124. Ibid., 214. For a valuable critique of Schillebeeckx's Christology, see Thomas Joseph White, OP, *The Incarnate Lord: A Thomistic Study in Christology* (Washington, D.C.: The Catholic University of America Press, 2015), 470–86.

125. Schillebeeckx, *Church*, 217.

of the gospel of Jesus Christ—which in today's world requires a fundamentally democratic Church—but also the Church has neglected the fact that "what the ministry says, even in dogmatic statements, about this offer of salvation in Jesus can only be understood in the totality of the whole of human history."[126] The latter point means that the actual truth-content of a dogmatic statement, including dogma about the Church (as taught in *Lumen Gentium*), will not be apparent until the eschaton, when the "totality of the whole of human history" will be known. This view severely relativizes the Church's dogmatic teaching, even if for Schillebeeckx dogmatic formulations, in their historical context, can be "a legitimate and even permanent milestone."[127]

In 1968, Congar's main concern is still the need for "co-responsibility" and for "the full participation of everyone in those affairs and activities that concern everyone."[128] He hopes that synods of bishops, councils of priests, and parish councils will solve many of the postconciliar (and preconciliar) problems, by re-instantiating the Church's tradition of "the coexistence of a hierarchical principle along with a communitarian framework in virtue of which all parties were invited to take part in the maturation of decisions by way of councils, discussions, and collegial gatherings (in the broad sense of the word)."[129] I agree with Congar that, within the context of the "hierarchical principle," discussions in which all parties are involved are important. He is certainly right that an overbearing exercise of ecclesial authority, such as he and his work were subject to in the 1950s, is neither appropriate nor charitable. I also agree with Congar that reform of the Church is constantly needed, in order to make clearer (rather than undermine or negate) the divine elements of the Church.

Congar recognizes in 1968, however, that "the church cannot admit a situation of being called into question all the time."[130] This is not because the Church does not dare to face questions or to change its prac-

---

126. Ibid., 224.
127. Ibid. Schillebeeckx concludes, "Community, ministry, theology: these three are themselves fundamentally dependent—in a process in which they are relativized—on the living God, who brings his creation in Jesus Christ, through our history, to a final consummation after history" (ibid., 228).
128. Congar, *True and False Reform in the Church*, 345.
129. Ibid., 346.
130. Ibid., 158.

tices, modes of expression, or nondefinitive teachings, but rather because the Church has been divinely commissioned to hand on divine revelation under the guidance of the Spirit and to mediate the means of salvation to the human race. If the Church's truthfulness is "called into question all the time" then this situation undermines the Church's evangelizing mission and makes conciliar texts such as *Lumen Gentium* useless.

Maureen Sullivan appropriately foregrounds Congar's contributions to *Lumen Gentium*.[131] But Sullivan's conclusion that Congar understood the Church as "divinely founded, but in the hands of humans" misses the true depth of Congar's theology of the Church.[132] For Congar, the Church is even now in divine "hands" (Christ and the Spirit), while at the same time being "in the hands of humans." It is divine not solely in its founding, but also now; and even in its founding, the human element was fully present.

In his 1978 book *Église catholique et France moderne*, Congar highlights this union of divine and human elements, in response to the one-sided perspective of some contemporary reformers: "This same Church whose human tares they condemn is from Jesus Christ, from the living and holy God. The Church is not a mere human creation. As the concrete form of Christianity she is *given* prior to Christians, namely in Christ."[133] Congar makes clear that Christ's Church possesses enduring truth about divine realities, so that Catholic theology cannot be envisioned as free to move in any direction but instead must be authoritatively governed by Scripture and Tradition. He emphasizes that the Church's "dogma and her theologies are radically given in the Word of God whose witness is the Scriptures."[134] In

---

131. For emphasis on the fact that in acknowledging the work of the individual drafters we should appreciate that the final texts are documents of the Church that transcend the individuals' viewpoints, see Innocent Smith, OP, "Ecclesial Authorship, the Council, and the Liturgy: Reflections on a Debate between Ratzinger and Lefebvre," *Angelicum* 92 (2015): 93–113. See also Gérard Philips, *L'Église et son mystère au IIe Concile du Vatican. Histoire, texte et commentaire de la Constitution* Lumen Gentium, 2 vols. (Paris: Desclée, 1967–1968).

132. Maureen Sullivan, OP, *The Road to Vatican II: Key Changes in Theology* (New York: Paulist Press, 2007), 19.

133. Yves Congar, OP, *Église catholique et France moderne* (Paris: Hachette, 1978), 13–14; cited in Nichols, *Yves Congar*, 181 (Nichols's trans.). See also Congar, "What Belonging to the Church Has Come to Mean," trans. Frances M. Chew, *Communio* 4 (1977): 146–60, where he seeks a solution to the current situation by proposing a "threshold Church," distinct from the Church in its fullness, but related to it in the way similar to how the catechumenate is related to the Church.

134. Congar, *Eglise catholique et France moderne*, 13–14 (Nichols's trans.).

this way, he insists upon the divine elements of the Church, upon which are grounded the Church's holiness: "There exists in the Church an element of transcendent purity."[135]

As Congar suggests in *Église catholique et France moderne*, if much preconciliar theology overemphasized the divine elements by neglecting the human aspects and disallowing reform, much postconciliar theology has overemphasized the human aspects by neglecting the divine elements and supposing that everything can or should be changed. At the outset of her exposition of *Lumen Gentium*, Sullivan sums up her view of its message: "We shall see that the church had changed—from a static, timeless entity to a dynamic, pilgrim people on a journey to their ultimate destiny, the fullness of truth found only in God."[136] For Congar, by contrast, there are "timeless" or divine elements present in a fully historical fashion within the "dynamic, pilgrim people on a journey." Congar does not historicize the divine elements of the Church, even while he locates them carefully in history.

Sullivan allows that "sin will never so dominate the church that it could be totally unfaithful to God's truth, a truth that unfolds ever more fully through history."[137] However, on the grounds that "all expressions of theological truth are conditioned by their moment in history," she observes that "our grasp of theological truths needs to be influenced by the council's acknowledgment of the church as an eschatological reality."[138] In her view, "theological articulations of the faith" are ever-changing and imperfect "attempts to articulate revelation in human words and systems of thought," so that dogmatic efforts "to articulate revelation" are not necessarily true—although, eschatologically speaking, "error will not have the final word."[139] She concludes that the Church's expressions of divine revelation are "simply the vehicles through which we attempt to bring God to birth again in each new generation."[140] Congar and *Lumen Gentium*,

---

135. Ibid. See also the analysis in Andrew Meszaros's "Vatican II as Theological Event and Text according to Yves Congar."
136. Sullivan, *The Road to Vatican II*, 91. 137. Ibid., 115.
138. Ibid., 109. 139. Ibid., 116.
140. Ibid. See also Christopher Cimorelli and Daniel Minch, "Views of Doctrine: Historical Consciousness, Asymptotic Notional Clarity, and the Challenge of Hermeneutics as Ontology," *Louvain Studies* 37 (2013): 327–63; and the response of Eduardo J. Echeverria, "The Essentialist

by contrast, teach that the Church's dogmas are Christ's enduring gifts of saving truth.

The ongoing theological event of *Lumen Gentium* today recalls believers to the nature and mission of the Church. Enlightened by Christ, the work of the pope, of the bishops, and of the whole people of God must "promote and defend the unity of faith and discipline common to the whole church" (§23), so that the world may be consecrated to God through the Spirit. The simple purpose of all of this is stated by Paul: "The grace of the Lord Jesus Christ and the love of God and the fellowship of the Holy Spirit be with you all" (1 Cor 13:14).

---

versus Historicist Debate about the Truth Status of Dogmatic Formulations: A Critique of the Cimorelli/Minch Proposal," *Louvain Studies* 38 (2014): 356–69. Echeverria observes that for Cimorelli and Minch (and, I would add, for many others), "inadequacy of expression seems to mean inexpressibility of divine truth. No, they do not deny the existence of divine or transcendent truth (C/M 344). Rather, they deny that divine truth may be determinately and hence truly known, inadequately, but not falsely, analogically, but no less meaningfully. Therefore, since C/M posit a radical epistemic break here between dogmatic formulations and reality, or concepts and reality (C/M 356), such that divine truth is unformulatable, we are not surprised to hear them claim that 'there is no constant, asymptotic progression towards Truth or full possession of the divine through certain knowledge of revealed truths'" (Echeverria, "The Essentialist versus Historicist Debate about the Truth Status of Dogmatic Formulations," 357–58).

CHAPTER 4

NATURE AND GRACE

Gaudium et Spes in Context

As Susan Wood has observed, Henri de Lubac drew a "clear connection ... between his own work on the supernatural and themes developed in *Gaudium et Spes*."[1] In his work on the nature-grace relationship, de Lubac sought to articulate the intimacy of the relationship between human nature as created and the divine gift of grace: grace is no mere add-on.[2] In

---

1. Susan K. Wood, SCL, "Henri de Lubac and the Church-World Relationship in *Gaudium et Spes*," in *The Legacy of Vatican II*, ed. Massimo Faggioli and Andrea Vicini, SJ (Mahwah, N.J.: Paulist Press, 2015), 226–47, at 227. Rightly, in my view, Wood argues that *Gaudium et Spes* §22's use of the term "vocation" avoids certain pitfalls that would otherwise be associated with de Lubac's approach. She remarks, "Since a person's supernatural vocation is only known through revelation, vocation sidesteps the problem of exigencies of nature.... In the theological controversy this exigency was understood as an exigency on the part of the human person, which became a right the person claimed from God. The notion of vocation prevents this kind of misunderstanding" (ibid., 235).

2. The recognition that human nature desires a happiness that no created reality can satisfy is contained in chapter 7 of the Preparatory Theological Commission's (neo-scholastic) *Schema de deposito fidei pure custodiendo*, titled "De ordine naturali et supernaturali," which was delivered to all the Council Fathers in late summer 1962. For discussion see Giovanni Turbanti, *Un concilio*

introducing *Gaudium et Spes* as an ongoing theological event by reference to de Lubac's *The Mystery of the Supernatural*, as I will do in this chapter, I do not mean to imply that *Gaudium et Spes* reprises the preconciliar controversy over nature and grace or even that *Gaudium et Spes* must be read in light of de Lubac's book. After all, *Gaudium et Spes*, like the other conciliar texts we have studied, ranges quite widely, displays a diversity of formative influences (including Pope John XXIII's encyclicals), and does not attempt to resolve the finer points of theological controversies. Instead, in choosing de Lubac's book for the present chapter, I seek to draw attention to a point made by Pope John Paul II in his *Crossing the Threshold of Hope*: "The Council proposed, especially in *Gaudium et Spes*, that the mystery of redemption should be seen in light of the great renewal of man and of all that is human."[3] In his encyclicals, too, John Paul II frequently emphasized *Gaudium et Spes*'s presentation of Christ vis-à-vis human nature. For example, with reference to *Gaudium et Spes* §22, John Paul II insists in *Dives in Misericordia* that "man cannot be manifested in the full dignity of his nature without reference—not only on the level of concepts but also in an integrally existential way—to God" (§1).[4] For John Paul II, the reality that human nature is fueled by the desire for union with God is "one of the basic principles, perhaps the most important one, of the teaching of the last Council [Vatican II]" (§1), and this insight should affect our understanding of *Gaudium et Spes* as an ongoing theological event.

Henri de Lubac does not appear to have had a great deal of direct influence on *Gaudium et Spes* (other than on its section about atheism), even if one may rightly posit significant indirect influence.[5] In his 1985

---

per il mondo moderno. La redazione della constituzione pastorale "Gaudium et spes" del Vaticano II (Bologna: Il Mulino, 2000); see also Jared Wicks, SJ, "More Light on Vatican Council II," *Catholic Historical Review* 94 (2008): 75–101. De Lubac responded critically to one passage in the *Schema de deposito fidei pure custodiendo*, but his criticism had to do with a passage related to his work on development of dogma, not to his work on the relationship of nature and grace.

3. John Paul II, *Crossing the Threshold of Hope*, trans. Jenny McPhee and Martha McPhee, ed. Vittorio Messori (New York: Alfred A. Knopf, 1995), 48. Bishop Karol Wojtyła, the future Pope John Paul II, befriended de Lubac during the Council.

4. This observation leads John Paul II to conclude: "The more the Church's mission is centered upon man—the more it is, so to speak, anthropocentric—the more it must be confirmed and actualized theocentrically, that is to say, be directed in Jesus Christ to the Father" (*Dives in Misericordia*, Encyclical Letter, November 30, 1980, §1).

5. For discussion, see Jared Wicks, SJ, "Further Light on Vatican Council II," *Catholic Histori-*

interview *Entretien autour de Vatican II: Souvenirs et reflections*, de Lubac mentions that he worked on the text of *Gaudium et Spes* "only in its later stages."[6] He was a *peritus* attached to the Mixed Commission that, beginning in early 1963, worked upon what eventually became *Gaudium et Spes*. Notably, *Gaudium et Spes* §22 paraphrases a central passage from de Lubac's 1938 book *Catholicism*.[7] De Lubac and *Gaudium et Spes* strongly agree that the mystery of humanity can be understood only through the mystery of Christ. In *Entretien autour de Vatican II*, de Lubac observes approvingly with regard to *Gaudium et Spes* (and to the Council as a whole): "Without any exaggeration, one can say that the Council broke away from extrinsicism which (was) the illness of modern Catholicism 'which had misunderstood the full character of the desire of nature' (Congar) purposefully avoiding the vocabulary of the two 'orders.'"[8]

In this chapter, then, de Lubac's *The Mystery of the Supernatural* will serve as an entrance point for exploring *Gaudium et Spes* as an ongoing theological event. De Lubac published this book in 1965, apparently in part as a response to criticisms of his *Surnaturel* during the conciliar debate over the document that would become *Gaudium et Spes*.[9] According

---

cal Review 95 (2009): 546–62, a review essay treating Henri de Lubac's posthumously published *Carnets du Concile*, ed. Loïc Figoureux, 2 vols. (Paris: Cerf, 2007). Wicks describes three "moments" in which de Lubac tried to directly influence *Gaudium et Spes* during its development.

6. See Henri de Lubac, *Entretien autour de Vatican II. Souvenirs et reflections* (Paris: Cerf, 1985), 45. See also his *Carnets du Concile* as well as his *At the Service of the Church: Henri de Lubac Reflects on the Circumstances That Occasioned His Writings*, trans. Anne Elizabeth Englund (San Francisco: Ignatius Press, 1993), chapter 7 and Appendix 7. For reflection on de Lubac's experience of the Council, see Loïc Figoureux, "Henri de Lubac et le concile Vatican II, espoirs et inquiétudes d'un théologien," *Cristianesimo nella Storia* 34 (2013): 249–71.

7. See David L. Schindler, "Introduction," in Henri de Lubac, SJ, *The Mystery of the Supernatural*, trans. Rosemary Sheed (New York: Crossroad, 1998), xi–xxxi, at xxvii.

8. De Lubac, *Entretien autour de Vatican II*, 28, cited in Wood, "Henri de Lubac and the Church-World Relationship in *Gaudium et Spes*," 237 (Wood's translation).

9. That is the contention of Karl Heinz Neufeld, SJ, "In the Service of the Council: Bishops and Theologians at the Second Vatican Council (for Cardinal Henri de Lubac on His Ninetieth Birthday)," trans. Ronald Sway, in *Vatican II: Assessment and Perspectives: Twenty-Five Years After (1962–1987)*, vol. 1, ed. René Latourelle, SJ (Mahwah, N.J.: Paulist Press, 1988), 74–105, at 91, citing *Acta Synodalia S. Concilii Oecumenici Vaticani II*, 26 vols. (Vatican City: Libreria Editrice Vaticana, 1970–1980), III/V, 519ff.; and H. Fesquet, *Diario del Concilio* (Milan: 1967), 621. Neufeld states that during discussions on Schema 13 (the future *Gaudium et Spes*), "A speaker launched into an offensive against ideas that he attributed to de Lubac in *Surnaturel* concerning the relationship between nature and the supernatural, or, more precisely, against the signification he gave to the 'natural desire'

to de Lubac, *The Mystery of the Supernatural* develops "point by point, in the same order and without changing the least point of doctrine, the article published under that title [by de Lubac] in *Recherches* in 1949."[10] The *Mystery of the Supernatural* therefore provides us with a synthesis of his influential view of the relationship of nature and grace—and of Church and world—as he understood it in the years before and during the Council.

After surveying *The Mystery of the Supernatural*, I summarize *Gaudium et Spes* in the second section of the chapter. *Gaudium et Spes* emphasizes the centrality of Christ from a standpoint of appreciation for the modern world's existential aspirations and dialogic spirit, alongside an awareness of the many challenges that threaten the modern world. Insisting both upon the integrity of human nature's capacities (even though wounded by sin) and upon human nature's God-given orientation toward graced fulfillment in Christ, *Gaudium et Spes* proposes that the modern world and the Church mutually require each other for true human development, peace, and happiness.[11]

---

of man for God. What was at stake here was nothing less than the basic idea underlying the subsequent text of *Gaudium et spes*: the question of the correct understanding of being a Christian in the world" (Neufeld, "In the Service of the Council," 91). In response, says Neufeld, de Lubac produced "two new volumes, which appeared in 1965 and which attempted to give a clearer presentation of his position: *Augustinisme et Théologie moderne* and *Le Mystère du Surnaturel*. Had these two works been read attentively, there should have been no further misunderstandings concerning this question. Naturally, de Lubac also did what he could to exclude such misunderstandings as far as possible from the drafted text of *Gaudium et spes*" (Neufeld, "In the Service of the Council," 92).

10. De Lubac, *At the Service of the Church*, 123. See Henri de Lubac, SJ, *Surnaturel* (Paris: Aubier, 1946); de Lubac, "Le Mystère du surnaturel," *Recherches de science religieuse* 36 (1949): 80–121, which appears in English as "The Mystery of the Supernatural," trans. Anne Englund Nash, in de Lubac, *Theology in History* (San Francisco: Ignatius Press, 1996), 281–316. For further discussion of nature and grace, see Henri de Lubac, SJ, *A Brief Catechesis on Nature and Grace*, trans. Richard Arnandez, FSC (San Francisco: Ignatius, 1984). See also de Lubac's 1965 book—a companion to *The Mystery of the Supernatural*—titled *Augustinianism and Modern Theology*, trans. Lancelot Sheppard (New York: Crossroad, 2000). For a helpful introduction to and contextualization of the development of de Lubac's thinking on nature and grace, see Raul Berzosa Martinez, *La Teología del Sobrenatural en los Escritos de Henri de Lubac: Estudio Historico-Teologico (1931–1980)* (Burgos: Aldecoa, 1991). See also Georges Chantraine, SJ, "The Supernatural: Discernment of Catholic Thought according to Henri de Lubac," in *Surnaturel: A Controversy at the Heart of Twentieth-Century Thomistic Thought*, ed. Serge-Thomas Bonino, OP, trans. Robert Williams (Ave Maria, Fla.: Sapientia Press, 2009), 21–40. For further background see Bernard Comte, "Le père de Lubac, un théologien dans l'Église de Lyon," in *Henri de Lubac: La rencontre au coeur de l'Église*, ed. Jean-Dominique Durand (Paris: Cerf, 2006), 35–89.

11. Henri de Lubac's insistence upon the "natural desire for the supernatural," as distinct from

Henri de Lubac's *The Mystery of the Supernatural*

De Lubac opens *The Mystery of the Supernatural* by arguing that his view of nature and grace, a view that he contends simply is "the traditional idea" and "the old tradition" from the Fathers onward, is currently under threat from two directions.[12] First, there is the dualist, or separatist, view of nature and grace, which denies that grace bears any relation to nature. Even though this view no longer has many adherents, he says, it is still bearing bitter fruit "in the sphere of practical action," since the secular world proceeds as though grace did not exist.[13] Second, there is an immanentist conflation of nature and grace that supposes, as in Marxist or Hegelian theory, that the dialectic of history will produce from within itself the transcendence that we desire.

In order to understand how these two extremes arose and how they can be overcome, de Lubac reflects upon what he calls the "new theory" of

---

a natural desire for God or a natural desire to see the divine essence, was and is controversial because of the paradox contained in the phrase. Opponents of de Lubac's position recognize that human nature is ordered to Trinitarian communion (in the graced order that God has willed), and they also affirm that human nature, because of its rational dynamisms, can be satisfied with nothing less than God (distinct, however, from the supernatural gift of Trinitarian communion). For opponents of de Lubac's position, his formulation inevitably implies—despite his efforts to show the contrary—that human nature *as such* possesses a supernatural dynamism distinct from the dynamism of grace, which thereby risks making grace superfluous. The contemporary debate is too extensive for me to cite here, but see for example Steven A. Long, "Obediential Potency, Human Knowledge, and the Natural Desire for the Vision of God," *International Philosophical Quarterly* 37 (1997): 45–63; Nicholas J. Healy, Jr., "Henri de Lubac on Nature and Grace: A Note on Some Recent Contributions to the Debate," *Communio* 35 (2008): 535–64; Lawrence Feingold, *The Natural Desire to See God according to St. Thomas Aquinas and His Interpreters*, 2nd ed. (Ave Maria, Fla.: Sapientia Press, 2010); David Braine, "The Debate between Henri de Lubac and His Critics," *Nova et Vetera* 6 (2008): 543–90; Christopher J. Malloy, "De Lubac on Natural Desire: Difficulties and Antitheses," *Nova et Vetera* 9 (2011): 567–624; Edward T. Oakes, SJ, "The *Surnaturel* Controversy: A Survey and a Response," *Nova et Vetera* 9 (2011): 626–56; Reinhard Hütter, *Dust Bound for Heaven: Explorations in the Theology of Thomas Aquinas* (Grand Rapids, Mich.: Eerdmans, 2012), chapters 5 and 6; Thomas Joseph White, OP, "Imperfect Happiness and the Final End of Man: Thomas Aquinas and the Paradigm of Nature-Grace Orthodoxy," *The Thomist* 78 (2014): 247–89; David Grummett, "De Lubac, Grace, and the Pure Nature Debate," *Modern Theology* 31 (2015): 123–46.

12. Henri de Lubac, SJ, *The Mystery of the Supernatural*, trans. Rosemary Sheed (New York: Herder and Herder, 1967), xi. I have employed the 1967 edition rather than the 1998 Crossroad edition. The translation is the same in the two editions, with the exception that the Latin quotations are all translated (by John M. Pepino) in the 1998 edition.

13. Ibid.

"pure nature," which claims to be able to set forth the constitutive elements and dynamisms of a hypothetical human nature existing without grace and without sin.[14] This theory, absent among the Greek Fathers and absent also in the West (according to de Lubac) until the sixteenth-century Dominican Thomas de Vio Cardinal Cajetan, rose to preeminence in the Baroque period, although it was criticized even by some Baroque commentators such as Francisco Toletus. In the 1920s and 1930s, however, a number of theologians contested the theory of pure nature, or at least Cajetan's credibility, and in the 1950s further theologians did so, building upon the critique that de Lubac had issued in the 1940s. In his 1908 *L'intellectualisme de saint Thomas*, the Jesuit scholar Pierre Rousselot had already pointed out Cajetan's error. Still earlier, in the late nineteenth century Théodore de Regnon recognized that he could (in de Lubac's words) "find no explicit affirmation in St Thomas of the concrete possibility of a purely natural order—remembering always that this means a complete order, bearing within it its own final end, in the modern sense of the expression."[15]

It would seem that if for humans a "purely natural" end or "pure nature" is not even *hypothetically* possible, then the distinction between human nature and graced human nature would be impossible to describe.[16] Absent a concept of "pure nature," how could we know what human "nature" is, as fully differentiated from grace? De Lubac responds that the answer consists in accepting a paradox. He fully grants that created spirit, as such, is not naturally a supernatural reality: "The fact that the nature of spiritual being, as it actually exists, is not conceived as an order destined to close in finally upon itself, but in a sense open to an inevitably supernatural end, does not mean that it already has in itself, or as part of its basis, the smallest positively supernatural element."[17] Certainly, too, human nature has "its own proper stability and its own definite structure."[18] But, paradoxically, this does not mean that human nature, as graced, has a twofold ultimate end—that is to say, a proportionate natural end, identified through the hypothesis of "pure nature," and the graced end of beatific vision.

In explaining what he means here, de Lubac appeals to the perspec-

14. Ibid., 7.
16. Ibid., 15–17.
18. Ibid.

15. Ibid., 15.
17. Ibid., 41.

tive of the Fathers, which he thinks was shared by Thomas Aquinas.[19] He states, "In the old teaching, which remains for us the traditional one, the argument was based on no such duality of ends. The supernatural, which always represented God's will for the final end of his creatures, put no obstacle in the way of the normal development or activity of nature in its own order."[20] Thus there was never a need to dissociate "the two orders completely," because grace permits the activity of nature in such a way that this activity need not constitute an end in its own right.[21] The greatness of grace means that it can never be simply "juxtaposed" with nature (as in the case of two ends), as though nature and grace were "contained in the same genus, of which they form as it were two species."[22] Grace is infinitely above nature, and therefore it will not work simply to align humans' graced end with a natural end as though we were speaking of the same kind of thing, or as though humans could in fact theoretically be perfected without divine assistance. As soon as such a supposition is entertained, the absolute necessity of grace for human perfection is impaired, and the meaning of "beatitude" is naturalized in an unacceptable fashion. De Lubac's concern is that setting up a natural beatitude alongside a supernatural beatitude inevitably flattens the latter, so that nothing "remains peculiar to the supernatural order, except the word."[23] As examples of this problem, he mentions theories of a "direct natural vision of God" and of a "natural possession" of God.[24]

Against such univocal understandings of nature and grace, de Lubac insists that nature cannot produce a "beatitude" in any way comparable to the God-given beatitude for which God made humans. For his opponents, he states, "the two series—'pure nature' and supernaturalized nature, or nature called to the supernatural—flowed along parallel channels in complete harmony.... Without anything apparently to distinguish them, one is called 'natural', the other 'supernatural.'"[25] On such a view,

---

19. According to de Lubac, Aquinas never accepted "a completely natural perfection [of the human person] which can be adequately defined by pure philosophy" (ibid., 49).
20. Ibid., 45.   21. Ibid., 46.
22. Ibid., 48.   23. Ibid., 52.
24. Ibid., 52–53. He credits these phrases, with which he obviously disagrees, to his Jesuit contemporaries Pedro Descoqs and Charles Boyer.
25. Ibid., 53.

grace presents God as the "supernatural good" of humans, whereas nature presents God as the "natural good." This distinction involves a merely nominal difference, since grace has here become a mere parallel nature. Furthermore, postulating God as the "natural good" or proportionate end of humans presumptuously offers God to humans through the work of human nature itself, in a way that patristic thinkers would not have dared to suppose could be done without God's own free gift, since (after all) God "dwells in unapproachable light" (1 Tm 6:16).

What about the distinction between seeing God's essence (the gift of beatific vision) and seeing God as first cause (the proportionate end of human nature)? Here, citing Bernard of Clairvaux, de Lubac questions whether the distinction can really be effectively conceived in this way. What would it mean to be blessed by seeing God as first cause, without seeing God's essence? Furthermore, de Lubac argues that the fact that our soul is an image of the Trinity indicates that in the highest aspect of our humanity, we are made for the enjoyment of the Trinity. The idea that any human, however hypothetical, could be happy without God's aid, simply by the exercise of natural powers, strikes de Lubac as not only mistaken, but as the source of a false view of the sufficiency of natural morality.

Does this mean, however, that the supernatural (i.e., grace) is *required in justice* by created human nature, so that grace can no longer be God's free gift but instead becomes merely a requisite of nature? De Lubac answers no: in fact the central problem with the hypothesis of pure nature is that it leads precisely to a God whose giving of himself to humans is no longer free, but pertains to a natural order that requires it (the *debitum naturae*, that is, the debt that the Creator God owes himself in justice once he determines to create humans). Even if the "formal hypothesis" of pure nature is "legitimate," it is so only when devoid of content and when it points to an abstract "human nature" that is utterly inconceivable in light of the actually existing human nature that we know.[26]

---

26. Ibid., 64. Étienne Gilson, with whom de Lubac was in correspondence and who shared de Lubac's concerns regarding nature and grace, likewise feared that "modern Scholasticism" (from Francisco Suárez onward) focuses on essence (possible being) rather than on existence (actual being). See for instance his remark in his *Being and Some Philosophers*, 2nd ed. (Toronto: Pontifical Institute of Mediaeval Studies, 1952), 119.

If we have only the end of supernatural beatitude, however, this would seem to entail that our spiritual powers—our intellect and will, which belong to our natural constitution—have supernatural beatitude as their end, toward which they (as natural powers, rather than by grace) are ordered. If this is so, however, it seems impossible to preserve the gratuity of grace, since the dynamism toward the supernatural end would be built into human nature, whose exigencies would be profoundly and unjustifiably frustrated were grace not available. In *The Mystery of the Supernatural*, de Lubac seeks to answer this question at length. He argues that in the task of theologizing, we have to begin from humans as humans actually are; and this means starting from humans as constitutively called by God to supernatural beatitude, rather than from possible worlds. As de Lubac states, "My finality, which is expressed by this desire, is inscribed upon my very being as it has been put into this universe by God."[27] Given the kind of creatures that we actually are, is grace (or the supernatural) freely given? De Lubac insists that this question must have to do not with hypothetical humans who never have existed, but with "the being whose finality is 'already', if one can say so, wholly supernatural—for such is the case with us.... [T]here is only one end, and therefore I bear within me, consciously or otherwise, a 'natural desire' for it."[28] At our existential core, we do not wait for knowledge of divine revelation and only then experience a desire for supernatural union with God. Rather, supernatural union with God—the vision of God—is the only end for which God has made us, and since God has made us for this end, we desire it and we would suffer if we failed to attain it. De Lubac comments, "That is why, if I fail to achieve this which is my end, it may be said that I have failed in everything; if I lose it, I am 'damned'; and to be aware of such a situation is for me the 'pain of damnation.'"[29]

On this basis, de Lubac arrives at the next step of his argument, namely the task of showing "how, even for a being animated with such a desire, there still is not and cannot be any question of such an end being 'owed.'"[30] Ruling out any appeal to a hypothetical "pure nature," which has never ex-

---

27. De Lubac, *The Mystery of the Supernatural*, 70.
28. Ibid., 71–72.
29. Ibid., 73.
30. Ibid., 75–76.

isted, is there a way of answering this question regarding whether grace is owed to the person who naturally desires the vision of God? De Lubac proposes that we approach this question from the side of God: does God, having from the outset given humans their ultimate end (beatific vision), give this beatific vision freely, or is God compelled? Put another way, in the present order of things, in which we desire to see God and this vision is in fact our divinely ordained ultimate end, can grace still be a free gift? Reflecting on this question, de Lubac rejects the supposition that "an end cannot be given freely for a definite being, existing here and now, unless there had first of all been a different end for him that was objectively, concretely realizable."[31] He insists that God never willed any other end than beatific vision for humans, that indeed humans were created solely for this end and are not (without ceasing to be humans) abstractable from this end, and that God nonetheless gives the end with utter freedom. Human finality is deeply inscribed in what it means to be human; if humans had a different finality, they would not remain the same qua human. We must not conceive of finality in so extrinsic a manner.

How then to resolve the question of God's freedom in giving the gift, if the gift is naturally desired? According to de Lubac, we must recognize that God's gift of grace is utterly transcendent; it is not like our gifting, but indeed the only gifting to which it can be compared is the gift of creation. Certainly grace must not be conflated with the gift of creation, since grace is "wholly distinct" and "wholly super-eminent."[32] The danger comes, however, when we look to creation and see a twofold gift, of natural being (creation) and of finality (grace): it seems that our being precedes its finality, which leads both to a false extrinsicism and to an anthropomorphic notion of the power of the divine Giver. We should see instead the radical contingency and freedom of both gifts. God gives no "exterior" gifts to us; and therefore our being and our finality are given in a twofold way *and* (paradoxically) given at once, with utter gratuitousness.[33] There are indeed two gifts, but the second gift cannot be rightly conceived as a mere sequel of the first, as though they were on the same ontological level. Grace radically transcends nature.

31. Ibid., 88. 32. Ibid., 98.
33. Ibid., 101.

We should also appreciate that the longing or desire for the supernatural present in the first gift (nature) expresses a lack, not a possession or a natural power. Thus the natural desire for the supernatural "does not constitute as yet even the slightest positive 'ordering' to the supernatural."[34] Only grace can order us to our ultimate end, and yet we can long for it and be inclined to it, even if not in a proportionate or efficacious way. De Lubac insists, "Man's longing for God is in a category of its own; we cannot apply univocally to it any of the patterns of thought which we generally use to try to define relationships between beings in this world."[35] Since our longing is expressive of a lack, not expressive of a positive power or faculty (or even an "ordering"), and since this longing "is in a category of its own," de Lubac concludes that the natural desire for the supernatural does not mean that God owes us grace in order to do justice to what he has created. Contrasting his position with the condemned viewpoint of Michael Baius, de Lubac holds that created nature can recognize a lack and express a longing for its supernatural ultimate end, but cannot rise to the radically transcendent level of grace. Since grace utterly transcends nature, it cannot be owed to nature. Again, human nature contains "no slightest element of the supernatural in it," but the supernatural nonetheless summons human nature through nature's God-given supernatural finality.[36] God's will is primary, and God's will is perfectly free in giving us this summons: "His sovereign liberty encloses, surpasses and causes all the bonds of intelligibility that we discover between the creature and its destiny."[37]

De Lubac goes on to differentiate human nature from lower natures, insofar as humans desire the infinite. Humans have a *spiritual* "nature," and so that term ("nature") needs to be taken in an analogous sense. Our nature is not stable, but reaches beyond itself, and also reaches lower than itself. While retaining the notion of human nature, de Lubac seeks to undermine the view that a spiritual nature must have an end that corresponds to its powers. This is why human nature is a paradox, always reaching above itself without thereby being divine in any way. De Lubac grants

---

34. Ibid., 111.
35. Ibid., 114.
36. Ibid., 124.
37. Ibid., 129.

that "the idea of a gift coming gratuitously from above to raise up that needy nature, at once satisfying its longings and transforming it—such an idea remains wholly foreign to all whose minds have not been touched by the light of revelation."[38] And yet, God has inscribed in human nature "a certain innate openness ... to that superabundance," a hidden "call within nature," "with its roots lying deeper than any tendency or commitment of man's free will."[39] Ancient civilizations experienced this, but did not know how to interpret it. This "call within nature," since it is not a positive power, does not compel God in justice to satisfy it; but God placed it within us because he does will to satisfy it, by raising human nature above itself. In recognizing divine revelation, humans recognize our "capacity for God and ... the 'natural' desire corresponding to it."[40]

Here de Lubac's fundamental point has to do with the meaning of the "obediential potency" for grace that Aquinas locates in humans. The key question is whether grace is a new finality, opposed to an already present natural finality in human nature. De Lubac's argument is that "obediential potency" is in fact expressive of a "call within nature," a natural desire, even though this "inscribed" finality cannot be a positive power in the human spirit. As a spiritual nature reaching out to an end beyond its powers, human nature never tends simply to a proportionate end, despite Cajetan's effort "to see in the human *spirit* no more than the *human* spirit," capable of being truly fulfilled (theoretically at least) by a proportionate end.[41] It is a mistake to require of human nature, which is intrinsically paradoxical, the proportionality (of powers and ends) that Aristotle imagines to hold for all natures.

De Lubac concludes, "The desire to see him [God] is in us, it constitutes us, and yet it comes to us as a completely free gift. Such paradoxes should not surprise us, for they arise in every mystery; they are the hallmark of a truth that is beyond our depth."[42] Our very nature, then, is a paradox. Faced with two seemingly contradictory truths—the constitutive character (for human nature) of the supernatural end and its status as free gift—theologians have sought to reconcile the two; and they were right not to drop

---

38. Ibid., 168.
39. Ibid., 168, 170, 177.
40. Ibid., 179.
41. Ibid., 187.
42. Ibid., 217–18.

the gratuitousness of grace. Yet in de Lubac's view, choosing between the two exhibited a failure of understanding, which a better reading of Aquinas could have avoided. In affirming the gratuitousness of grace, one need not reject the natural desire for the supernatural. Here de Lubac also discusses the tendency to see "the call to the supernatural and the offer of grace in a chronological series, as though the second is governed by the first."[43] If this were the case, then all humans, given the interior dynamism to the supernatural, would necessarily rise to beatitude. In fact, the offer of grace remains completely gratuitous, and our will remains fully free to reject grace, even though all humans possess the natural desire for the supernatural.

As a deep neediness rather than a positive possession, the natural desire cannot be defined more closely except in the light of revelation, even when evidence of the desire manifests itself (ambiguously) in non-Christian philosophies or religions. This is so not least because the "desire," far from mandating a particular divine response, becomes clear only in the light of God's utterly free gift of self in love. As de Lubac remarks, therefore, "such a 'desire', even before the transformation which it must undergo in order to attain its goal, is different in kind from all the desires of our common experience."[44] The revelation of Jesus Christ shows that God's utter freedom in love is at the root of everything. Revelation also shows that the utterly gratuitous "vision of God face to face is the only genuinely final end for any created spirit, since it is the only end which can totally satisfy its desires."[45] Yet God is bound by our natural desire, since, after all, it is God who freely "awakens the desire": reason alone cannot demonstrate that we desire the beatific vision (although this desire, de Lubac specifies again, is natural rather than "elicited").[46] De Lubac remarks that "[c]ertain depths of our nature can be opened only by the shock of revelation. Then, with a new clarity, deep calls upon deep."[47]

My view is that we must not attribute modally supernatural elements to human nature as such, and I think that de Lubac's position cannot avoid doing this. I advocate retrieving the concept of obediential potency

---

43. Ibid., 239.
45. Ibid., 262.
44. Ibid., 301.
46. Ibid., 272, 289.
47. Ibid., 282; cf. 294: "revelation cannot help at the same time transforming and completing our idea of man and his desire, and ultimately, at least if we consent to it, of the desire itself."

along lines that differ from de Lubac's suggestion. But rather than setting forth my own position, I will proceed to the text of *Gaudium et Spes*, whose concerns are anticipated in important ways by de Lubac. Even if the conundrums that de Lubac poses can be answered in ways that differ from his own solution, de Lubac nicely describes the existential condition of fallen human nature embedded in a graced historical economy of salvation. When thinking in concrete historical terms (as *Gaudium et Spes* does), it is necessary to hold human nature and the grace of the Holy Spirit together, under the rubric of what all parties agree is our graced supernatural orientation toward fulfillment in Christ. The salutary insistence that nature and grace ought never to be separated (even though they can be distinguished) profoundly informs *Gaudium et Spes*'s reflections on the relationship of the Church to the aspirations, advances, and challenges of the modern world. Unlike *The Mystery of the Supernatural*, of course, *Gaudium et Spes* is not seeking to resolve a clash of philosophical-theological theories. But in accord with the main intention of de Lubac's work, *Gaudium et Spes* makes clear how, in the sphere of human action (the world), we "live and move and have our being" (Acts 17:28) in the risen Christ, the supernatural source and goal of true human fulfillment.

Gaudium et Spes

In its opening paragraph, *Gaudium et Spes* states that "[n]othing that is genuinely human fails to find an echo" in the hearts of Christian believers, and so Christians—as befits those who bear a "message of salvation intended for all men"—possess "a feeling of deep solidarity with the human race and its history."[48] At the same time, Christians are "united in Christ and guided by the Holy Spirit" (§1). Paragraph 2 observes that "the world ... has been created and is sustained by the love of its maker" and "has been freed from the slavery of sin by Christ, who was crucified and rose again in order to break the stranglehold of the evil one." The world, therefore, must

---

48. Quotations of the preface, introduction and part 1 are from *Gaudium et Spes*, in *Vatican Council II*, vol. 1: *The Conciliar and Post Conciliar Documents*, rev. ed., ed. Austin Flannery, OP (Northport, N.Y.: Costello Publishing, 1996), 903–1001.

"be fashioned anew" and "brought to its fulfillment" (§2). In paragraph 3, *Gaudium et Spes* specifies that since "it is mankind that must be renewed" and redeemed, the key to the discussion of the contemporary situation of the world—and the Church's role in it—is "man considered whole and entire, with body and soul, heart and conscience, mind and will." Paragraph 3 also notes that, in service to human brotherhood, the Church proclaims the "noble destiny of man" and affirms "an element of the divine in him." When the human person is considered "whole and entire," one finds inserted in the human person an element that cannot be reduced to matter and that has a transcendent vocation to union with God.

Gaudium et Spes next speaks about "the aspirations, the yearnings, and dramatic features" (§4) that characterize the world today even more than in the past. It states dramatically: "Ours is a new age of history with critical and swift upheavals spreading gradually to all corners of the earth" (§4). Humans are becoming much more powerful, and yet questions of how to use this power justly and of how to share resources equitably are even more pressing. Technological advancement is ongoing but "without a parallel spiritual advancement" (§4). In paragraph 5, *Gaudium et Spes* notes the expansion of the power of the mind due to technological advancement. We now experience the world as a unity; regions are no longer cut off from one another as they once were. As a result of these changes, "nature" (including human nature) is seen as "dynamic" and "evolutionary" rather than as "static" (§5). Paragraph 6 addresses industrialization, urbanization, and the growth of the mass media,[49] and paragraph 7 points out that many young people no longer accept traditional religion and morality. Paragraph 8 examines imbalances that have become commonplace: between the practical/particular and the contemplative/whole; between generations and between the sexes; and between wealthy and poor nations; and between peace-making international organizations and aggressor nations. At the same time, today the human person demands "a life that is full, autonomous, and worthy of his nature as a human being" (§9).

Given this portrait of modern life, *Gaudium et Spes* argues that "[t]he dichotomy affecting the modern world is, in fact, a symptom of the deeper

---

49. See Vatican II's *Inter Mirifica*.

dichotomy that is in man himself. He is the meeting point of many conflicting forces" (§10). We are finite and limited creatures, but we have "unlimited ... desires" and feel ourselves "summoned to a higher life" (§10). *Gaudium et Spes* calls modern humans to face the age-old existential questions rather than imagining that humans can build a satisfying earthly paradise or devise a satisfying meaning of life that excludes God. Among these age-old questions are "What is man?" and "What happens after this earthly life is ended?" (§10). To these questions and others like them, *Gaudium et Spes* argues that Jesus Christ shows the answer. The Church's voice should be welcomed by the world, because Jesus offers satisfying answers to the world's questions. Thus, for *Gaudium et Spes* §10, it is only in light of Christ that we can rightly apprehend and interpret "the mystery that is man."

Gaudium et Spes §11 is the opening paragraph of part 1. The paragraph expresses the Church's desire, under the guidance of the Spirit "who fills the whole world," to assist the world in finding "solutions that are fully human" (§11). These fully human solutions are knowable through faith, which "throws a new light on all things and makes known the divine plan for the integral vocation of man [divinum propositum de integra hominis vocatione manifestat]" (§11).[50] This "integral vocation of man" is a supernatural one. From this soteriological perspective, the paragraph then suggests that faith needs to be put into action, helping to purify the values of modern societies—values that "stem from the natural talents given to man by God" and that are therefore "exceedingly good," but that must be seen always in relation to God. The paragraph concludes that part 1 of *Gaudium et Spes* will seek to demonstrate that "the people of God, and the human race which is its setting, render service to each other; and the mission of the Church will show itself to be supremely human by the very fact of being religious."

Paragraph 12 inaugurates chapter 1 of *Gaudium et Spes*, on "The Dignity of the Human Person." Sometimes humans conceive of themselves as utterly exalted, sometimes as utterly debased. Fortunately, divine revelation teaches "the true state of man" and explains his infirmities, "in such

---

50. I have modified the Flannery translation here, which reads "makes known the full ideal which God has set for man."

a way that at the same time his dignity and his vocation may be perceived in their true light" (§12). *Gaudium et Spes* then presents the basic components of this revealed teaching on the human person: humans are created in the image of God, so as to worship God and share in God's wise and loving rule over creatures; humans are created male and female and are made for communion with God and each other; sin alienates humans from God and each other and thereby turns humans away from the ultimate end of union with God. Sin mires humans in evil, which only God's grace can overcome.

Gaudium et Spes §14 explores human nature in more detail. Human nature is a body-soul unity, and the body is good, though both body and soul are rebellious through sin. Since humans are embodied creatures, through us the entire material cosmos praises God. We have an immortal, spiritual soul, which manifests itself through our power to know ourselves, to encounter God, and to determine our own destiny by free moral choices. Our minds have the power to go beyond the limits of sense observation and to obtain certitude about invisible realities, such as God. We can attain to a life of contemplative wisdom. We experience within ourselves a law of right and wrong, conscience, through which we encounter God. We enjoy freedom, the ability to choose the good; we can rise above passion and instinct. Thus far our natural rational powers can go; but to know and obey God's plan, we need grace.

Paragraph 18 takes up the problem of death—is death natural to humans? *Gaudium et Spes* goes right to the heart of the matter, namely "the dread of forever ceasing to be" (§18). Alongside this dread, as *Gaudium et Spes* says, there is a counter-intuition: "a deep instinct leads him [man] rightly to shrink from and to reject the utter ruin and total loss of his personality" (§18). Humans possess a spiritual soul, which *Gaudium et Spes* calls "the seed of eternity" (§18). Building upon our soul's spiritual nature, we have a graced ultimate end: "God has created man in view of a blessed destiny" that will not only restore our bodily integrity, but will also establish us "in the perpetual communion of the incorruptible divine life [in perpetua incorruptibilis vitae divinae communione]" (§18).[51] Paragraph 19

---

51. I have modified the Flannery translation here, which reads "a life that is divine and free from all decay."

rests human dignity primarily upon our supernatural ultimate end, which defines all humans from the outset of their existence, even when grace has been lost by original sin: "The dignity of man rests above all on the fact that he is called to communion with God. The invitation to converse with God is addressed to man as soon as he comes into being" (§19). The reason for this invitation to divine communion is God's love, and humans can respond to this invitation because their created nature is rational. Paragraph 19 specifies that to live "fully according to truth" requires that humans know and love God.

The nuanced discussion of the reasons for atheism that follows in paragraph 19 make clear that human reason itself—and not solely the rejection of grace—is implicated in atheism, insofar as some atheists "try to drive God from their heart and to avoid all questions about religion, not following the biddings of their conscience." Yet, atheism also can arise from a reaction to unfaithful teaching or practice on the part of believers. A key point here is that atheism is not the natural condition of human nature: it "is not present in the mind of man from the start" (§19), despite the fallen human drive for autonomy and self-sufficiency that makes atheism so prevalent today (as paragraph 20 describes). *Gaudium et Spes* §21 reiterates some points made earlier, including the point that human dignity arises both from human intelligence and freedom (nature) and from the call to share in God's own happiness (grace). In response to Marxism, it adds that the hope for eternal life does not take away from the significance of the present life. Paragraph 21 also affirms that "all men, those who believe as well as those who do not, should help to establish right order in this world where all live together."

The final sentences of paragraph 21 emphasize that the gospel message of grace does not impair human nature but instead bestows "light, life, and freedom," since "[a]part from this message nothing is able to satisfy the heart of man." Paragraph 21 ends by citing the famous line from Book I of Augustine's *Confessions*, "Thou hast made us for thyself, O Lord, and our heart is restless until it rest in thee."

Building upon paragraph 21's insistence that only the gospel can satisfy the yearning of the human heart, paragraph 22 states that "it is only in the mystery of the Word made flesh that the mystery of man truly becomes clear." This claim echoes paragraph 10's statement that "the key, the center and the purpose of the whole of man's history is to be found in its Lord and Master," as well as paragraph 10's promise to "unfold," on the basis of Jesus Christ, "the mystery of man." It also echoes a well-known statement made by de Lubac in *Catholicism*: "By revealing the Father and by being revealed to him, Christ completes the revelation of man to himself. By taking possession of man, by seizing hold of him and by penetrating to the very depths of his being Christ makes man go deep down within himself, there to discover in a flash regions hitherto unsuspected."[52] After remarking in Pauline fashion that Adam, the first human, was a type of Christ, paragraph 22 adds that Christ, "in the very revelation of the mystery of the Father and his love, fully reveals man to himself and brings to light his most high calling." Here we should also recall paragraph 11's teaching that "faith throws a new light on things and makes known the divine plan for the integral vocation of man."

The remainder of paragraph 22 speaks of Jesus Christ. It observes that he is the "perfect man" who thereby restores human nature in the fullness of the image of God, and also, as the incarnate Son, elevates human nature "to a dignity beyond compare." By dying for our sins and rising from the dead, Jesus opened up the path of eternal life. Even though we must die, we have sure hope of the resurrection when we are configured to him through faith and love. Paragraph 22 notes that Christ died for all and that all have the same supernatural calling; therefore "we must hold that the Holy Spirit offers to all the possibility of being made partners, in a way known to God, in the paschal mystery." The unity of the human race consists both in sharing human nature and in sharing the same ultimate end (although we can rebel against it). Insisting upon the necessity of Christ for understanding the meaning of suffering and death, which otherwise would be overwhelming, paragraph 22 makes one final reference to "the nature and the greatness of the mystery of man as enlightened for the faithful by the Christian revelation."

Paragraph 23 inaugurates chapter 2, on "The Community of Mankind." The paragraph encourages all humans to undertake a "genuine fra-

---

52. Henri de Lubac, SJ, *Catholicism: Christ and the Common Destiny of Man*, trans. Lancelot C. Sheppard and Elizabeth Englund (San Francisco: Ignatius Press, 1988), 339.

ternal dialogue" through personal friendships, which require "mutual respect for the full spiritual dignity of men as persons" rather than dividing humans into some who merit respect and others who do not. Paragraph 24 reiterates that all humans "are destined to the very same end, namely God himself." It adds that all have the same end because "they have been created in the likeness of God" (§24). Paragraph 24 distinguishes nature and grace when it comes to the Trinitarian and ecclesial communion: Jesus "has opened up new horizons closed to human reason by implying that there is a certain parallel between the union existing among the divine persons and the union of the sons of God in truth and love." Without revelation, reason could not have known of this deepest sense of communion. Given this truth about communion, paragraph 24 states that "man can fully discover his true self only in a sincere giving of himself." Human nature has to be self-giving in order to find itself, since love must be ecstatic; and our "true self" is found in the supernatural order revealed by Christ.

Gaudium et Spes §§25–28 treat the human person in relationship to life in society, the common good, respect for the life and well-being of all other humans, and love for enemies and for those who differ from us (including in religious conviction). Paragraph 29 reiterates the unity of the human race, both with regard to nature and with regard to destiny: "All men are endowed with a rational soul and are created in God's image; they have the same nature and origin and, being redeemed by Christ, they enjoy the same divine calling and destiny." On the basis of the equality of all humans, *Gaudium et Spes* defends human rights and rules out such things as racism, sexism, and religious discrimination. It critiques economic disparities and, in paragraph 30, calls for obedience to social obligations such as payment of taxes and observance of speed limits. Paragraph 31 commends the free and full involvement of citizenry in public life, and calls for broader and better education. Capping chapter 2 of *Gaudium et Spes*, paragraph 32 explores the communal life of Jesus: Jesus observed the law, sanctified the bond of family, and feasted with friends as part of "revealing the Father's love and man's sublime calling." Jesus sought to restore the unity of the human race, and he "established, after his death and resurrection, a new brotherly communion among all who received him in faith and love" (§32). Just as human nature requires life in society, so does grace establish the society of the Church, rooted in supernatural self-giving love and solidarity.

Chapter 3, which includes paragraphs 33–39, examines "Man's Activity in the Universe." On the one hand, *Gaudium et Spes* wants to affirm the value of human work and of science and technology insofar as they lead to better living conditions. God created the human race with intellectual ability, and it was God's plan that we should exercise this ability. Yet work and advances in science and technology are not ends in themselves, but are good only insofar as they serve human goals such as personal development, justice, brotherhood, and social progress. Thus, on the other hand, *Gaudium et Spes* denies that work or science and technology can be autonomous from God. This is consistent with *Gaudium et Spes*'s understanding of human nature as always related to and dependent upon God. Paragraph 36 adds that "once God is forgotten, the creature is lost sight of as well." The human tendency to seek autonomy from God is a mark of the sinfulness that afflicts the world. In speaking to the world, the Church proclaims that human activities "must be purified and perfected by the cross and resurrection of Christ" (§37).

Indeed, *Gaudium et Spes* is well aware that there is no natural realm or "world" that is not profoundly in need of the healing and elevating power of grace. Paragraph 38 states that love is "the fundamental law of human perfection, and consequently of the transformation of the world." Jesus' commandment of love and his exercise of the power of love by his Cross are not simply for our spiritual transformation in the life to come. Here and now, the glorified Jesus at the right hand of the Father is the source of grace that makes the world a better place: "Christ is now at work in the hearts of men by the power of his Spirit; not only does he arouse in them a desire for the world to come but he quickens, purifies, and strengthens the generous aspirations of mankind to make life more humane and conquer the earth for this purpose" (§38). *Gaudium et Spes* describes various vocations inspired by the Holy Spirit, some of which are directed toward focusing attention upon our heavenly goal, while others are directed toward service on earth. In every case, grace inspires a willingness "to put aside love of self and integrate earthly resources into human life, in order to reach out to that future day when mankind itself will become an offering accepted by God" (§38). The grace of the Holy Spirit heals and elevates our nature so that we can love, and this love is transformative of the world. Paragraph 38 speaks of this graced transformation as promised and nourished by "the sacrament of faith, in which natural elements, the fruits of man's cultivation, are changed into His glorified Body and Blood, as a supper of brotherly fellowship and a foretaste of the heavenly banquet."

Paragraph 39 concludes this chapter of *Gaudium et Spes* by reflecting upon how the activities that occupy us in this life are related to the full establishment by God of his kingdom at the end of time. Does the kingdom of God undermine the meaningfulness of the works to which much of our lives are devoted? By no means: grace transforms these works necessitated by the needs of nature, so that "[w]hen we have spread on earth the fruits of our nature and our enterprise—human dignity, brotherly communion, and freedom—according to the command of the Lord and in his Spirit, we will find them once again, cleansed this time from the stain of sin, illuminated and transfigured, when Christ presents to his Father an eternal and universal kingdom" (§39). In other words, works done in charity will remain in a transformed way in eternal life, since the works we do for the building up of the human family will be supernaturally crowned in the final consummation. Thus, far from there being a separation of our natural needs and the life of grace, it is already true that "[h]ere on earth the kingdom is mysteriously present; when the Lord comes it will enter into its perfection" (§39).

The last chapter of part 1 of *Gaudium et Spes* is chapter 4, on "The Role of the Church in the Modern World." Paragraph 40 begins with the point that Christ founded the Church by the eschatological outpouring of the Holy Spirit, and so the Church has "a saving and eschatological purpose which can be fully attained only in the next life." Until Christ comes in glory, members are to be added to his family the Church; indeed the spreading of this family of Christ, through the Holy Spirit, is the very purpose of the Church (rather than any worldly or secular purpose). These members, of course, live in the world and share in the movement of history, and they are called "to be a leaven and, as it were, the soul of human society in its renewal by Christ and transformation into the family of God" (§40). Grace does not liberate humans from their natural (created) constitution, nor from their place in the world with its various needs. They are called to take part in the world and to transform it by the grace of the Spirit acting in and through them. Paragraph 40 states, "In pursuing its own salvific purpose not only does the Church communicate divine life to men but in a certain sense it casts the reflected light of that divine life over all the earth, notably in the way it heals and elevates the dignity of the human person" and "in the way it consolidates society."

To make this general claim more specific, paragraph 41 addresses the benefits that revelation brings to individual humans by healing and elevating their natural constitution. In a manner reminiscent of paragraphs 10–11 and 21–22, paragraph 41 notes that by revealing the triune God, who is the supernatural finality of human life, revelation "opens up to him [man] the meaning of his own existence, the innermost truth about himself." Much like paragraph 21, paragraph 41 states that "God alone, whom it [the Church] serves, can satisfy the deepest cravings of the human heart, for the world and what it has to offer can never fully content it." Paragraph 41 continues by observing that "man is continually being aroused by the Spirit of God" so as never to be "utterly indifferent to religion." This point stands in sharp contrast to the contention of Cold War Communist governments. Paragraph 41 adds, "For man will ever be anxious to know, if only in a vague way, what is the meaning of his life, his activity, and his death. The very presence of the Church recalls these problems to his mind." *Gaudium et Spes* is willing to admit that in our fallen condition, we do not think of God or consciously desire God as much as we should. The Holy Spirit must stimulate our attention by giving us grace, not least through the evangelizing presence of the Church.

Paragraph 41 underscores that our fallen nature needs to be humanized; human nature profoundly needs grace. It promises that "[w]hoever follows Christ the perfect man becomes himself more a man" (§41). Far from wishing to override the proper "autonomy of the creature," the Church contributes to the world by making the world more truly the world (§41). Contrary to what may have been supposed when the phrase "the rights of man" was popularized, the gospel enables and requires the Church to proclaim "the rights of man" (§41). Paragraph 41 supports the spread of "these rights all over the world," even while warning against "all traces of false autonomy" that would in fact undermine true human rights. Those who hold themselves above divine law inevitably trample upon the human dignity of others. In this fallen world, therefore, it is the graced "spirit of the Gospel" that ensures the natural "rights of man" (§41).

While paragraph 41 focuses upon the ways in which the Church benefits individual humans in the world, paragraph 42 focuses upon the ways in which the Church benefits societies in the world. The Church itself does not have "a mission in the political, economic, or social order"; theocracy, or the instantiation of any particular political or economic system, is not the Church's goal (§42). But this does not mean that the Church, in proclaiming the gospel, has nothing to contribute in these areas. On the contrary, the Church undertakes works of mercy and promotes social unity, not least by its example of unity (enabled by the Holy Spirit). *Gaudium et Spes* is eager to emphasize that the Church does not seek to influence modern societies by gaining an "external power exercised by purely human means" (§42). Here *Gaudium et Spes* seeks to show appreciation for the natural order as natural, even if fallen: "Whatever truth, goodness, and justice is to be found in past or present human institutions is held in high esteem by the Council" (§42). Paragraph 42 also proposes that the Church can be a mediating bond between the various social entities, helping to reduce conflict and to "consolidate legitimate human organizations." What the Church requires from societies is freedom to serve the gospel, as well as a just recognition of "the basic rights of the person and the family, and the needs of the common good." This paragraph is particularly careful to stake out space for natural human institutions, and to show how the Church can benefit such institutions insofar as they are committed to justice.

By contrast, the next paragraph (§43) warns against the state's effort to restrict religion to a private sphere of personal piety, an effort that is mirrored in the lives of believers who separate their private piety from their public lives. Although there are natural institutions, there can be no natural realm that is separated or isolated from grace. Paragraph 43 warns, "Let there, then, be no such pernicious opposition between professional and social activity on the one hand and religious life on the other." Every this-worldly enterprise undertaken by a believer is necessarily suffused by the power of grace; if not, then the person is not truly in a state of grace. The laity thus must not imagine that their piety is for Sundays, and that the rest of the week is a godless sphere. In cases where members of the laity disagree with each other over prudential matters in the world, *Gaudium et Spes* reminds such persons that "no one is permitted to identify the authority of the Church exclusively with his own opinion" (§43). The key point is that the (fallen) natural realm is precisely where the laity is expected to manifest the power of the grace of the Gospel, although the laity also bear witness within the Church to this grace.

Do bishops and priests also bear witness in the world, or is that solely the province of the laity? Paragraph 43 answers that it is the task of bishops and priests to prepare and nourish the laity, and it is also the task of bishops and priests to show "[b]y their words and example" that the Church is "an inexhaustible font of all those resources [virtutum] of which the modern world stands in such dire need." Yet, as paragraph 43 goes on to indicate, the Church cannot overrun the legitimate autonomy of the world, despite the world's fallenness. Bishops and priests must engage "in dialogue with the world" rather than trying to dictate terms on this-worldly matters (§43). Above all, bishops and priests must foster true unity, in the Church and in the world.

Is the Church, then, immune to the perils that afflict the fallen world? Paragraph 43 observes that although "[b]y the power of the Holy Spirit the Church is the faithful spouse of the Lord and will never fail to be a sign of salvation in the world," nonetheless its members include some who have rebelled against the Holy Spirit. Further, paragraph 43 notes that the doctrine of the Church's relationship to the world has developed over the centuries. In these ways, *Gaudium et Spes* recognizes the faulty witness of some members of the Church and of the Church itself in particular prudential situations over the centuries. The grace of the gospel is communicated without fail by the Church, and yet the fallenness of human nature inevitably affects the Church, which therefore is always in need of renewal.

In addition, as paragraph 44 says, the Church and world should mutually acknowledge not only each other's failings but each other's gifts: "Just as it is in the world's interest to acknowledge the Church as a social reality and a driving force in history, so too the Church is not unaware how much it has profited from the history and development of mankind." As an example of the latter, paragraph 44 mentions the use of Greco-Roman philosophy in the communication of the gospel. Paragraph 44 acknowledges that evangelization today must likewise involve inculturation, not simply so that our contemporaries can understand the gospel, but indeed so that the meaning of the gospel itself can be "more deeply penetrated."[53] The Church not only employs cultural resources, but also is changed by them in positive ways. For instance, the development of the Church's visible form—not a rupture with the constitution given the Church by Christ, but a deepening of the Church's understanding of this constitution and a fitting adaptation of this constitution to our times—benefits from "the evolution of social life" (§44). Developments in the realm of reason (nature), including political philosophy, enrich the community of grace, just as the community of grace enriches the realm of reason. Paragraph 44 adds that God ensures that even the opposition of the Church's enemies enriches the Church.

Is the purpose of the Church, then, to assist the world, and to receive benefits from the world in turn? No, because the Church truly is an eschatological community, awaiting Christ's coming in glory and the new creation. The Church's purpose, which only God can bring about, is the salvation of the world. Any lesser purpose would deform the Church. This does not mean that the Church does not benefit the world, but it does mean that all benefits that flow from the Church are rooted in the gospel of the kingdom. These benefits are not alien to the world, however, because the world was created by and for Jesus Christ. *Gaudium et Spes* §45 describes the incarnate Word as "a perfect man" and states, in accord with paragraph 41 (and 10–11, 21–22): "The Lord is the goal of human history, the focal point of the desires of history and civilization, the center of mankind, the joy of all hearts, and the fulfilment of all aspirations" (§45). The concluding sentences of paragraph 45, which bring to a close part 1 of *Gaudium et Spes*, emphasize that Christ (with the Father and the Holy Spirit) is the creative source and ultimate end of all things, "'the Alpha and the Omega, the first and the last, the beginning and the end' [Rev 22:13]."

---

53. See also Vatican II's *Ad Gentes*.

Part 2 treats various urgent problems of the present day. Chapter 1 identifies the first urgent problem as that of the status and stability of marriage and the family—both a natural and a supernatural reality. For *Gaudium et Spes*, "The wellbeing of the person and of human and christian society is intimately connected with the healthy state of the community of the family" (§47).[54] What then are the problems that beset this crucial community? *Gaudium et Spes* names polygamy, divorce, free love, "selfishness, pleasure-seeking and wrongful practices against having children" (§47). Economic and social conditions, including "problems arising from increasing population," are also placing stress upon the family (§47).

In response to these problems, *Gaudium et Spes* devotes five lengthy paragraphs to setting forth a theology of marriage as rooted in both nature and grace. Paragraph 48 explains that "[t]he covenant, or irrevocable personal consent, of marriage sets up an intimate sharing of married life and love as instituted by the creator and regulated by God's laws." The bond of marriage is not a mere human invention. Rather, the Creator God is its author, and it is directed first and foremost to the begetting and raising of children. The sacrament of marriage enables marriage—which otherwise would be solely a natural bond pertaining to the order of creation—to be in the order of grace a sign of Christ's union with his Church. By the grace of the sacrament, the married couple is strengthened to live out the responsibilities of marriage and to serve each other and their children in the path of sanctification.

In making decisions about whether to have more children, the married couple should exercise careful prudence while also being "aware that they cannot just do as they please, but ought always to be ruled by a conscience in conformity with the divine law, and be docile to the magisterium of the church which authentically interprets the divine law under the light of the gospel [dociles erga ecclesiae magisterium, quod illam sub luce evangelii authentice interpretatur]" (§50).[55] *Gaudium et Spes* notes

---

54. Quotations of part 2 and the conclusion are from *Gaudium et Spes*, in *Decrees of the Ecumenical Councils*, vol. 2, *Trent to Vatican II*, ed. Norman P. Tanner, SJ (Washington, D.C.: Georgetown University Press, 1990), 1069–1135.

55. I have modified the Tanner translation here, which reads "be attentive to the church's teaching authority which officially interprets that law in light of the gospel."

that the Church's laws for the transmission of life serve the good of true married love, despite the sacrifices that couples often face; and *Gaudium et Spes* adds that, with regard to the transmission of life, "the moral character of the behaviour does not depend simply on good intention and evaluation of motives, but ought to be determined by objective criteria, derived from the nature of the person and its acts, which take account of the whole meaning of mutual giving and human procreation in the context of true love" (§51). Abortion receives condemnation as a grave crime, and with regard to contraception *Gaudium et Spes* states simply: "It is not permitted to daughters and sons of the church who rely on these principles to take steps for regulating procreation which are rejected by the teaching authority [magisterium] in its explanation of the divine law" (§51). Having a large family is commendable, but *Gaudium et Spes* makes clear that in cases where the couple are unable to have children, "marriage remains as a sharing and communion for the whole of life and retains its goodness [valorem] and indissolubility" (§50).

Gaudium et Spes calls for the state to "consider it its sacred duty to recognise, protect and advance the true nature of marriage and the family, to safeguard public morality and to promote family prosperity" (§52). Married couples should collaborate in raising their children, and *Gaudium et Spes* suggests that it remains preferable for mothers to care for young children at home, without thereby denying women their proper advancement in society. *Gaudium et Spes* encourages scientists who are studying "the various conditions which favour the virtuous control of procreation" (§52). The section on marriage concludes by urging that married couples "be united in equal regard, similarity of mind and mutual holiness so that, following Christ the beginning [principium] of life in the joys and sacrifices of their vocation, they may become through their faithful love witnesses to that mystery of devoted love which the Lord in his death and resurrection revealed to the world" (§52).

Chapter 2 discusses "The proper development of culture," that is to say, the proper task of the cultivation, development, and perfecting of "the goods of nature and values" (§53). The development of natural and social science, technology, and the modes of communication has produced "a new age of human history," and "a more widespread form of human culture" is emerging (§54). Indeed, paragraph 55 holds that the growing sense of personal responsibility for "building a better world in terms of truth and justice" means that "a new humanism is being born in which the human is defined above all in terms of our responsibility to our sisters and brothers and to history." How does the Church contribute to this "new humanism"? *Gaudium et Spes* notes that a key problem facing the development of culture consists in how to unite scientific and technological growth with the "capacities for contemplation and wonder which lead to wisdom" (§56), in other words, how to ensure that nature remains open to the supernatural call (grace).

Gaudium et Spes appreciates culture's ability to serve the human mission of "subduing the earth and completing creation" and of "raising the human family to higher planes of truth, goodness and beauty, and to judgments of universal value, thus further enlightening it with the wonderful wisdom which was with God at the beginning" (§57). But *Gaudium et Spes* warns that modern science and technology, by focusing solely on the empirical, can lead to a reductive agnosticism or to a view of humans as self-sufficient without God. Even so, *Gaudium et Spes* notes that such negative consequences are not inevitable, and it focuses on the positive dimensions of modern culture, "including scientific study and scrupulous respect for truth in scientific enquiry, the need to work in collaboration with others, a feeling of international solidarity, a daily increasing awareness of the responsibility of experts to help and also protect others, and a wish to improve the living conditions of all" (§57).

In paragraph 58, *Gaudium et Spes* observes that just as God revealed himself to Israel—and preeminently in Christ—from within a variety of cultural contexts, so also the Church has made use of the gifts of numerous cultures in performing its graced task of spreading the gospel. The Church does not commit itself to any particular culture, ancient or recent, but instead gladly enters "into a communion with different forms of culture" over the centuries, to the benefit of both the Church and the cultures (§58). *Gaudium et Spes* remarks that the gospel "attacks and dispels the errors and evils which flow from the ever-threatening seduction of sin" and "ceaselessly purifies and enhances the ways of peoples" by grace (§58). The Church insists that culture should be directed toward the good of human persons and communities, and thus should truly cultivate the mind and heart by fostering contemplative wonder and "a religious, moral and social sense" (§59). Approving of the "legitimate autonomy of human culture and especially of the sciences," *Gaudium et Spes* proclaims that "while observing the moral order and the common benefit, people should be able to seek truth freely, to express and publicise their views, to cultivate every art" (§59).

Gaudium et Spes goes on to urge that action be taken "to recognise and implement throughout the world the right of all to human and civil culture appropriate to the dignity of the person" (§60). In this context, *Gaudium et Spes* mentions the full part that women should be able to play in every sphere of life, the need for education and for appreciation of "the collective cultural expressions and activities of our day" (§61),[56] the need for theologians to continually seek better ways "of communicating doctrine to the people of their time" (§62) in accord with the distinction between the truths of faith and the manner in which the truths are expressed, the value of psychology and sociology for pastoral care, and the need for the Church to appreciate new forms of art and to "receive them into the sanctuary when their idiom is suitable and in conformity with the needs of the liturgy" (§62). *Gaudium et Spes* urges members of the Church, filled with grace, not to shy away from the world: "The faithful should live in the closest contact with others of their time, and should work for a perfect understanding of their modes of thought and feeling as expressed in their culture" (§62). Theologians should collaborate with scholars in other fields, even while pursuing "a deep knowledge of revealed truth" (§62). Lay people are encouraged to study theology and to become theologians, and theologians are granted "a just freedom of enquiry, of thought and of humble and courageous expression in those matters in which they enjoy competence" (§62).

Chapter 3 treats economics. Paragraph 63 warns against disparities of wealth and against the reduction of humanity to economic factors, and it opposes both unfettered capitalism and socialism. Paragraph 64 encourages the ongoing agricultural and industrial (technological) growth and

---

56. See Vatican II's *Gravissimum Educationis*.

creativity needed to provide for an increasing human population. The pursuit of economic productivity, however, must not lose sight of the fact that its goal cannot be mere profit but instead must be "the service of humanity and of the whole human person," integrating nature and grace by fully "taking into account material needs and the requirements of intellectual, moral, spiritual and religious life" (§64).

The paragraphs that follow make this point concrete. Paragraph 65 urges that all citizens and nations should be included in guiding and contributing to economic progress. Paragraph 66 denounces economic inequality, addresses the situation of migrant or immigrant laborers, calls for professional training for those put out of work by technological advances, and commends programs for people who cannot work because of old age or illness. Paragraph 67 demands that workers not be "made slaves of their work," but should instead have time for family and leisure, and paragraph 68 approves labor unions because they give workers an active participation in the shared enterprise. Paragraph 69 affirms private property, but notes that property is ultimately for the common good and so a person "in extreme need has the right to procure from the riches of others what is necessary for personal sustenance." Paragraph 69 also approves of new social welfare programs with the proviso that such programs not be allowed to make citizens passively dependent upon society. Nor should citizens suppose that their own good works are no longer necessary now that society is taking on a greater role. Paragraphs 70 and 71 depict investment and private poverty in a positive light, so long as the common good is kept in view by those who have resources. Paragraph 72 concludes *Gaudium et Spes*'s discussion of economics by stating that "Christians taking an active part in modern socioeconomic progress, and campaigning for justice and charity, should be convinced that they have much to offer to the prosperity of humanity and and to the peace of the world."

Turning to politics, chapter 4 suggests that the world today has "a clearer awareness of human dignity" (§73), in accord with the exigencies of both nature and grace. It finds that "there is growing concern to protect the rights of minorities in any country without prejudice to their duties to the political community; there is increasing respect for people professing a different opinion or a different religion; and greater cooperation is being established so that all the citizens ... can in fact enjoy their personal rights" (§73). Political structures that "obstruct civil or religious liberty" or serve only a particular faction receive condemnation (§73).[57] In paragraph 74, *Gaudium et Spes* observes that the political community arises in order to serve the common good of individuals, families, and associations. The political community has its "foundation in human nature" and thus in "the order established by God," though the particular form of government varies according to the will of the people (§74).

Gaudium et Spes discusses the rights and duties of citizens, and states that "[c]itizens individually and together should take care not to concede too much power to the public authority, nor to make inappropriate claims on it for excessive benefits and services, in such a way as to weaken the responsibilities of individuals, families, and social groupings" (§75). It favors welfare programs but warns that the state should not become too big or dominant over the rights of the citizens. It urges that citizens should combine loyalty to their own country with concern for all nations, that political parties should serve the common good rather than merely their own interests, that politicians should not seek their own gain, and that dictatorship or the permanent rule of one political party should be avoided. While paragraph 76 notes that the Church transcends the state and any political system, it also encourages cooperation between the Church and state, as the Church ministers to the graced calling of human beings. Although the Church grants the state's independence, the Church insists upon its own freedom to proclaim the gospel and to minister to people, and the Church also insists upon its ability "to pass moral judgment even on matters belonging to the political order when this is demanded by the fundamental rights of the person or the salvation of souls" (§76). In its graced mission of evangelization, the Church encourages all elements of truth, goodness, and beauty and fosters peace.

Chapter 5 addresses peace, understood "not merely [as] the absence of war" but as a just order (§78). As followers of Christ, Christians should "work with all people in order to consolidate peace in mutual justice and love and to prepare instruments of peace" (§77). Paragraph 78 notes that,

---

57. See Vatican II's *Dignitatis Humanae*.

in the face of the power of sin, peace does not simply arise from natural justice and lawful authority, important though these are, but also requires that people trust one another and respect one another's human dignity, which means that peace (as a fruit of grace) "emerges as the fruit of love which goes beyond what justice is able to provide" and "is an expression and result of the peace of Christ which flows from God our Father." Paragraph 78 adds that even in situations of self-defense where violence is permissible, persons should strive to avoid violence, so long as this renunciation of violence "can be done without harm to the rights and obligations of others or of the community." Paragraph 79 stresses "the permanent force of the natural international law and its binding principles," and it condemns genocide, with the Nazis in view. It accepts that "once all means of peaceful negotiations are exhausted, the right of legitimate defence cannot be denied to governments" (§79).

Detailing the requirements of natural justice among nations, *Gaudium et Spes* condemns acts of "total war," which aim to obliterate whole cities (§80), and equally condemns the "arms race" of stockpiling nuclear weapons (§81). It calls for the world's security to be safeguarded by "the establishment of a universal public authority" (§82) vested with power sufficient to accomplish its aims, and it encourages international cooperation with the goal of removing "the causes of discord among people on which war feeds" (§83). With regard to the establishment of a just world order, it approves of the effort by international institutions to assist poorer countries in development and to relieve the "distress of refugees" and migrants (§84). It advocates the emergence "of a true universal economic order," which will require grace to accomplish "the abolition of excessive profit-motive, national ambitions, the will to political domination, military considerations, and schemes to spread and impose ideologies" (§85). It argues that the developed countries should assist "developing nations" especially by helping them to cultivate their citizens' economic abilities and by ensuring that international trade is set up in favor of developing nations, while at the same time no development program should be tied to anything that harms the "spiritual nature and development" of the citizens (§86). It accepts that governments have the right to address population problems, though not in ways contrary to God's law. With regard to methods for regulating the number of children, it appreciates "scientific advances that are well proven and are found to be in accordance with the moral order" (§87). It praises "those Christians, especially the young, who freely volunteer to bring aid to others and to whole peoples" (§88). It insists that the Church, as an instrument of God's grace, "ought to be present in the community of nations in order to encourage and stimulate universal cooperation" (§89), and it establishes "an organisation of the universal church" whose purpose will be "to stimulate the catholic community to the promotion of progress in poor areas and of social justice among nations" (§90).

Finally, given modern people's ambition to achieve "a universal fellowship with deeper foundations" (§91) and in view of the Church's "mission to spread the light of the gospel's message over the entire globe" (§92), *Gaudium et Spes* urges that human unity be sought not least through the promotion of "genuine dialogue" (§92). Such dialogue should characterize the life of the Church, through "mutual esteem, respect and harmony, with the recognition of all legitimate diversity, in the Church itself, in order to establish ever more fruitful exchanges among all who make up the one people of God, both pastors and the rest of the faithful" (§92). Here *Gaudium et Spes* affirms the principle that in the Church "there should be unity in essentials, freedom in doubtful matters, and charity in everything" (§92). The unity of Catholics with non-Catholic Christians must be fostered as much as possible, so as to show the unity and peace of Christians.[58] Likewise, *Gaudium et Spes* encourages dialogue with "all who recognise God and whose traditions contain precious religious and human elements," and also dialogue with those who do not believe in God and who may even be persecuting the Church (§92).[59] *Gaudium et Spes* concludes by emphasizing the need for grace-filled love as the mark of the Church's engagement with the world: "The Father wishes us to recognise and extend active love in word and deed to Christ our brother in people everywhere, thus witnessing to the truth, and to share with others the mystery of our heavenly Father's love" (§93).

---

58. See also Vatican II's *Unitatis Redintegratio*.
59. See also Vatican II's *Nostra Aetate*.

Conclusion: *Gaudium et Spes* as an Ongoing Theological Event

In light of *Gaudium et Spes* §§10, 22, and 45, Antonio López remarks: "To the council's mind, Christ illumines the mystery of man, his truth, by accompanying him."[60] Although there are different emphases in various parts of *Gaudium et Spes*, it should be clear that *Gaudium et Spes* insists upon both the created goodness of the fallen world and its urgent need for the grace of the Holy Spirit through Jesus Christ. The conflicts and existential threats present even at the height of the world's scientific and technological progress show the world's need for grace. Although there are "natural" spheres of life that are not governed by the Church, there is no sphere of strict autonomy from God, since human nature seeks and desires God as its proper fulfillment and since the true dignity of human nature can be known only through Jesus Christ.

Like *Gaudium et Spes*, de Lubac insists over and over again upon the centrality of Christ for the Church and the world. In his seminal 1938 volume *Catholicism: Christ and the Common Destiny of Man*, de Lubac responds forcefully to contemporary thinkers who argue that Christianity lacks concern about the earthly conditions of human life and has an individualistic piety in which each person is concerned solely with his or her eternal destiny. He repeatedly emphasizes "the unity of the human race"; humans are "one spiritual family intended to form the one city of God."[61] It follows that there can be no strict separation between the Church and the world, or even the Church and non-Christians, because "[n]o one is a Christian for himself alone."[62]

In *Catholicism*, de Lubac responds at length to those who consider that the Christian claim to be the perfect religion, the one Church into which God is uniting everyone, is dismissive of other religions. He emphasizes that God's pedagogical plan, in preparation for Christ's coming (and second coming), always had in view the salvation of the nations

---

60. Antonio López, FSCB, "Vatican II's Catholicity: A Christological Perspective on Truth, History, and the Human Person," *Communio* 39 (2012): 82–116, at 106.
61. De Lubac, *Catholicism*, 25, 29.
62. Ibid., 245.

and not solely the salvation of those visibly united to the Church. As he observes, "Peace upon the world, unity of all peoples in the service and praise of Yahweh! That is no dream, it is the word of God. No afflictions and disappointments can ever make us doubt it."[63] Catholicism does not mean compelling everyone to be Catholic. On the contrary, the Catholic vision of human unity, toward which the Church works constantly, is an eschatological one in service of all the nations: only God will bring about the final unity. Thus de Lubac affirms the need to respect non-Christian religions, even while also insisting upon the truth that only Christ fulfills the desires of the human race.

In his *The Drama of Atheist Humanism* (1944), de Lubac observes that "the peoples of the West are denying their Christian past and turning away from God," and he also perceives—well before many others did—that the atheism of the 1940s had moved beyond its strictly negative Enlightenment posture and become "increasingly positive, organic, constructive."[64] Its constructive power flows from an anti-Christian posture: it aims to develop a way of life that has no need for anything belonging specifically to Christianity. The atheistic movements that have developed around the ideas of Auguste Comte, Ludwig Feuerbach, Karl Marx, and Friedrich Nietzsche seek to remove humans from contact with the Christian God. De Lubac notes that although man can "organize the world without God," nonetheless "without God, he can ultimately only organize it against man. Exclusive humanism is inhuman humanism."[65] This point is at the center of *Gaudium et Spes* as well. De Lubac also strives to show that Christianity is not the path of sleepy and parochial retreat nor atheism the path of bold advance. Rather, Christianity itself contains the bold element, the God who goes all the way to the Cross out of love for us, the God who demands holiness of us and who offers us a share in his own life. Compared to this, atheism is self-contented and self-enclosed; it cannot truly meet our spirits' desire for going beyond ourselves, for transcendence and true life. Thus de Lubac, like *Gaudium et Spes*, is constantly examin-

---

63. Ibid., 247.
64. Henri de Lubac, SJ, *The Drama of Atheist Humanism*, trans. Edith M. Riley, Anne Englund Nash, and Marc Sebanc (San Francisco: Ignatius Press, 1995), 11.
65. Ibid., 14.

ing the world's concerns and showing the intersections with Christianity.

William Portier has shown that for de Lubac, the Council's "christological focus illuminates the question, at the center of much contemporary strife in the Church, about how, or in what senses, the world is graced.... The first four chapters of *Gaudium et spes* make clear that the world is graced in and through the Divine Word become incarnate in Jesus Christ."[66] Portier recalls that in a 1969 lecture at Saint Louis University, de Lubac raised the concern that postconciliar Catholics are again separating faith from life in the world, this time rejecting not life in the world (as in the papal response to the modernist crisis) but rather faith itself. Portier comments that in 1969 "de Lubac saw the christological anthropology of Part 1 of *Gaudium et spes* being separated from the concerns of Part 2 about urgent problems of the world. The 'world' of Part 2 swallowed up in a new secularization Part 1's Christ-centered interior life in the Church."[67]

Arguably, then, de Lubac's postconciliar writings shed important light upon the ongoing theological event of *Gaudium et Spes*. For example, in his strikingly titled "The Council and the Para-Council," de Lubac observes: "Just as the Second Vatican Council received from a number of theologians instructions about various points of the task it should assume, under pain of 'disappointing the world', so too the 'post-conciliar' Church was immediately and from all sides assailed with summons to get in step, not with what the Council had actually said, but with what it should have said."[68] De Lubac particularly has in mind theologians who have misread *Gaudium et Spes*, either by reading only certain portions of it or by reading it in isolation from the other Constitutions. According to de Lubac, such theologians argue that in order to attain credibility with the modern world and to bring Vatican II to culmination, the Church "must no longer pretend to interpret the world to us in terms of the Christian faith; she

---

66. William L. Portier, "What Kind of a World of Grace? Henri Cardinal de Lubac and the Council's Christological Center," *Communio* 39 (2012): 136–51, at 137.

67. Ibid., 142.

68. Henri de Lubac, SJ, "The Council and the Para-Council," appendix to *A Brief Catechesis on Nature and Grace*, trans. Richard Arnandez, FSC (San Francisco: Ignatius Press, 1984), 235–60, at 235.

must cease considering herself 'as the depositary of the truth'" and "must give herself a 'democratic structure.'"[69] Here nature and the world have subsumed grace and the Church, despite *Gaudium et Spes*'s intentions.

Along the same lines, in his "The 'Sacrament of the World,'" de Lubac responds to Edward Schillebeeckx's 1967 claim that, according to the Council, the Church is the "sacrament of the world." De Lubac's concern here is that for Schillebeeckx, "the role of this Church of Christ is only to 'manifest' a 'progressive sanctification of the world (as a profane reality)', a sanctification which seems to take place without her."[70] Schillebeeckx attributes the phrase "sacrament of the world" to *Lumen Gentium* and *Gaudium et Spes*, but in fact it is found in neither document. The key issue, as de Lubac shows, is that for Schillebeeckx the eschatological kingdom appears (in de Lubac's words) "as the culmination of our 'earthly expectations', as their supreme fulfillment and consummation."[71] On this view, Jesus Christ and the Church serve the purpose of revealing and ratifying what belongs immanently and always to the world in its history. For Schillebeeckx, according to de Lubac, the nature-grace distinction is eliminated in a manner that does away with the Christological integration found in *Gaudium et Spes*, since for Schillebeeckx nature itself is already intrinsically graced and Christ simply manifests the inherent kingdom-dynamism of the world (of which the Church is the sacrament).[72]

---

69. Ibid., 257.

70. Henri de Lubac, SJ, "The 'Sacrament of the World'?," appendix to *A Brief Catechesis on Nature and Grace*, 191–234, at 194. See also Jared Wicks, SJ, "Vatican II in 1964: Major Doctrinal Advances, but Also Fissures on Addressing the Modern World," *Josephinum Journal of Theology* 20 (2013): 4–19, at 17–19. See also the issues raised in Joseph A. Komonchak, "Le valutazioni sulla *Gaudium et Spes*: Chenu, Dossetti, Ratzinger," in *Volti di fine concilio. Studi di storia e teologia sulla conclusion del Vaticano II*, ed. Joseph Dore and Alberto Melloni (Bologna: Il Mulino, 2000), 115–63.

71. De Lubac, "The 'Sacrament of the World'?," 225. See also the emphasis on the distinction between nature and grace found, in the same postconciliar context, in de Lubac's "The 'Supernatural' at Vatican II," appendix to *A Brief Catechesis on Nature and Grace*, 177–90. For the nuances of Schillebeeckx's anthropological method and account of salvation, see for example Schillebeeckx, "Questions on Christian Salvation of and for Man," in *Toward Vatican III: The Work That Needs to Be Done*, ed. David Tracy, Hans Küng, and Johann B. Metz (New York: Seabury Press, 1978), 27–44.

72. See also Richard R. Gaillardetz, *An Unfinished Council: Vatican II, Pope Francis, and the Renewal of Catholicism* (Collegeville, Minn.: Liturgical Press, 2015), 117; cf. 51. Of course salvation history takes place in the midst of and in dialogue with sociocultural histories. No one disputes

In a brief 1968 commentary on *Gaudium et Spes*, titled "The Total Meaning of Man and the World," de Lubac emphasizes the importance of *emboldening* the Church to evangelize the world with the gospel of Christ, since it is in fact the gospel of Christ that fulfills human nature and the world.[73] In Christ, and in cultures transformed by faith in Christ, true human progress will be found. Rather than imagining *Gaudium et Spes* to be a mere embrace of the world, de Lubac argues that *Gaudium et Spes* aims to show that "the faith in fact contains the only hope for a truly spiritual integration of man and his world."[74] Faith in Christ transforms humanity and the world rather than merely ratifying or expressing an experiential datum found in the world; the gospel of the Cross requires repentance and conversion. De Lubac remarks that Christian hope "presupposes a transfiguration that passes through the Cross, and it reminds us how the Church is the matrix in which this cosmic rebirth begins to take place."[75]

De Lubac is correct that for *Gaudium et Spes*, commitment to the Church's role in history and to the Church's dialogue with the world is built upon the distinction (not separation) of nature and grace, Church and world. Neither de Lubac nor *Gaudium et Spes* can be classified as darkly "neo-Augustinian" or optimistically "neo-Thomist," since this would be to overlook the Christological standard by which both de Lubac and *Gaudium et Spes* value and judge the world in its history and culture.[76] To-

---

that point. But the priority of divine revelation (God's Word) to merely human words, and divine revelation's ability to address us authoritatively with judgments of truth that hold across diverse sociohistorical contexts, is crucial. Otherwise, we simply accommodate the "gospel" (whatever the "gospel" is, since if its truth does not transcend its sociohistorical context, then it is merely a wax nose) to whatever socio-historical context we find ourselves in, rather than both appreciating and critically judging our sociohistorical context on the basis of the enduring truth of the gospel (God's Word addressing us). The Barmen Declaration penned by Karl Barth against the Nazis is a central example of the importance of this point.

73. See Henri de Lubac, SJ, "The Total Meaning of Man and the World," trans. D. C. Schindler, *Communio* 35 (2008): 613–41.

74. Ibid., 641.

75. Ibid.

76. See Thomas Gertler, *Jesus Christus—Die Antwort der Kirche auf die Frage nach dem Menschsein* (Leipzig: St. Benno-Verlag, 1986). For the opposition between "neo-Augustinian" and "neo-Thomist," see Michael G. Lawler, Todd A. Salzman, and Eileen Burke-Sullivan, *The Church in the Modern World:* Gaudium et Spes *Then and Now* (Collegeville, Minn.: Liturgical Press, 2014), 14.

day, our task is to retrieve the ways in which *Gaudium et Spes* offers a vision of the whole world created by and for Christ, a world that, in both its wonderfully positive gifts and its deep neediness, calls out for the fulfillment and truth given only by the grace of the gospel. In the ongoing theological event of *Gaudium et Spes*, in which the debate remains as intense as it was in the early 1970s, the Church must proclaim anew, for the sake of the world, the Creator who is the Redeemer: "The true light that enlightens every man was coming into the world. He was in the world, and the world was made through him, yet the world knew him not.... But to all who received him, who believed in his name, he gave power to become children of God; who were born, not of blood nor of the will of the flesh nor of the will of man, but of God" (Jn 1:9–13).

The authors use these terms to replace another deficient polarity, "conservative" and "liberal." The misleading character of the authors' use of their terms is evident not least in their claim regarding the struggle at the outset of the Council: "The sides were those that had already emerged during the preparatory phase, the Roman classicist neo-Augustinian theologians who had prepared the schemas for discussion, and the historically conscious neo-Thomist bishops and their theologians who were critical of the prepared schemata" (Lawler, Salzman, and Burke-Sullivan, *The Church in the Modern World*, 19).

CHAPTER 5

VATICAN II AS AN ONGOING THEOLOGICAL EVENT

The Way Forward

This final chapter contrasts two representative approaches to Vatican II as an ongoing theological event, namely the approaches of Robert Imbelli and Massimo Faggioli. In light of the preceding chapters, I argue that Imbelli's focus on Jesus Christ is the proper way to receive Vatican II as an ongoing theological event, in accord with Pope John XXIII's insistent pastoral emphasis that "the Church should bring Christ to the world."[1]

---

1. Pope John XXIII, Radio Message of His Holiness John XXIII a Month before the Opening of the Second Vatican Council, September 11, 1962, at www.vatican.va (my translation from the Spanish text). See Jared Wicks, SJ, "Vatican II Taking Hold of Its (and Pope John's) Council

By focusing on Christ as faithfully known and mediated by the Church, and on the world's need for Christ as well as the Church's need to be centered anew upon Christ, Imbelli avoids the danger—present, I argue, in Faggioli's approach—of a historicist reception of the Council, a reception that undermines the possibility of enduring dogmatic truth and thereby inevitably makes power relations the central theme of the Council. Imbelli's approach illumines the Council's path to a "renewed discovery of [the Church's] vital bond of union with Christ," as Pope Paul VI described the Council's work in his 1964 encyclical *Ecclesiam Suam*.² Focusing on

---

Goals, September 1962–May 1963," *Josephinum Journal of Theology* 19 (2012): 172–86. See also Pope John XXIII's "Gaudet Mater Ecclesia," English translation at https://jakomonchak.files.wordpress.com/2012/10/john-xxiii-opening-speech.pdf. In this important speech on October 11, 1962, at the solemn opening of the Second Vatican Council, Pope John affirms, "The very serious matters and questions which need to be solved by the human race have not changed after almost twenty centuries. For Christ Jesus still stands at the center of history and life: people either embrace him and his Church and so enjoy the benefits of light, goodness, order, and peace or they live without him or act against him and deliberately remain outside the Church, so that confusion arises among them, their relationships are embittered, and the danger of bloody wars impends" (§4). At the same time, he warns strongly against the false nostalgia that some people have for the past and their correspondingly overly negative view of the present: "These people see only ruin and calamity in the present conditions of human society. They keep repeating that our times, if compared to past centuries, have been getting worse. And they act as if they have nothing to learn from history, which is the teacher of life, and as if at the time of past Councils everything went favorably and correctly with respect to Christian doctrine, morality, and the Church's proper freedom" (§8). He goes on to describe the central goal of the Council: "The greatest concern of the Ecumenical Council is this, that the sacred deposit of Christian doctrine should be more effectively defended and presented" (§11), for the enrichment of both the Church and the whole world. With an eye to both *ressourcement* and *aggiornamento*, he adds: "But for this teaching to reach the many fields of human activity which affect individuals, families, and social life, it is first of all necessary that the Church never turn her eyes from the sacred heritage of truth which she has received from those who went before; and at the same time she must also look at the present times which have introduced new conditions and new forms of life, and have opened new avenues for the Catholic apostolate" (§12).

2. Pope Paul VI, *Ecclesiam Suam*, Encyclical Letter, August 6, 1964, §35, at www.vatican.va. In accord with Imbelli's approach, Gerald O'Collins, SJ (who, like Imbelli, was a seminarian during the Council, though in Australia and Germany rather than in Rome) describes his "greatest debt to Vatican II" as the prompting that he received from the Council "to center my theological work on Jesus in an unqualified way" (O'Collins, *Living Vatican II: The 21st Council for the 21st Century* [New York: Paulist Press, 2006], 17). O'Collins speaks beautifully about the Christocentricity of *Gaudium et Spes*: "What I treasured in *Gaudium et Spes* was its capacity to hold together various themes about Jesus: his role as both creator and redeemer (no. 45), his life, death, and resurrection (no. 22), his inseparable relationship with the Father and the Holy Spirit (nos. 22, 92–93), and his vital link with every human being (no. 22)" (O'Collins, *Living Vatican II*, 17). Indeed, with regard to the purpose of his *Living Vatican II*, O'Collins states: "If by this present work, I help readers to 'know Jesus more clearly, love him more dearly, and follow him more nearly' (from a prayer of

Christ as the measure of true reform also enables Imbelli to avoid privileging the contemporary sociohistorical context of the secular West, as though it embodied the graced future toward which the Church must now catch up. At the same time, Imbelli does not ignore or dismiss that context.

I should note at the outset that the alternative I wish to expose is not between "Christ-centered" on the one hand and "historical" on the other (since Christ obviously cannot be known outside of history!), but between a Christological interpretation of both history and the Council and a historicist interpretation of both history and the Council. The latter turns the meaning of Vatican II into a mere struggle for power, whether between neo-scholastics and the *nouvelle théologie*, clergy and laity, traditionalists and progressives, conservatives and liberals, and so on. The former places the focus upon Jesus Christ crucified and risen and upon how Christ wishes us to share in his life today in the modern world and for the salvation of the world. Imbelli, who has constantly sought dialogue and healing among contesting groups in the Church throughout his long career, makes clear that his Christological interpretation is not a power play. Rather, Imbelli simply wishes for Jesus Christ, the "bridegroom" and divine Son incarnate in history, to "increase" (Jn 3:29–30) in the Church of the Second Vatican Council.

A Christological interpretation of Vatican II will not put an end to theological controversies or power struggles, but it will mean that these controversies proceed on the basis of shared Christ-centered frameworks: divine revelation through Christ, liturgical participation in Christ, ecclesial mediation of Christ, and evangelizing mission for the world's fulfillment in Christ. This is the path that the Constitutions of Vatican II encourage, and it is the path that the Council Fathers themselves took in arriving at their teachings. Guided by the conciliar Constitutions, we

---

St. Richard of Chichester), I will be more than satisfied. I passionately believe that the teaching of Vatican II can help bring about that happy result" (O'Collins, *Living Vatican II*, 18). O'Collins differs from Imbelli (and from me) in his sharply negative view of the encyclical *Humanae Vitae* and the Congregation for the Doctrine of the Faith's *Dominus Iesus*: for the latter, see Imbelli's "The Reaffirmation of the Christic Center," in *Sic et Non: Encountering Dominus Iesus*, ed. Stephen J. Pope and Charles Hefling (Maryknoll, N.Y.: Orbis Books, 2002), 96–106.

should follow this Christological path today for the sake of the renewal—symphonic rather than monotone—that Vatican II continues to inspire.

Robert Imbelli: Christ the Center

Many leading commentators on the Council have emphasized the significance of *Dei Verbum*. Giuseppe Alberigo, for example, finds it "significant that *Dei Verbum* was one of its [the Council's] major and most telling documents, and the only one the composition of which lasted through the entire duration of the assembly, from 1962 to 1965."[3] Gerald O'Collins notes that the four Constitutions provide a "hermeneutical key" to the Council, and he then asks: "does one of them, as a kind of '*primus inter pares*,' enjoy a certain 'primacy' over the other three when we set ourselves to interpret Vatican II and its teaching?"[4] He answers his question in the affirmative: "Many scholars and others have assigned this primacy to *Lumen Gentium*, but, given the priority of divine revelation over the doctrine of the Church (which is derived from revelation), it might be preferable to name *Dei Verbum* in first place."[5] In support of this view, O'Collins cites Jared Wicks and Christoph Theobald, both of whom are known for their expertise in the study of the Council. From a similar perspective, Godfried Cardinal Danneels has recently remarked: "The Constitution on Divine Revelation is perhaps the most important doctrinal document of the Council.... *Verbum Dei*, which consumed so much time and discussion, is unfortunately barely read today. This Constitution is however a pillar for conciliar work and, from a doctrinal point of view, is the crown of Vatican II."[6]

In his *Rekindling the Christic Imagination*, Robert Imbelli likewise observes that "not all the documents of the council are of equal weight," even

---

3. Giuseppe Alberigo, "Vatican II and Tradition," in *History of Vatican II*, ed. Giuseppe Alberigo, vol. 5, *The Council and the Transition: The Fourth Period and the End of the Council, September 1965–December 1965*, trans. Matthew J. O'Connell, English version ed. Joseph A. Komonchak (Leuven: Peeters, 2006), 592–95, at 594.

4. Gerald O'Collins, SJ, *The Second Vatican Council: Message and Meaning* (Collegeville, Minn.: Liturgical Press, 2014), 141.

5. Ibid.

6. Gottfried Cardinal Danneels, "The Ongoing Agenda: A Council Unlike Any Other," in *The Second Vatican Council: Celebrating Its Achievements and the Future*, ed. Gavin D'Costa and Emma Jane Harris (London: Bloomsbury, 2013), 19–34, at 26.

though we must "appropriate the texts of the council in a comprehensive way that does justice to all of the documents it [the Council] bequeathed the church."[7] Holding up the four Constitutions as "the interpretive keys to the council's intentions,"[8] Imbelli considers that these Constitutions should be read together, in an intertextual fashion, so as to expose their shared principles and thereby to perceive how to interpret the Council's teachings as a whole. He finds *Dei Verbum* to be "first among equals" with respect to the conciliar Constitutions.[9] As he remarks, *Dei Verbum* has priority because without divine revelation, the Council could have no real warrant. If God had not revealed himself, and if the cognitive content of divine revelation could not be or had not been faithfully transmitted by the Spirit-guided Church in Scripture and Tradition, then Vatican II's teachings about the liturgy or about the Church would be no more than human constructions, unanchored by any real connection to the living God or the risen Christ. Imbelli nicely articulates what is at stake: "Unless God has revealed himself fully through Jesus Christ in the Holy Spirit, then the church is without foundation and the liturgy a merely human construct. *Dei Verbum* makes this foundational claim: 'By this revelation the deepest truth, both about God and about human salvation, shines forth for us in Christ, who is himself both the mediator and the fullness of all revelation' (2)."[10]

Imbelli identifies the Council's two fundamental intentions—united in a "creative tension"—as *ressourcement* (the "effort to rediscover, with fresh eyes, the wellsprings of the faith, in particular the Scriptures themselves and the reception of and reflection upon the Scriptures by the early bishops and theologians of the church") and *aggiornamento* (the "intention to bring the Good News of Jesus Christ proclaimed by the tradition into the world of today, addressing the aspirations and concerns of contemporary men and women in language that speaks to them in a way both intelligible and pastorally inviting").[11] Both of these intentions,

---

7. Robert P. Imbelli, *Rekindling the Christic Imagination: Theological Meditations for the New Evangelization* (Collegeville, Minn.: Liturgical Press, 2014), xiv.
8. Ibid., xv.
9. Ibid.
10. Ibid. See also Eric de Moulins-Beaufort, "Henri de Lubac, Reader of *Dei Verbum*," *Communio* 28 (2001): 669–94.
11. Imbelli, *Rekindling the Christic Imagination*, xiii–xv. In 1961, addressing a group of the

clearly, depend upon divine revelation, in which the Triune God reveals himself and his plan of salvation in and through Jesus Christ and the Holy Spirit. The rediscovery of Scripture and of Scripture's dogmatic and pastoral reception in the early Church would be of mere historical import if Scripture and dogma did not authoritatively teach saving truth about divine mysteries. Likewise, the communication of the gospel to our contemporaries in fresh and inviting ways, with appreciation for the modern world's advances and challenges, would be of little use if the gospel did not teach us truly about the nature of God, Christ, and humanity.

Imbelli then asks whether the Council's intentions regarding *ressourcement* and *aggiornamento* have been adequately received, in light of the ongoing conflicts within the Church today. He grants that "[p]artial and partisan readings of the council and its documents account for some of the fragmentation and polarization we have experienced" since the Council.[12] But he emphasizes that if we keep our eyes focused on the surface-level debates between so-called liberals and conservatives, we will miss the deeper problem that has surfaced in the reception of the Council. Put succinctly, a crisis of faith in Jesus Christ, and not mere battles over liberal and conservative emphases, is what ails the Church today. This is so especially in Europe and North America, but elsewhere as well. As Imbelli states, the liberal-conservative partisan battles "are symptoms of a more severe crisis: an eclipse of the enlivening and unifying center of the faith. That center is Jesus Christ himself, crucified under Pontius Pilate, risen and present as Lord and head of his body, the church."[13] The Church

---

Blessed Sacrament fathers, Pope John XXIII expressed the hope that the coming Council would accomplish the updating or *aggiornamento* (an Italian term) of the Church. In his 1964 encyclical *Ecclesiam Suam*, Pope Paul VI strongly affirms John XXIII's hope that the Council would accomplish *aggiornamento* (see especially §50), and he frames *aggiornamento* within the context of a *ressourcement* that leads the Church deeper into the sources of faith, requiring the Church to embrace a deeper charity (see §56). *Ecclesiam Suam* devotes much of its space to distinguishing between true and false reform and to describing the rationale and conditions of true dialogue.

12. Ibid., xv.
13. Ibid., xv–xvi. In his essay on "Vatican II as an 'Event,'" in *Vatican II: Did Anything Happen?*, ed. David G. Schultenover (New York: Continuum, 2007), 24–51, Joseph Komonchak portrays the postconciliar situation this way: "Within five years, articles and books began to be written, some of which enthusiastically spoke of the 'new Church,' 'the Church of the future,' 'a new Christendom,' while others noted with displeasure what they variously called decomposition, crisis, disaster, apostasy, etc." (Komonchak, "Vatican II as an 'Event,'" 29). This way of phrasing it can make

is built not by us, but by Jesus Christ, who pours out the Spirit and unites disciples to his saving work.

The Constitutions of Vatican II are rooted in this vision of the living Christ, the Messiah of Israel, at the head of his Church and at the center of all history. Imbelli notes, however, that "in some theological circles, an odd aversion to affirmations of the uniqueness and universality of Jesus Christ has taken hold," and he suggests that this aversion to "the revelatory primacy of Jesus Christ" is the root cause of the "relative neglect" of *Dei Verbum* since the Council.[14] In support of his view that faith in Christ is the real issue in the reception of the Council today, he cites Joseph Ratzinger (Pope Benedict XVI), Luke Timothy Johnson, and Avery Dulles.[15] Like Ratzinger/Benedict and Johnson, he points to the challenge that historical-critical biblical scholarship poses to believers' ability to know Jesus Christ and to assent to the truth of the gospel—although Imbelli certainly values historical-critical scholarship. Like Dulles, he notes that some influential theologians "hold that each religion has its own way of salvation. Jesus may be the savior for Christians, but this confession need not preclude the acknowledgement of other savior figures."[16] This position, as Imbelli observes, is fatal for the Council's "Christic center of faith" and for the Council's emphasis on the Church's evangelizing mission—the proclamation of the gospel of Christ as good news for the whole world.[17]

With beautiful simplicity, getting right to the heart of things, Imbelli

---

it sound as though those who responded with "displeasure" were made grumpy by the speed of change in the Church, that is to say by the "event-character of the council" as "a watershed" (ibid.). Komonchak might add that one cause of concern, for Congar, de Lubac, Ratzinger, and other leading figures of the Council, was the massive exodus of laity and clergy from the Church, especially in Europe and Canada.

14. Imbelli, *Rekindling the Christic Imagination*, xvi; see also Imbelli, "The Reaffirmation of the Christic Center." Already in 1972 Yves Congar spoke of a troubling silence about and forgetfulness of *Dei Verbum*: see Congar, "Le chrétien, son présent, son avenir et son passé," *Lumière et vie* 21/108 (1972): 72–82, at 80. In 1985, the Extraordinary Synod of Bishops, meeting in order to discuss the Council, likewise underscored in its Final Report "the importance of the Dogmatic Constitution, *Dei Verbum*, which has been too neglected" (The Synod of Bishops, "'Final Report,' December 7, 1985," in *The Extraordinary Synod—1985: Message to the People of God* [Boston, Mass: St. Paul Editions, 1986], 37–68, at 49).

15. See also Robert P. Imbelli, "The Christocentric Mystagogy of Joseph Ratzinger," *Communio* 42 (2015): 119–43.

16. Imbelli, *Rekindling the Christic Imagination*, xvii.

17. Ibid.

offers a plan for contemporary reception of the Council: we need to recognize "in Jesus, crucified and risen, the Word of God in person";[18] we need to confess anew with *Dei Verbum* that "Jesus completes the work of revelation ... above all by his death and his glorious resurrection from the dead, and his sending of the Spirit of Truth" (*Dei Verbum* §4); and we need to recall that "revelation," far from being something narrow, partisan, or marginalizing, is nothing less than "the joyful realization that in Christ 'God is with us, to free us from the darkness of sin and death, and to raise us up to eternal life' (4)."[19] Jesus Christ, fulfilling in the history of Israel God's covenantal promises to make his people holy and to bring blessing to all nations, mercifully heals, restores, and enlightens us so that we might, in the Holy Spirit, follow his path of self-giving love and be joined everlastingly to the Trinity in the new creation, whose pattern is love. Imbelli makes clear that the "Christocentric approach" he advocates is not "Christomonism," because "one cannot do justice to Jesus short of seeing him within a fully trinitarian frame of reference," and furthermore because the recognition that Christ is the center entails the equal recognition that "the eschatological goal is the 'recapitulation of all in Christ' (Eph 1:10) in the Church as the *"totus Christus* ... enlivened by the Holy Spirit."[20]

Although Imbelli prioritizes *Dei Verbum* on the grounds that "from God's revelation the identity [*Lumen Gentium*], mission [*Gaudium et Spes*], and worship [*Sacrosanctum Concilium*] of the church proceed," he devotes much of his book to *Lumen Gentium* and *Gaudium et Spes*.[21] His central argument throughout is that "the deepest *ressourcement* the coun-

18. Ibid.
19. Ibid. See also Imbelli's remark elsewhere that "[a] truly Eucharistic grounding of priestly identity is founded upon the real presence of the risen and ascended Jesus Christ in Church and world. Therefore, it does not support retrenchment, but engagement, not withdrawal, but missionary advance. The love of Christ, experienced above all in the Eucharist, impels Christian and priestly existence" (Imbelli, "The Identity and Ministry of the Priest in the Light of Vatican II: The Promise and Challenge of *Presbyterorum Ordinis*," forthcoming in the *Josephinum Journal of Theology*). Although he is speaking here of ordained priests, his words equally apply to the priesthood of all believers. Gerald O'Collins offers four helpful questions or "tests" for receiving the Council faithfully: "(1) a deeper experience of salvation that comes through real sensitivity to the work of Christ and the Holy Spirit; (2) a richer experience of life-giving worship in the community; (3) fidelity to biblical witness; and (4) a generous service of those who suffer" (O'Collins, *Living Vatican II*, 60), though I would add to these experiential "tests" Newman's seven "notes" of true doctrinal development.
20. Imbelli, *Rekindling the Christic Imagination*, xviii.
21. Ibid., 76.

cil engaged in was a re-Sourcement: a return to the unique Source who is Jesus Christ."²² Beginning with *Dei Verbum*'s insistence that divine revelation is ultimately centered in a Person (Christ), Imbelli insightfully draws the connection to the ecclesiology of *Lumen Gentium* and to the evangelizing mission of *Gaudium et Spes*: "the church is not a self-contained institution, but witnesses to what God has done and is doing in Jesus Christ."²³

It is significant for Imbelli, and rightly so, that *Lumen Gentium*—indebted to Henri de Lubac's *Méditation sur l'Église*—emphasizes the Church's character as mystery and sacrament of Jesus Christ. In this light, the Church's "institutional" (and hierarchical) character can be seen for what it is: an instrument, rooted in cruciform service, by which the Holy Spirit builds up the Church. When the Church is built up, its purpose is not power but praise: its goal (and its source) is "relation with Christ" in Eucharistic worship and mission (*Sacrosanctum Concilium*).²⁴ True reform of the Church, then, is a matter of the holiness of all the members of the Church (laity, religious, clergy), their configuration to Christ's self-sacrificial love in true worship. As Imbelli states, "Entering into the mystery of the church at a contemplative, mystical depth and thirsting for the transformative holiness to which Christ summons the whole people of God—lay women and men, religious, priests, bishops (the *universal* call to holiness!)—is the royal road to the reform of the church."²⁵ Imbelli makes clear, as I have also sought to do in the preceding chapters, that a necessary part of reading and receiving Vatican II is to thirst for transformation and conversion of heart, so that we no longer use and

22. Ibid., 79.
23. Ibid., 78.
24. Ibid., 79. See Christopher Ruddy, "'In my end is my beginning': *Lumen Gentium* and the Priority of Doxology," *Irish Theological Quarterly* 79 (2014): 144–64.
25. Imbelli, *Rekindling the Christic Imagination*, 80. The emphasis on "mystical, contemplative depth" is a trademark of Imbelli's work. For background to Imbelli's perspective, see Frans Jozef van Beeck, SJ's remark: "The mystic leads the Church to trust the deeper source of unity: One Father, one Lord, one Holy Spirit—Triune Source of the varieties of energies, services, and gifts.... Only the mystic knows God, that is to say, he or she desires to be known by God, and so he or she loves" (van Beeck, *Catholic Identity after Vatican II: Three Types of Faith in the One Church* [Chicago: Loyola University Press, 1985], 66–67). Van Beeck concludes that "the Catholic faith and identity experience after Vatican II stands to gain decisively from *liturgical spirituality*" (Van Beeck, *Catholic Identity*, 67).

abuse our neighbors or ourselves, and so that our hearts and minds are filled in Christ with the grace of the Holy Spirit. According to *Lumen Gentium*, as Imbelli points out, the model of such holiness is Mary, precisely because of her intimate relationship with her Son and her unique participation in his work: "Of all the members of the church, Mary has lived most intimately and fully the mystery of the church, the sacrament of the paschal mystery of her Son."[26] Thus Imbelli identifies "Christification," the participation of Christians in the very life of Christ, as the central theme—including the central ecclesiological theme—of Vatican II.[27]

Given Imbelli's salutary insistence upon the centrality of Christ, he resists separating the "pastoral" from the "dogmatic," without thereby denying the distinction. As he shows, *Gaudium et Spes* contains many dogmatic elements, and *Lumen Gentium* many pastoral ones (not least the universal call to holiness).[28] The justice, peace, and dialogue that the Church in the world seeks are, on Imbelli's reading, inseparable from the light of the salvation won by the crucified and risen Christ, as can be seen not least in *Gaudium et Spes* §22's teaching that Christ reveals the source, nature, and fulfillment of humankind. God's grace is available to all persons, yet "all grace is paschal, and, therefore, Christic."[29] When Christ is excluded from the world, the world suffers, because even in our most mundane activities we need the healing from sin and the elevation to eternal life that Christ brings. Imbelli summarizes: "The church's only goal, the council claims, is that the reign of God may come and that the salvation of humankind may be realized."[30] The Church works to serve this goal, but only Christ can bring it about, since indeed the goal is none other than everlasting union with Christ that fulfills every human desire

---

26. Imbelli, *Rekindling the Christic Imagination*, 82.
27. Ibid., 83.
28. For the link between "pastoral" and "doctrinal" (and the distinction of both from "dogmatic"), see Yves Congar, OP, "A Last Look at the Council," in *Vatican II Revisited by Those Who Were There*, ed. Alberic Stacpoole, OSB (London: Geoffrey Chapman, 1986), 337–58, at 345–48. For the French version of this essay, see Congar's *Le Concile de Vatican II. Son église: Peuple de Dieu et corps du Christ* (Paris: Beauchesne, 1984), 49–72. See also the Synod of Bishops, "Final Report," in *The Extraordinary Synod—1985*, 41: "It is not licit to separate the pastoral character from the doctrinal vigor of the documents."
29. Imbelli, *Rekindling the Christic Imagination*, 86.
30. Ibid., 87.

for wisdom, love, and joy. After quoting Pope Benedict XVI and Pope Francis (and noting the debt of both to de Lubac), Imbelli concludes, "Unless united intimately to Jesus on the one Way he has shown, the Way who he himself is, the church inevitably goes astray."[31] That this fact is at the heart of Vatican II's Constitutions has also been the theme of my own book.

Massimo Faggioli: Historical Consciousness and Ecclesiastical Decentralization

In his recent essay "Vatican II: The History and the Narratives," the Vatican II scholar Massimo Faggioli notes that "after Vatican II, the Catholic Church took unambiguous steps to help Catholics remember the council," such as Pope Paul VI's decision "to collect and publish the proceedings of the plenary congregations celebrated in the Basilica of St. Peter, the different *schemas* in the redaction history of each final conciliar document, and the minutes of the conciliar and preconciliar commissions."[32]

---

31. Ibid., 88. Already in 1964, de Lubac wrote: "Reform, *aggiornamento*, openness to the world, ecumenism, religious freedom, and so on: that is all to be understood within the faith, as a present requirement of the purified and deepened Christian spirit. Now all that, distorted, is nearly equivalent in the mind of many to carelessness, indifference, amorphous liberalism, concessions to the 'spirit of the world' and almost an abandonment of faith and of morals. I well know that this is in part the effect of propaganda coming from opposition that is bent on presenting things that way. But doesn't the language of many of the partisans of *aggiornamento* also contribute to it? They speak, for example, of 'conservatives' and 'progressives'; greater emphasis on a return to traditional positions (on the Church, on Revelation, and so forth) is presented as the victory of new ideas; few serious efforts are made to explain in the press the principal subjects treated or to justify the orientations adopted: even all the Catholic journalists whom I had occasion to read declared, on the day the discussion of *de Revelatione* was opened, that the Council was entering into 'ultra-technical questions', thereby discouraging readers from taking an interest in it, even though this subject is the source and center of our faith. On the contrary, what would have been simpler, or more necessary, than to remind everyone of the proclamation of the Good News through the revelation of God in Jesus Christ, the essential subject of this schema" (de Lubac, *At the Service of the Church: Henri de Lubac Reflects on the Circumstances That Occasioned His Writings*, trans. Anne Elizabeth Englund [San Francisco: Ignatius Press, 1993], 340–41). See also Matthew L. Lamb, "Vatican II after Fifty Years: The Virtual Council versus the Real Council," in *The Second Vatican Council: Celebrating Its Achievements and the Future*, 7–17.

32. Massimo Faggioli, "Vatican II: The History and the Narratives," in *50 Years On: Probing the Riches of Vatican II*, ed. David G. Schultenover (Collegeville, Minn.: Liturgical Press, 2015), 61–81, at 62. This essay appeared earlier in *Theological Studies*. Note that, of the minutes of Commissions' meetings, only those of the Central Preparatory Commission have appeared in print, but the Vati-

Faggioli appreciates the Church's original and indeed "continuing trust in the community of scholars of Vatican II."[33] By this community of scholars, Faggioli means professional Church historians with specific expertise in the Second Vatican Council. Although Imbelli was in Rome during the four conciliar years as a seminarian, and although Imbelli has an extensive knowledge of the Council's texts, he would not claim that he is a historian, nor does he analyze the Constitutions of Vatican II from the perspective of the historical formation of the texts. Since Imbelli freely reads the Council's texts through the lens of later papal teaching (for example, Pope Benedict and Pope Francis), it may seem that Imbelli's Christocentric interpretation of the Constitutions has been ahistorically shaped by "a particular 'institutional interpretation' of the council," given (in Faggioli's words) "the organizational dominance of one center of power [the Vatican] that announces the event, manages it, and after its ending determines the process of the event's evaluation and concretization of its resolutions."[34]

In fact, Faggioli warns in sharp terms against the rise, since the 1980s, of unapologetically (even proudly!) ahistorical readings of the Council's documents. He remarks, "What we have seen emerge in the last few decades is a new prominence for narratives about Vatican II and the shape of contemporary Catholicism that take no account of the historical research on the council produced during this same period. We are left with narratives innocent of historical studies and even inimical to them."[35] Faggioli points out that at the very same time (1985) that the Extraordinary Synod issued its authoritative interpretative lens for the Council—emphasizing the "ecclesiology of communion"[36]—Giuseppe Alberigo began his massive five-volume project of surveying the history of Vatican II. The 1985 Extraordinary Synod taught that a "deeper reception of the Council" is needed, and the Synod proposed that this "deeper reception," one that gets to the real heart of the Council as both a historical and an ongo-

---

can Archives' vast holdings of all the rest is, by Paul VI's decision, open to scholars and not limited by the normal time limits of the Archive.

33. Faggioli, "Vatican II," 62.   34. Ibid., 63.
35. Ibid., 64.
36. The Synod of Bishops, "Final Report," in *The Extraordinary Synod—1985*, 54.

ing event, should be undertaken by giving hermeneutical primacy to the four Constitutions and by refusing to disjoin either the doctrinal from the pastoral, or the spirit from the letter.[37] As we saw, Imbelli reiterates and confirms the urgency of precisely this approach, which I follow in this book.[38] But in Faggioli's view, it is the particular historical approach exemplified by Alberigo that will in fact lead to a deeper reception of the Council. Faggioli bemoans "the gap between Catholic church historians on one side (and historians of the councils in particular) and theologians, magisterium, and 'secular historians' on the other side."[39]

This gap, Faggioli contends, has led to the flourishing of misleading macronarratives and subnarratives about the Council. He first describes the traditionalist narrative, which he finds to have become increasingly influential under the pontificate of Benedict XVI. He then summarizes the liberal narrative, represented by Hans Küng. Thirdly, he treats the neoconservative narrative that in his view combines aspects of "the ultratraditionalist and the ultraliberal" and is found in the writings of George Weigel, Richard John Neuhaus, and Michael Novak. After his critique of these metanarratives, Faggioli puts forward one that he favors, which builds upon the distinction (in my view a deeply ahistorical one) that some scholars have made between the "Thomistic" Karol Wojtyła and the

---

37. Ibid., 41. For a largely appreciative response to the 1985 Extraordinary Synod's Final Report, see Avery Dulles, SJ, "The Reception of Vatican II at the Extraordinary Synod of 1985," in *The Reception of Vatican II*, ed. Giuseppe Alberigo, Jean-Pierre Jossua, and Joseph A. Komonchak (Washington, D.C.: The Catholic University of America Press, 1987), 349–63. See also the essays in *Synod 1985: An Evaluation*, ed. Giuseppe Alberigo and James Provost (Edinburgh: T. & T. Clark, 1986), especially Jean-Marie Tillard, OP's generally positive "Final Report of the Last Synod," 64–77 and Avery Dulles, SJ's "Catholic Ecclesiology since Vatican II," 3–13.

38. Yves Congar, too, emphasizes the centrality of "communion" for the Council: see his "Moving Towards a Pilgrim Church," in *Vatican II Revisited by Those Who Were There*, 129–52, at 136–37. With regard to the mystery of the Church, Congar states that "the most suitable concept is undoubtedly that of 'communion' and Paul VI loved it. I well remember the way in which he spoke to me about it, quoting from J. Hamer's book, *The Church is a communion* (1962)! It is true, of course, that the Council did not go as far as it might have gone in working out this idea. As Antonio Acerbi has pointed out, it retained some elements of a juridical ecclesiology" (ibid., 136). Congar adds, "'Communion' is a key concept in the ecumenism of Vatican II and Paul VI continued to use it again and again after the Council" (ibid., 137). Congar goes on to note approvingly that the concept of a hierarchical, unequal society "was not rejected by Paul VI, the Council or the post-conciliar Church. On the contrary, they reaffirmed it. They did not, however, regard it as of first importance or as the door by which one had to enter ecclesiology" (ibid., 141).

39. Faggioli, "Vatican II," 65.

"Augustinian" Joseph Ratzinger. Faggioli argues that the Church's official reception of the Council since 1978 has been "characterized by two partially conflicting visions: John Paul II's fundamentally positive view of the council and Ratzinger's decidedly pessimistic reading of the post–Vatican II period. This 'dialogue' of interpretations—at the beginning under some control of the pope [John Paul II]—gradually ceded place to Ratzinger's views."[40]

It quickly becomes clear that in Faggioli's view, Ratzinger/Benedict's vision, beloved of Imbelli, is in fact at the service of the American neoconservative distortion of the Council, which Faggioli warns has roots in "recent converts to Catholicism" who use Catholicism for their own political ends.[41] In response, Faggioli promotes the "historicization" of Vatican II achieved by Alberigo, a historicization that works at two levels: to ward off apologetic or reactionary metanarratives, and to contribute to the historicizing of the Church's doctrinal, moral, and scriptural tradition. Admittedly, Alberigo's five principles of interpretation do not themselves explicitly advocate "historicization." Faggioli lists the five principles as the "event" character of the Council, Pope John XXIII's intention for the Council, the pastoral goal of the Council, *aggiornamento* as the "key goal" of the Council, and the conciliar compromises among theological schools.

Faggioli is more explicit in his *Pope Francis: Tradition in Transition*. After rejecting "the simplistic myth of the 'anticonciliar' Joseph Ratzinger," he goes on to attack Benedict XVI's "fundamentally pessimistic Augustinian anthropology, a world view that sees the world and the Church as two forces in opposition," by sharp contrast to *Gaudium et Spes*.[42] Faggioli warns against thinking of the Council in terms of "continuity" with Tradition, an approach associated with Ratzinger/Benedict as well

---

40. Ibid., 71.

41. Ibid. The implicit questioning of the sincerity of the faith of such persons as Richard John Neuhaus strikes me as unfortunate and wrong. If one removes the ad hominem attack, moreover, the Catholic "neoconservatives" in America seem more closely aligned to Pope John Paul II than to Joseph Ratzinger/Pope Benedict XVI, as shown by *Caritatis in Veritate*'s (2009) differences from *Centesimus Annus (1991)*, for example.

42. Massimo Faggioli, *Pope Francis: Tradition in Transition*, trans. Sean O'Neill (New York: Paulist Press, 2015), 23.

as with figures such as Yves Congar and Avery Dulles.[43] Faggioli suggests that both before and after Vatican II, the Church has always been in constant change, and so the very notion of "continuity" requires an ideal or ahistorical history that has never existed, by contrast to the historicist history that actually exists.[44]

In his "Vatican II: The History and the Narratives," Faggioli grants that more than historical studies are needed for understanding a Council.

43. See, for example, Congar, "A Last Look at the Council," 351; Congar, "Moving Towards a Pilgrim Church," 129; Avery Dulles, SJ, "The Reception of Vatican II at the Extraordinary Synod of 1985," appendix to *The Reception of Vatican II*, ed. Giuseppe Alberigo, Jean-Pierre Jossua, and Joseph A. Komonchak, trans. Matthew J. O'Connell (Washington, D.C.: The Catholic University of America Press, 1987), 349–63, at 350; Dulles, "Nature, Mission, and Structure of the Church," in *Vatican II: Renewal within Tradition*, ed. Matthew L. Lamb and Matthew Levering (Oxford: Oxford University Press, 2008), 25–36; Pope Benedict XVI, "A Proper Hermeneutic for the Second Vatican Council," in *Vatican II: Renewal within Tradition*, ix–xv, at xi; excerpted from Pope Benedict XVI's December 22, 2005 address to the Roman Curia, "Ad Roman Curiam ob omnia natalicia," *Acta Apostolicae Sedis* 98 (6 January 2006): 40–53. Dulles concludes, "The teaching of Vatican II on the nature, mission, and structures of the Church should by rights have brought about a peaceful consensus within the Church and launched a new era of confident evangelization. In point of fact the council was followed by several decades of contestation, polarization, and confusion. Often enough, dissenters tried to justify their stance by appealing to Vatican II, as though it had broken sharply with the past and ushered in a new era of critical thinking and innovation. Such appeals to the council were hollow and unwarranted. With a sounder hermeneutic, it may still be possible to retrieve the council's actual teaching. If so, the Church may appear more radiantly as the sacrament of Christ, who remains forever the light of the nations" (Dulles, "Nature, Mission, and Structure of the Church," 34–35). See also Peter Walter's study, "Kontinuität oder Diskontinuität? Das II. Vaticanum im Kontext der Theologiegeschichte," in *Das II. Vatikanische Konzil und die Wissenschaft der Theologie*, ed. Ansgar Kreutzer and Günther Wassilowsky (Frankfurt: Peter Lang, 2014), 11–31.

44. For Congar, change does not negate continuity: "Vatican II was intentionally in continuity with the previous councils of the Church and with Tradition. Paul VI himself insisted on its continuity with Vatican I. As every historian knows, everything is always changing and at the same time there is in many ways a deep continuity" (Congar, "Moving Towards a Pilgrim Church," 129). Although the Church often breaks with aspects of its past, the issue is whether such breaks involve a false teaching that was previously taught authoritatively, as part of the deposit of faith, by the Magisterium. For the latter view, which I find unpersuasive, see for example Francis Oakley, "History and the Return of the Repressed in Catholic Modernity: The Dilemma Posed by Constance," in *The Crisis of Authority in Catholic Modernity*, ed. Michael J. Lacey and Francis Oakley (Oxford: Oxford University Press, 2011), 29–56, especially 46–49. See also along the same lines Terrence W. Tilley's *Inventing Catholic Tradition* (Maryknoll, N.Y.: Orbis Books, 2000) and Edward Schillebeeckx, OP's *Church: The Human Story of God*, trans. John Bowden (New York: Crossroad, 1993), as well as Daniel Speed Thompson, *The Language of Dissent: Edward Schillebeeckx on the Crisis of Authority in the Catholic Church*, with a Foreword by Edward Schillebeeckx, OP (Notre Dame, Ind.: University of Notre Dame Press, 2003). See also, on the relationship of change and continuity, Paul VI's important 1976 letter to Archbishop Lefebvre.

He argues, however, that the problem is that the metanarratives—such as Ratzinger/Benedict's—have wrongly become "detached from the kind of historical studies dedicated to the councils and cultivated by the church that celebrated them."[45] Here he specifically has in mind Alberigo's historiography. Making negative reference to Agostino Marchetto, he warns that "[a]lready in 1997 members of the entourage of the Roman Curia, feeling more secure in the decline of John Paul II's pontificate, began expressing more vocally their prior criticism of the volumes of *History of Vatican II* edited by Giuseppe Alberigo, because *History of Vatican II* challenged their favorite narrative."[46] After the papal election of Joseph Ratzinger, this vocal criticism grew even stronger. Faggioli explains that the "initially quiet reaction against the international, multiauthored, and respected historiographical work on Vatican II (polemically labelled 'the Bologna School') became gradually more visible over time and especially after 2005."[47] Fortunately, says Faggioli, no serious historians criticized Alberigo's work, and so the criticism "never acquired a real scholarly standing as an alternative to the international research on Vatican II."[48] Even so, during the pontificate of Pope Benedict, "Catholic ultratraditionalist intellectuals, ideologi-

---

45. Faggioli, "Vatican II," 77.
46. Ibid. See Agostino Marchetto, *The Second Vatican Ecumenical Council: A Counterpoint for the History of the Council*, trans. Kenneth D. Whitehead (Scranton, Penn.: University of Scranton Press, 2010). Marchetto's book amply demonstrates the theological perspectives present in the historiography of the Council, including in Alberigo's volumes. Indeed, we should expect that works of Church history will be colored by particular theological perspectives, and whenever the presence of such perspectives is denied, we should worry. Here I agree with Joseph Komonchak that "the question of how the Church ought to be at once faithful to Christ and an effective sign and instrument of him in the world or worlds of today continues. It is only natural that disagreements about these matters will affect one's initial interest in the council, the questions one asks, the elements one assembles in order to answer them, the story one decides to tell, and, above all, one's *evaluation of* the conciliar event. I do not believe that there is any way in which these larger issues can be wiped from a historian's mind, nor do I think that anything but a purely mythical ideal of 'presuppositionless history' should require one to try to do so. But I do think that it might help if we were to acknowledge that the last thing to which I referred above—the evaluation of the council—represents a different level of the historian's existential involvement in his project and that gross differences on this level will not be resolved by the same criteria by which the historian attempts to say 'what really happened at Vatican II.' It is too much to expect that mere history will suffice to overcome those differences, which have other causes and require other solutions" (Komonchak, "Vatican II as an 'Event,'" 44–45).
47. Faggioli, "Vatican II," 77–78.
48. Ibid., 78.

cally much closer to the Lefebvrites than to the Roman 'official' interpretation of Vatican II as an event of 'continuity and reform,' have been given honors and venues by prelates of the Roman Curia."[49]

While complaining that the historians by whom he was trained have not been appreciated for their even-handed historiography, Faggioli at the same time does not hesitate to show his own theological positions, in a manner that is in tension with his ideal of a normatively objective historiography. He criticizes the centralizing tendencies of the pontificates of John Paul II and Benedict XVI (who had not yet resigned at the time Faggioli first published his "Vatican II" essay). He states, "So many expectations regarding the power of Vatican II to reform the church have been disappointed, such that it has become easy for the ones who never believed in Vatican II as a real reform council to blame it for what happened *after* Vatican II."[50] On this view, "what happened *after* Vatican II" is considered blameworthy by those who, Faggioli thinks, actually "never believed in Vatican II as a real reform council"—while at the same time Vatican II's real reforms were never implemented or barely implemented (thus producing the disappointment "regarding the power of Vatican II to reform the church"). Here Faggioli does not pause to define what "reform" would mean in terms of Vatican II's own teachings; instead he seems to take it for granted that the Council's "real reform" must be political in nature.

Faggioli's position raises two concerns. First, the way that he speaks about Vatican II's goal of reform does not touch upon the cruciform charity that Imbelli identifies as the center of Vatican II's call for "Christification." Certainly, as Imbelli recognizes, Vatican II promoted reforms in the Church's institutional power relations. But to describe the "reform" advocated by Vatican II fundamentally in terms of power rather than fundamentally in terms of cruciform love suggests that one has not adequately apprehended the centrality of Christ for Vatican II. Second, Faggioli's essay warns about "the escalating risk of leaving church history, and especially Vatican II, in the hands of 'theological pundits' (journalists in the best of cases; bloggers in the worst) whose agenda is far more influenced

---

49. Ibid. He does not name these intellectuals, but he points the reader to Giovanni Miccoli's *La chiesa dell'anticoncilio: I tradizionalisti alla riconquista di Roma* (Rome: Laterza, 2011), 234–334.
50. Faggioli, "Vatican II," 79.

by nontheological factors."⁵¹ Opposed to this nontheological or ideologically theological punditry, Faggioli sets the work of Alberigo and also his own work. He puts Alberigo's work, and the work of those whose approaches accord with Alberigo's, beyond the ability of non-historians to criticize. For Faggioli, the real experts on Vatican II must not be criticized by theologians who lack historical expertise in the field of Vatican II historiography, because "[a]ll the experts know that there is no trustworthy alternative, at least so far, to the history of Vatican II written in the last 20 years and represented by Alberigo, Komonchak, and O'Malley."⁵²

Of course, the most prominent theologian criticizing the basic approach that Faggioli adopts has been Joseph Ratzinger/Benedict XVI.⁵³ This is no mere journalist or blogger, ignorant of the real history of the Council, let alone a mere "pundit." As we have seen, however, Faggioli identifies Ratzinger with the promotion of the American neoconservative metanarrative, and Faggioli responds sharply (though implicitly) to Pope Benedict XVI's 2005 suggestion that the historiography of Vatican II has been taken over by theorists of doctrinal rupture. Faggioli states that "church historians have been accused of 'discontinuism,' of being uninterested in the tradition, that is, in Catholicism's past. But it is clear now, at 50 years from the opening of Vatican II, that those not interested in recovering the past—as well as tradition in its entirety—are actually the

---

51. Ibid., 80.
52. Ibid.
53. In his "Benedict XVI and the Interpretation of Vatican II," in *The Crisis of Authority in Catholic Modernity*, 93–110, Joseph A. Komonchak suggests (probably rightly) that Pope Benedict XVI's December 22, 2005, speech to the Roman Curia on the proper interpretation of Vatican II did not have Alberigo's approach in view, but instead aimed to persuade the small band of Lefebvrist traditionalists. Thus, Komonchak observes regarding the five-volume history of the Council edited by Alberigo, "There are reasons to think that this work is not the chief target [of Benedict XVI's speech] and certainly not the only one. Neither the editors nor the authors of individual chapters in the five volumes entertain the exaggerated hermeneutics of discontinuity that the pope criticizes. None of them denies the church's continuity in the faith. They do point to rupture or discontinuity in two areas. First, the council represented a departure from the tight system of thought and discipline that in the decades before the council had cast suspicion on most of the movements of *ressourcement* and aggiornamento, of renewal and reform, that made the council possible. Second, these authors found discontinuity precisely where the pope has placed it: in the council's effort at a more successful engagement with the modern world than had been achieved by the antimodern attitudes and strategies adopted by the papacy since the French Revolution" (ibid., 104). Certainly, if this is all that is meant by "rupture or discontinuity," then it was present at the Council (and is present in the Council's documents).

ideologues of the 'narratives' on Vatican II."⁵⁴ The assumptions here are manifold: not only that the expert Church historians have risen above the theological and ideological blinders that have led great theologians such as Benedict XVI (despite his *historical* role in the drafting of the Council's documents) into the punditry of false metanarratives, but also that historicist retrieval of "the past" is sufficient for understanding continuity within Tradition—precisely the point that Maurice Blondel, a key source for many of the leading contributors to the Council's documents, took great pains to deny.⁵⁵ In short, Faggioli both sets forth an understanding of "reform" according to Vatican II that revolves around the distribution of power rather than Christic love, and offers a vision of experts whose historical knowledge of Vatican II makes them theologically unassailable even by theologians whose knowledge of the Council is rooted in actual high-level participation in the Council.

According to Faggioli, "church historians try, with their own scientific method, to remind the church 'how much purposeful forgetting—repression or amnesia—is required to make a case for continuity.'"⁵⁶ Faggioli

54. Faggioli, "Vatican II," 80.
55. See Maurice Blondel, *History and Dogma*, trans. Alexander Dru, in Blondel, *The Letter on Apologetics and History and Dogma* (Grand Rapids, Mich.: Eerdmans, 1994), 221–87.
56. Faggioli, "Vatican II," 81, citing Stephen Schloesser, "Against Forgetting: Memory, History, Vatican II," *Theological Studies* 67 (2006): 275–319, at 277. Arguing in favor of "radical historicity" of human reality and of Vatican II as a "revolution" in the Church's understanding of divine revelation, John W. O'Malley, SJ, grants that "there *is* a strong continuity in history, whether we are speaking of history as past human reality itself or as historians' understanding of the past reality" (O'Malley, "Reform, Historical Consciousness, and Vatican II's Aggiornamento," in *Tradition and Transition: Historical Perspectives on Vatican II* [Wilmington, Del.: Michael Glazier, 1989], 44–81, at 77, 79). The problem comes in O'Malley's understanding of the handing on of the gospel: "At the core of Christianity lies the belief in a message—'the Gospel', 'the Good News'. That belief postulates that the message has a validity that transcends the ages and transcends the limitations of any culture in which it finds itself, even the culture in which it first took expression.... The charge of the Church was to 'hand on' that message, not adulterate or change it. But the very transcendence of the message implies that it perforce will be variously articulated and that every articulation will but imperfectly realize it" (O'Malley, "Tradition and Traditions," in *Tradition and Transition*, 32–43, at 33). I note that the "message" is a Person, Jesus Christ, and even if "every articulation" of the mysteries revealed in Christ is imperfect in the sense of not exhausting the mystery, nonetheless the articulations are either true or false. The Niceno-Constantinopolitan Creed confesses that the divine Son is "consubstantial with the Father," and this is either true about God or not. The question, therefore, is not whether there are changes and discontinuities (since, of course, development of doctrine would be impossible without changes and discontinuities), but whether the handing on of divine revelation is subject to revolutions that contradict a truth that the Church has definitively

considers that the scientific method of historians has made clear that claims to doctrinal "continuity" (such as Benedict XVI's or, for that matter, Congar's) are built upon a highly negative "purposeful forgetting" that, since it is purposeful, must in fact be "repression" rather than "amnesia." Faggioli's contention, then, is that those who criticize the conclusions of Alberigo and Faggioli not only are non-experts who have no right to criticize the reputable results of historical scholarship—despite their own historical involvement during the Council at the highest levels—but also are persons engaged in an intellectual act of "repression" which is the only way, as historians know, that the theological claim of doctrinal "continuity" across the vicissitudes of history can be advanced.

In his 2012 book *True Reform: Liturgy and Ecclesiology in* Sacrosanctum Concilium, Faggioli argues in favor of reading Vatican II largely in terms of historical consciousness (historicism) and ecclesiastical decentralization: "Among the elements of the 'transition age' of Vatican II, there is definitely a change in the categories of thinking, which implies—to take just two examples—a modern critical approach to exegetical interpretation of the Scriptures and a relationship between pope, bishops, and laity characterized ... by freedom and responsibility."[57] Certainly, the Council affirms both historical-critical exegesis and "freedom and responsibility," but these need to be distinguished from a philosophically naïve historicism and from a muting of the authority of the gospel over our lives.[58] Imbelli's concern needs to be highlighted here: without *Dei Verbum*'s full account of divine revelation, we will find that "the church

---

taught about the content of the gospel, that is, about faith and morals. (Note that such definitive teaching does not require dogmatic definition: many truths of faith and morals, such as the Resurrection of Jesus Christ, have not been dogmatically defined but have been definitively taught by the Church through the "ordinary" Magisterium.) Thus, O'Malley's distinction between a transcendent "message" and its imperfect articulations does not get to the heart of the matter, which has to do with whether God can reveal enduring truths about himself in history and in human words.

57. Massimo Faggioli, *True Reform: Liturgy and Ecclesiology in* Sacrosanctum Concilium (Collegeville, Minn.: Liturgical Press, 2012), 156.

58. See Joseph Ratzinger, "Biblical Interpretation in Conflict: On the Foundations and the Itinerary of Exegesis Today," trans. Adrian Walker, in *Opening Up the Scriptures: Joseph Ratzinger and the Foundations of Biblical Interpretation*, ed. José Granados, Carlos Granados, and Luis Sánchez-Navarro (Grand Rapids, Mich.: Eerdmans, 2008), 1–29; Joseph Ratzinger, "Foreword," in Ratzinger, *Jesus of Nazareth: From the Baptism in the Jordan to the Transfiguration*, trans. Adrian J. Walker (New York: Doubleday, 2007), xi–xxiv.

is without foundation and the liturgy a merely human construct."[59] After all, given a historicized understanding of Scripture and Tradition, the terms "freedom and responsibility" can possess only the meaning that they have in this-worldly institutions, not the meanings that they would have within the Christologically grounded ecclesiology and theology of mission one finds in *Lumen Gentium* and *Gaudium et Spes*.[60]

Theologically, Faggioli's *True Reform* proposes that the liturgical reform found in *Sacrosanctum Concilium* embodies and undergirds the decentralized, lay-empowering, world-affirming, change-embracing ecclesiology that, in his view, is found in the other documents of the Council. As a theologian, Faggioli advocates political decentralization in ecclesiology, dissent from magisterial teaching (especially from moral teachings), and the need to re-interpret the Church's authority and structure in a historicist manner. Faggioli is therefore particularly concerned about the way that Ratzinger/Benedict and others, when discussing Vatican II, imply "the catholicity of continuity and the 'un-catholicity' of discontinuity and change in the Church."[61] He finds this "simplistic distinction" to be

---

59. Imbelli, *Rekindling the Christic Imagination*, xv

60. Consider, for example, the similar claim made by Michael G. Lawler, Todd A. Salzman, and Eileen Burke-Sullivan that "[i]t is never enough simply to read the text to find out what it says about morality. Its original sociohistorical context must first be clarified and then the text can be translated, interpreted, and applied in a contemporary context" (Lawler, Salzman, and Burke-Sullivan, *The Church in the Modern World:* Gaudium et Spes *Then and Now* [Collegeville, Minn.: Liturgical Press, 2014], 99). This position supposes that the "original sociohistorical context," determined by modern historical-critical research, has a foundational priority over all other interpretative tools or contexts (for example, providentially ordered canonical context and context within the ecclesial Tradition guided by the Holy Spirit). Although Lawler, Salzman, and Burke-Sullivan consider themselves to be interpreting *Dei Verbum* §12 here (specifically its second and third sentences), the actual text of *Dei Verbum* §12 paints a more complex portrait. Thus *Dei Verbum* §12 goes on to say that "holy scripture requires to be read and interpreted in the light of the same Spirit through whom it was written. Consequently a right understanding of the sacred texts demands attention, no less than that mentioned above, to the content and coherence of scripture as a whole, taking into account the whole church's living tradition and the sense of analogy of faith" (*Dei Verbum*, in *Decrees of the Ecumenical Councils*, vol. 2: *Trent to Vatican II*, ed. Norman P. Tanner (Washington, D.C.: Georgetown University Press, 1990), 971–81, at 976; translation slightly modified). In discussing marriage in light of *Gaudium et Spes*, Lawler, Salzman, and Burke-Sullivan argue for the separation of the unitive and procreative ends of sexual intercourse, so that the goodness of a particular act of sexual expression depends entirely on what it may contribute to a relationship—a position that is quite different from that which is found in Scripture and Tradition (and in *Gaudium et Spes* itself!).

61. Massimo Faggioli, *A Council for the Global Church: Receiving Vatican II in History* (Minneapolis, Minn.: Fortress Press, 2015), 276.

"one of the most disturbing elements of today's scenario," since he thinks that it ahistorically rules out the possibility of change and grants to today's magisterial teaching an inviolable authority.[62]

Faggioli goes on to argue: "One implication of the paradigmatic shift at Vatican II from a metaphysics theology to a more historical understanding of the truths of Christian faith is that the conciliar teaching is not abstract, but something that must be understood in the world of today."[63] On this basis, he reads the texts looking for "the ways the Church of Vatican II has (or has not) been able to reform itself in order to be a credible witness of the changes announced by the council."[64] It is these changes, both particular ones (such as the liturgy, ecumenism, interreligious dialogue, and decentralization of authority) and general ones (most importantly the embrace of the Church's radical historicity and of the Church's embeddedness within the modern world), that for Faggioli make up the heart of the Council. From this perspective, he considers that in receiving the Council, Catholics must receive not merely fifty-year-old propositional teachings that may or may not retain their value today, but rather a heart for further change in response to discernment of the needs of our time. As he puts it with reference to the shift of tone under Pope Francis: "Vatican II was an act, and the reception of Vatican II is an act. Looking for it only in written documents reveals a scant understanding of the profound nature of that moment—and of the Church in general."[65] The spirit of this "act," which flows from but is not limited to the actual conciliar texts, is found for Faggioli in "[e]cumenism, interreligious dialogue, an ecclesiology of the Church 'that goes forth,' a Church of mercy and for the poor."[66]

All of these elements—ecumenism, interreligious dialogue, a missiological ecclesiology, mercy, and the preferential option for the poor—are good and, indeed, necessary. For Faggioli, "the council is a solemn moment of rejection of the temptations to make of the Catholic Church

---

62. Ibid. He cites in this regard the book I co-edited with Matthew L. Lamb, *Vatican II: Renewal within Tradition.*
63. Faggioli, *A Council for the Global Church*, 330.
64. Ibid.
65. Ibid., 334. By contrast, see Andrew Meszaros's "Vatican II as Theological Event and Text according to Yves Congar," forthcoming in the *Josephinum Journal of Theology.*
66. Faggioli, *A Council for the Global Church*, 334.

an inward-oriented community,"⁶⁷ and certainly Imbelli would agree, so long as one emphasizes (by contrast to an inward-looking focus on decentralization, dissent, and discontinuity) that the Church must be an outward-looking community whose eyes are focused on Jesus Christ. Indeed, what I find largely missing in Faggioli's work on Vatican II is attention to Jesus Christ, who according to Vatican II is the measure, source, and center of all things. I do not find Faggioli giving an account of Christ or setting forth his salvific significance and the mode of the mediation of the transformative truths of his gospel. Faggioli's concerns, instead, are primarily political, in the sense that it is the distribution of power in the Church, illumined by historicist modes of critical thought (as distinct from Ratzinger/Benedict's Blondelian historical engagement), that most attracts Faggioli's attention and that, crucially, bears the burden of defining what "true reform" means.

Consider his way of unfolding his contention that "[t]he vision of Vatican II is crucial ... for the viability of theology in modernity."⁶⁸ He explains this viability in two ways. First, he notes (quite rightly) that "clearly long overdue were the shifts about biblical hermeneutics, theology and modern science, interreligious and the ecumenical dialogue."⁶⁹ Second, he sums up the "other theological issues" by stating that "Vatican II opened a path toward the future of the Church: a more communional and less juridical ecclesiology, a new understanding of the relationship between laity and ministry, and Church reform."⁷⁰ In other words, his view of Vatican II's theological contributions ultimately reduces to the Council's approval of modern modes of critical thought (certainly a good thing, but—I would emphasize—in need of Christological reference) and the Council's redistribution and reconceptualization of ecclesiastical power in the light of religious pluralism. Faggioli seems to think that these two dimensions—modern hermeneutics and democratized power (both of which can be recognized as beneficial in their proper context, but which must be measured by and centered in Christ)—largely suffice for describing the way in which the Council "is about recentering theology in the very roots of the

67. Ibid., 331.
68. Ibid., 285.
69. Ibid.
70. Ibid., 285–86.

Christian revelation without losing sight of the signs of our times."[71] The problem here is that "the very roots of the Christian revelation" are in fact discussed extensively and deeply by the Council, not least in the four Constitutions, in christologically specific ways that Faggioli almost completely ignores. With respect to the "signs of our times," the crucified and risen Christ so strongly proclaimed by Vatican II is, as Imbelli makes clear, too often no longer at the center of Catholic consciousness.

Faggioli concludes, "The interpretation of Vatican II as an exercise of textual exegesis made in a historical vacuum is not only a reduction of its meaning, it is also the subtlest form of rejection of the council."[72] Surely no one, let alone Ratzinger/Benedict, wishes to read Vatican II "in a historical vacuum" as though the historical contextualization of ecclesial texts did not matter. But a comparison of the theology of Vatican II uncovered by Imbelli with the theology of Vatican II uncovered by Faggioli makes evident that it is Faggioli who has produced "a reduction of its meaning" and who has not taken up the most central Christological and Trinitarian themes of the actual historical Council into his vision of Vatican II as the ongoing theological event of the decentralization and historicization of the Church.

In sum, Imbelli rightly perceives that the real ongoing theological event of the Council is the renewed biblical, liturgical, ecclesial, and missional ways by which—with ecumenical and interreligious outreach and with appreciation for the advances and challenges of the modern world— "the Church should bring Christ to the world" (as Pope John XXIII put it a month before the Council's opening).[73] The ongoing theological event of Vatican II is centered upon Christ.

Joseph Ratzinger and the Council: Brief Further Reflections

Faggioli, like Imbelli, is well aware of the significance of the figures of the *nouvelle théologie* for the composition of Vatican II. He presents the central debate in terms of a contrast between the perspectives of Henri de Lu-

---

71. Ibid., 287.   72. Ibid., 345.
73. Pope John XXIII, Radio Message, 11 September 1962 (my translation from the Spanish text).

bac and Joseph Ratzinger, on the one side, and Congar (joined by Chenu and Rahner) on the other. Faggioli considers de Lubac and Ratzinger to be theological pessimists who misdiagnosed the Council's aftermath as a return of immanentism or modernism, and who therefore consistently fought the true reforms called for by the Council. In his engagement with these figures, Faggioli highlights *Gaudium et Spes* rather than, as he does elsewhere, *Sacrosanctum Concilium*; but in both cases Ratzinger's oppositional perspective takes center stage. Faggioli states, "*Gaudium et Spes* was and still is at the very heart of the two major streams of interpretation of the council. Henri de Lubac and Joseph Ratzinger were the champions of a more Augustinian view of the modern world and therefore were not enthusiastic about *Gaudium et Spes*."[74]

74. Faggioli, *A Council for the Global Church*, 124. In his "A Council for All Peoples," Marie-Dominique Chenu, OP, criticizes "a particular, explicit or implicit, conception of Christian doctrine as focused on God as God, rather than on the Man-God Christ, upon God as involved in the history of humanity" (Chenu, "A Council for All Peoples," in *Vatican II Revisited by Those Who Were There*, 19–23, at 20). In Chenu's view, *Gaudium et Spes* rectifies this situation by focusing "upon God as involved in the history of humanity." Arguing that "[i]f the humanization of God is the constant axis of the theology of Vatican II, it is natural that man should be the common denominator of its analyses and decisions," he praises the fact that *Gaudium et Spes* "is headed by a long psychological and sociological analysis of the situation of mankind in the modern world. This is the first time in history that a Council has 'introduced' (the text is called an 'Introductory Statement') its doctrinal and institutional position by referring to the actual situation of the world. This is because this Constitution is built not on recourse to the eternal verities come down from heaven, but on constant reference to the dynamic of a 'new age' that calls the statements of faith into question. For the first time, the Church defines its own mystery through and in the movement of the world, in which it finds the setting for its existence and its self-understanding" (Chenu, "A Council for All Peoples," 20). Chenu links this Christian humanism to that found in Pope John Paul II's 1979 encyclical *Redemptor Hominis*, but if Chenu's emphasis on the Church defining "its own mystery through and in the movement of the world" were pressed further than he presses it here, it would be difficult to avoid a historicist account of the dogmatic teaching of the Church. Chenu is also somewhat too confident with respect to the ease of determining, prior to theological analysis, what "man" and "the world" are. For a movement along Chenu's lines, according to which one can speak of "concrete self-realizations of the Church" at particular historical times and places but not of "the Church" per se (thus leaving dogmatic theology deeply vulnerable to historicism), see Joseph A. Komonchak, *Foundations in Ecclesiology* (Chestnut Hill, Mass.: Boston College, 1995), although Komonchak does not go as far as does Roger Haight, SJ's *Christian Community in History*, 2 vols. (New York: Continuum, 2004–2005). For insight into the issues involved, criticizing the historicism that he identifies in Walter Kasper's 1967 book *The Methods of Dogmatic Theology*, trans. John Drury (Glen Rock, N.J.: Paulist Press, 1969), see Reinhard Hütter, "'A Forgotten Truth?'—Theological Faith, Source and Guarantee of Theology's Inner Unity," in his *Dust Bound for Heaven: Explorations in the Theology of Thomas Aquinas* (Grand Rapids, Mich.: Eerdmans, 2012), 313–48. As Hütter shows, for Kasper in 1967—and for numerous others following the same

A careful consideration of Ratzinger's statements shows the weakness of Faggioli's one-sided engagement with Ratzinger's perspective. For instance, commenting on *Gaudium et Spes*'s discussion of war and peace (and the anthropology therein), Ratzinger observes in his 1966 *Theological Highlights of Vatican II*: "If we meditate on the Council's statement, we become immediately aware how suited it really is to lead us from what seems to be an almost secular consideration into the very heart of Christianity."[75] What is this "very heart of Christianity"? Ratzinger answers that it is the inability of humans to redeem ourselves, to be holy by our own power. This perspective is not simply "Augustinian" but deeply Pauline, and it leads Ratzinger to emphasize that *Gaudium et Spes* draws us to the center of Vatican II: Jesus Christ. He remarks that *Gaudium et Spes*'s teachings on war and peace force us "to admit that our righteousness is nothing but a temporary expedient in the midst of unrighteousness. We find ourselves crying for mercy to him who makes just the unjust."[76] *Gaudium et Spes*'s proposals show us, as the document itself emphasized in earlier passages, that only Christ can satisfy the human heart and bring ultimate fulfillment and peace to the human race. Thus Ratzinger goes on to say, with a strong interreligious impulse that is deeply Christological: "The sincerity of the man who acknowledges reality with no excuses is itself a hidden appeal to the mercy of the mystery which has appeared to the faithful in Jesus Christ. The foremost intention of the Council was to reveal this need for Christ in the depth of the human heart so as to make man able to hear Christ's call."[77] Here, indeed, is the Ratzinger and the Vatican II about which Imbelli writes so beautifully.

---

path—"dogma is always relative to its particular time. All propositions are functions of the promise of a future that is not yet at hand, hence historically conditioned by this future and therefore to be interpreted in light of it. Because there is no perennial supernatural given of the faith, there can be no contemplation of the faith that rises above the flux of history toward God," with the result that "the theological enterprise cannot be correlated to the deliveries of the faith that essentially transcend the vagaries of historically conditioned understanding" (ibid., 329). See also Joseph A. Komonchak, "Le valutazioni sulla *Gaudium et Spes*: Chenu, Dossetti, Ratzinger," in *Volti di fine concilio. Studi di storia e teologia sulla conclusion del Vaticano II*, ed. Joseph Dore and Alberto Melloni (Bologna: Il Mulino, 2000), 115–63.

75. Joseph Ratzinger, *Theological Highlights of Vatican II*, trans. Werner Barzel, Gerald C. Thormann, and Henry Traub, SJ (Mahwah, N.J.: Paulist Press, 2009), 243.
76. Ibid.
77. Ibid., 243–44.

There are many other passages in Ratzinger's writings that praise *Gaudium et Spes*, such as one in his 1968 commentary on the document in which he states, with respect to paragraph 22, "We are probably justified in saying that here, for the first time in a document of the magisterium, a new type of completely Christocentric theology appears. On the basis of Christ this dares to present theology as anthropology and only becomes radically theological by including man in discourse about God by way of Christ."[78] This Christocentrism, and not a merely negative "Augustinianism" that seeks to do anything to counter the threats of modernity, is what drives Ratzinger's interpretation of the Council. The Council's texts correspond deeply, as Imbelli shows, to this Christ-centered vision. When Ratzinger criticizes certain statements in *Gaudium et Spes*, as he does in his 1968 commentary with respect to paragraph 12, it is because he fears that the paragraph retains traces of "a schematic representation of nature and the supernatural viewed

---

78. Joseph Ratzinger, "Part I, Chapter I," in *Commentary on the Documents of Vatican II*, ed. Herbert Vorgrimler, vol. 5, *Pastoral Constitution on the Church in the Modern World*, trans. W. J. O'Hara (New York: Herder and Herder, 1969), 115–63, at 159; cited in Imbelli, *Rekindling the Christic Imagination*, 87. See also Ratzinger's 1975 essay "On the Status of Church and Theology Today," in *Principles of Catholic Theology: Building Stones for a Fundamental Theology*, trans. Mary Frances McCarthy, SND (San Francisco: Ignatius Press, 1987), 367–93. Ratzinger praises *Gaudium et Spes* as "a revision of the *Syllabus* of Pius IX, a kind of countersyllabus" (Ratzinger, "On the Status of Church and Theology Today," 381). As he notes, *Gaudium et Spes* does not represent a sudden or unprepared shift in this regard: "The new ecclesiastical policy of Pius XI produced a certain openness toward a liberal understanding of the state. In a quiet but persistent struggle, exegesis and Church history adopted more and more the postulates of liberal science, and liberalism, too, was obliged to undergo many significant changes in the great political upheavals of the twentieth century. As a result, the one-sidedness of the position adopted by the Church under Pius IX and Pius X in response to the situation created by the French Revolution was, to a large extent, corrected *via facti*, especially in Central Europe, but there was still no basic statement of the relationship that should exist between the Church and the world that had come into existence after 1789" (Ratzinger, "On the Status of Church and Theology Today," 381–82). In the final section of this essay, Ratzinger examines the reception of *Gaudium et Spes*, both the embrace of the modern world (represented by the reception of the document in the Netherlands) and the radical critique of the modern world (represented by the reception of the document in Latin America). Although Ratzinger finds *Gaudium et Spes* to be in certain respects too hopeful (as shown by the events of the years 1966–1975) about the reconciliation of Church and world, he argues that "[w]hat devastated the Church in the decade after the Council was not the Council but the refusal to accept it. This becomes clear precisely in the history of the influence of *Gaudium et spes*. What was identified with the Council was, for the most part, the expression of an attitude that did not coincide with the statements to be found in the text itself, although it is recognizable as a tendency in its development and in some of its individual formulations. The task is not, therefore, to suppress the Council but to discover the real Council and to deepen its true intention in the light of present experience" (Ratzinger, "On the Status of Church and Theology Today," 390–91).

far too much as merely juxtaposed," not because of any goal of "imposing [upon the text] a pessimistic view of man or of constructing an exaggerated theology of sin."[79] Ratzinger adds that in fact the final form of paragraph 12 is greatly improved from earlier drafts, as a result of the introduction of a strongly Pascalian or phenomenological understanding of human nature's existential situation at the outset of the paragraph.

Ratzinger was aware that the Council's changes, whose purpose was to draw people closer to Jesus Christ, were not necessarily having the desired impact of reinvigorating the Church and its mission.[80] In his *Milestones:*

---

79. Ratzinger, "Part I, Chapter I," 120.

80. With regard to the impact that Vatican II has had, two recent articles in *First Things* draw different conclusions. In his "Reckoning with Modernity," *First Things*, no. 258 (December 2015): 23–30, Bruce D. Marshall argues that "the council channeled the torrent of modernity in a way that made the Church's ancient teaching on her relationship with the world especially clear" (Marshall, "Reckoning with Modernity," 30)—a relationship that includes Jesus' promise that "[i]f the world hates you, know that it hated me before you" (Jn 15:18), a hatred that arises from the love of creaturely goods above the love of God. Marshall finds that the Council came just at the right moment and accomplished evident good: "In 1960, it was increasingly evident, not least to people like Congar, that this anti-modernist discipline had become ineffective at coping with the flood of social, cultural, and intellectual forces that confronted the Church. Had this regime continued, while modernity—the bad along with the good—continued to take root among Catholics, unguided by the actions and decisions of an ecumenical council, the flood might simply have broken in on the Church willy-nilly, sweeping away the precious treasure Congar loved along with the anti-modernist regime he detested" (Marshall, "Reckoning with Modernity," 29). I agree with Marshall that "Vatican II did not, as some theologians still suppose, accommodate modernity by digging an ugly ditch between the Catholic Church and her past. It channeled the modern flood in a way that was beneficial to the Church just because it was faithful to her traditions" (Marshall, "Reckoning with Modernity," 29). In his "A Crisis of Conservative Catholicism," *First Things*, no. 259 (January 2016): 21–28, Ross Douthat observes (among other things) that "a major part of Vatican II's mission was to equip the Church to evangelize the modern world, and … five decades is long enough to say that in this ambition the council mostly failed. Since the close of the council, we've seen fifty years of Catholic civil war and institutional collapse in the world's most modern (and once, most Catholic) societies, fifty years in which only Africa looks like a successful mission territory, while in Asia and Latin American the Church has been lapped and lapped again by Protestants" (Douthat, "A Crisis of Conservative Catholicism," 27). As Douthat notes with regard to the United States, "Ex-Catholics are one of the country's largest religious groups, and without Hispanic immigration, trends in Catholic affiliation and practice would resemble Mainline Protestantism more than many would be eager to admit" (Douthat, "A Crisis of Conservative Catholicism," 22). Lest he be misunderstood, Douthat adds: "This doesn't mean the council was a failure in its entirety, or that arch-traditionalists are right to condemn it as heretical, or (as more moderate traditionalists would argue) that the council itself was primarily to blame for everything that followed. The experience of every other Christian confession suggests that some version of the same civil war and institutional crisis would have arrived with or without the council" (Douthat, "A Crisis of Conservative Catholicism," 27). Douthat concludes that "for all its future-oriented rhetoric, Vatican II's clearest achievements were mostly backward-looking. It dealt impressively with

Memoirs 1927–1977, Ratzinger recalls that by 1964 he encountered theological confusion in Germany, especially among faculties and students of theology: "Now and then, on returning from Rome, I found the mood in the Church and among theologians to be quite agitated. The impression grew steadily that nothing was now stable in the Church, that everything was open to revision. More and more the Council appeared to be like a great Church parliament that could change everything and reshape everything according to its own desires."[81] Rather than leading people to a deeper relationship with Jesus Christ, the danger was that the Council could undermine believers' sense of divine revelation.[82] Ratzinger suggests that already during the Council itself, the Council was being interpreted in a primarily hermeneutical and political way, as though the Church were simply coming to terms with its own hermeneutical backwardness

---

problems that came to the fore during the crises and debates of the nineteenth and early twentieth centuries (the Church's relationship to democracy, to religious liberty, to anti-Semitism). But its deliberations simply took place too soon to address the problems that broke across Catholicism and Christianity with the sexual revolution and that still preoccupy us now" (Douthat, "A Crisis of Conservative Catholicism," 27). I agree with Douthat so far as he goes, but I think that Marshall is more insightful on the crucial theological work done by the four Constitutions.

81. Joseph Ratzinger, *Milestones: Memoirs 1927–1977*, trans. Erasmo Leiva-Merikakis (San Francisco: Ignatius Press, 1998), 132. John O'Malley observes, "The impact of the media and the very content of the documents explain, therefore, why Catholics feel such a stake in the Council, and they further indicate why the interpretation of the Council has become so problematic. Christianity is by self-definition traditional. Its obligation is to 'tell the next generation' the message it has received. Any too sudden or too obvious change in practice or attitude is bound to be scrutinized for possible adulteration of that fundamental commission" (O'Malley, "Vatican II: Historical Perspectives on Its Uniqueness and Interpretation," in *Vatican II: The Unfinished Agenda. A Look to the Future*, ed. Lucien Richard, OMI, Daniel Harrington, SJ, and John W. O'Malley, SJ [Mahwah, N.J.: Paulist Press, 1987], 22–32, at 23). Writing in 1987, O'Malley speaks of "the present crisis" (O'Malley, "Vatican II: Historical Perspectives," 23), and he also speaks of "[t]he turmoil into which the Church was thrown in the aftermath of the Council" (O'Malley, "Vatican II: Historical Perspectives," 31).

82. In 1966, Karl Barth famously asked: "Are the adherents of the 'progressive' majority of the Council ... aware of the danger that this might result in an undesired repetition of the errors committed in modern Protestantism?" (Barth, *Ad Limina Apostolorum: An Appraisal of Vatican II*, trans. Keith R. Crim [Edinburgh: The Saint Andrew Press, 1969], 20). Barth had in view specifically the errors of Protestant liberalism, which, for those who embraced it, dissolved the sense of an authoritative divine revelation that we must hear and obey, and also dissolved the sense of real sin and real salvation by Christ. Ratzinger, like de Lubac and other members of the "progressive" majority, clearly seems to have been aware of this danger, but the threat that Barth identified emerged powerfully in the immediate postconciliar period and remains today, fifty years after the Council, the key struggle within the Catholic Church.

and its oppressively feudal structure. The Christological center of Vatican II's Constitutions was thereby being missed. Ratzinger recollects that in Germany during the later stages of the Council, "The disputes at the Council were more and more portrayed according to the party model of modern parliamentarianism."[83]

As a result, it began to seem in the popular imagination as though hermeneutics and power, rather than Jesus Christ, were the real issues of the Council. This result made faith in Christ seem like a human construct, changeable by whoever has the power. As Ratzinger puts it, "The faith no longer seemed exempt from human decision making but rather was now apparently determined by it."[84] This situation was the very opposite of the *nouvelle théologie*'s desire to draw people closer to Christ. Rather than finding Christ at the very center of everything, people found the human hermeneutical will to power at the center: a self-constituting Church with no real need for or access to Christ. Ratzinger adds that alongside a "tendency to dominance by specialists," so that "even the Creed no longer appeared untouchable but seemed rather subject to the control of scholars," there was emerging "the idea of an ecclesial sovereignty of the people in which the people itself determines what it wants to understand by Church."[85]

Conclusion

In his "Vatican II: For the Life of the World," James Hanvey articulates a common criticism of Ratzinger/Benedict XVI's approach, one that many other Catholic theologians find persuasive. He remarks that Benedict XVI's "hermeneutic of 'continuity,'" while correct so far as it goes, "cannot and should not be used to normalize the Council and minimize its achievements, its vision or the tasks which it sets for the Church and the creative challenges which it still continues to propose."[86] This remark deserves atten-

---

83. Ratzinger, *Milestones*, 132–33.
84. Ibid., 133.
85. Ibid., 134. As Bruce Marshall remarks, the key question became "what it really means for the Church to be 'updated' and open to the world" (Marshall, "Reckoning with Modernity," 26).
86. James Hanvey, SJ, "Vatican II: For the Life of the World," in *The Second Vatican Council: Celebrating Its Achievements and the Future*, 45–68, at 47.

tion, because many theologians today, as we have seen, fear that appeal to "continuity" is tantamount to neutralizing or even neutering the Council.[87]

The key question is what it would mean to "normalize the Council and minimize its achievements, its vision or the tasks which it sets." What kinds of things would we need to understand in order for the Council's achievements, vision, and tasks not to be minimized? For Hanvey, as for so many other theologians today, the answer is simply that we must recognize that the Council "commits us to the journey of history" and that the Council commits the Church to understanding "its own need to change in order to be faithful to Christ and the mission entrusted to it."[88]

In response, I observe that no one denies that the Church is on "the journey of history" or that the Church changes in significant ways. There are also some things in the Church that do not change: for instance, the Church has believed in Jesus Christ as Lord and Savior from the outset. This belief has been enriched by doctrinal development, but it is important to insist upon unchanging elements in the Church's faith, without which the communication of the apostolic deposit of faith would not make sense.

Hanvey argues that "the Council must be read as the beginning of a new phase in the Church's self-understanding and development for which the theology is still being worked out."[89] The danger here is that by maximizing this "new phase ... for which the theology is still being worked out," one could end up radically *minimizing* the new phase by separating it too sharply from the vast riches of preconciliar theology—including the theological teachings of Scripture and the luminous theological writings produced in the twenty centuries during which Christians have reflected upon the biblical testimony to Jesus Christ. For example, Hanvey observes that "[b]efore Vatican II, the Church was predominantly thought of as a *perfecta societas*" and as a "Mystical Body" in a manner

---

87. In his December 22, 2005, address to the Roman Curia, of course, Benedict XVI contrasted the "hermeneutic of discontinuity and rupture" not with the "hermeneutic of continuity" but with the "hermeneutic of reform": see Benedict XVI, "A Proper Hermeneutic for the Second Vatican Council," in *Vatican II: Renewal within Tradition*, ed. Matthew L. Lamb and Matthew Levering, ix–xv, at x–xi; excerpted from Benedict XVI's "Ad Roman Curiam ob omnia natalicia," *Acta Apostolicae Sedis* 98 (6 January 2006): 40–53. On the "hermeneutic of reform," see also Kurt Koch, *Das zweite Vatikanische Konzil: Eine Bilanz. Die Hermeneutik der Reform* (Augsburg: Sankt Ulrich Verlag, 2012).

88. Hanvey, "Vatican II," 47.

89. Ibid., 49.

that "emphasized its hierarchical constitution, governed by the Pope, and sanctified through the proper administration of the sacraments."[90] But by citing only Robert Bellarmine and Pius XII's encyclical *Mystici Corporis*, Hanvey inadvertently presents a truncated view of the resources of pre-1962 theology, a truncated view against which the *nouvelle théologie* fought strenuously and which Vatican II sought to correct. The resources of the *entire* ecclesiological tradition, rooted in the wide array of biblical images and certainly not downplaying the role of the Petrine office and the sacraments ("the Eucharist builds the Church"), provide Vatican II with its ecclesiological vision.

Despite the weakness of some of his formulations, Hanvey's insistence upon "the journey of history" strikes me as in a certain way quite appropriate for the interpretation of Vatican II. The four themes that I highlighted in the preceding chapters—personal encounter with the self-revealing Lord, active participation in Christ's sacrificial self-offering, true reform so as to deepen communion with Christ, and the fulfillment of all created things in Christ—all emphasize the historical context and historical dynamic by which faith in Jesus Christ arises and grows. In the contrasting visions of Imbelli and Faggioli, however, we find two alternative ways of construing "the journey of history" and two alternative ways of conceiving of how historical and theological scholarship should join together in the interpretation of Vatican II's texts. For Imbelli, the center of history is Jesus Christ, and the Church must meet him—and draw the whole world to him—in a historical journey fueled by encounter with divine Mystery, by Eucharistic participation, by reform rooted in the Church's response to Christ's universal call to cruciform holiness, and by an evangelizing mission. In this history, it is not ecclesiastical power—whether during Vatican II or after it—that takes center stage. Imbelli does not deny the importance of ecclesiastical power, and he gladly supports Vatican II's call for the greater participation of laity and of diocesan bishops in the governance and mission of the Church, even while he rejects efforts to undermine the authority that Vatican II accords to the pope or to undermine the obedience of faith. But power structures do not stand at the core of Imbelli's

90. Ibid., 50.

vision of Vatican II. While the history of the power struggles and complex drafting of documents during the Council interests him, he points firmly to the historical and trans-historical Mystery made present afresh by the documents and preeminently by the Constitutions, the same Mystery to which Scripture testifies: Jesus Christ crucified and risen.

By comparison, Faggioli's work presents "the journey of history" with a much different focus. In the journey of history, according to Faggioli, Vatican II finally has enabled the Church itself to recognize how profoundly historically conditioned (in a historicist sense) its teachings and structures are. The Church no longer supposes that the answers to contemporary theological problems are readily available from Scripture or Tradition. Given how radically historically conditioned the teachings of Church and Scripture are, we cannot really know what the Church should teach in the future, since it is the act of change rather than the content of texts that now is determinative. As a result, intra-ecclesiastical power politics takes center stage. This is especially so with regard to the need to weaken hierarchical power to command obedience about matters of faith and morals. For Faggioli, each of us, along with our local, regional, and worldwide communities, strives toward a truth that will be knowable only at the end of history. The center of Vatican II, on this view, is the journeying community and its awakening to its real freedom. From this perspective, the center of the study of Vatican II should not be the salvific realities taught anew by the Council, but rather the struggles and behind-the-scenes influences that portend further decentralization and historicization.

I hold that Imbelli's approach to Vatican II is correct. Christ crucified and risen, faithfully mediated to us through Church and Scripture and participated in through faith and sacramental worship, is the very center of the Second Vatican Council. The ongoing event of Vatican II consists primarily in learning from the Council how better to encounter and know the love of Christ, how to participate actively in the liturgy in Christ's supreme act of love, how to understand what is reformable and what is unchanging in the Church's witness to Christ, and how to lead the whole world "to live for the praise of his glory" (Eph 1:12) and to be "filled with the fruits of righteousness which come through Jesus Christ, to the glory and praise of God" (Phil 1:11).

CONCLUSION

On December 1, 1965, as the Second Vatican Council approached its end, Henri de Lubac wrote in a letter to his Jesuit Superiors in France: "In the coming months and years, it will be necessary to study seriously the overall work of the Council. One must know how to take the dogmatic constitutions as the center of perspective, for they are in fact at the center of everything."[1] The present book has tried to implement this advice, from a perspective of profound appreciation for the teachings of the Council. The great themes of the Council are dogmatic and pastoral at the same time: personal encounter with the mystery of Jesus Christ through Scripture and Tradition; active participation in Christ's Paschal mystery; the Church as comprising divine constitutive elements (dogma, sacraments, offices) and human elements that are in constant need of reform; and the connection of nature and grace so as to show that Jesus Christ is the very center of history. These great themes make clear why de Lubac, in his letter to his Jesuit Superiors, strongly opposes "placing too much emphasis on a distinction between 'doctrine' and 'pastoral.'"[2] Doctrine has as its source and goal the living Christ, and therefore it is not cut off from the

---

1. Henri de Lubac, SJ, *At the Service of the Church: Henri de Lubac Reflects on the Circumstances That Occasioned His Writings*, trans. Anne Elizabeth Englund (San Francisco: Ignatius Press, 1993), 345.
2. Ibid., 342.

pastoral dimensions of Christ as the Good Shepherd and of the Church as God's sheepfold.

De Lubac was an advocate of reform, but reform of a particular kind, namely reform that unites us more tightly with the Person of Christ and thus with divine revelation as faithfully handed on in Scripture and Tradition. He would have resonated with Lawrence Cunningham's observation fifteen years after the Council, "If by fiat the Vatican assented to all the demands of every reform group of every persuasion (hardly a possibility because reform groups are headed by Archbishop Lefebvres and well as Hans Küngs), the fundamental issue would still remain: How is the Gospel to be lived and why should it be followed?"[3] It should be followed because it is true and fulfills our deepest yearnings, and it should be lived in repentance and love of Christ. When we look at the conciliar reforms of the ways that the Church communicates the truths of faith, we find personal encounter with Christ emphasized in *Inter Mirifica*, *Gravissimum Educationis*, and *Optatam Totius*. Likewise, the reforms of the Church's hierarchical order emphasize the need for all believers to actively participate in Christ, as can be seen in *Christus Dominus*, *Presbyterorum Ordinis*, and *Apostolicam Actuositatem*. In the reform of the relationship of Latin Catholics to Eastern Catholics, the reform of consecrated religious life, and the reform of the relationship of the Catholic Church to non-Catholic Christians—found respectively in *Orientalium Ecclesiarum*, *Perfectae Caritatis*, and *Unitatis Redintegratio*—we observe the effort to retain the divine elements of the Church while removing certain human elements that weaken the power of the divine elements given by Christ. Finally, in the reform of the Church's missionary activity (*Ad Gentes*), the reform of the Church's relationship with the Jewish people and with other religions (*Nostra Aetate*), and the reform of the Church's relationship with the state (*Dignitatis Humanae*), we find Christ at the center but not in a punitive or condemnatory way.

At the outset of the Council, the great figures of the *nouvelle théologie* were united by a shared experience of misunderstanding, and in some cases real persecution, by neo-scholastic authorities in Rome (both Cu-

---

3. Lawrence S. Cunningham, *The Meaning of Saints* (San Francisco: Harper and Row, 1980), 171.

rial authorities and the leaders of the religious orders). Joseph Ratzinger describes an oppressive atmosphere of "anti-ism."[4] Many exemplary theologians, including de Lubac, were removed in the 1950s from teaching positions or forbidden to write on particular topics. This situation rapidly changed under Pope John XXIII, and by 1963 the Council was clearly being shaped theologically by representatives of the *nouvelle théologie*. Though the great figures of the *nouvelle théologie* each had disagreements with certain passages in particular conciliar documents, as a whole the documents of Vatican II embody what they had hoped to accomplish.

Thus, at the conclusion of the Council, Yves Congar reported in his journal, "A great many bishops congratulated me, thanked me. To a good extent, it was my work, they said."[5] Ratzinger, too, expresses pleasure in 1966 about the outcome of the Council: "the overall result can be summed up in line with what Oscar Cullmann, the Protestant exegete from Basel, said to the German Council conference on December 2, 1965. After a careful analysis he said that, looking at the Council in retrospect, 'on the whole our expectations ... were fulfilled and in some respects surpassed.'"[6] In a letter written on July 26, 1966, de Lubac underscores his appreciation for "the authentic sense of the Council and of true aggiornamento."[7] Describing the admiration that Pope Paul VI had for de Lubac, Karl Neufeld reports that following the ecumenical celebration of the end of the Council, Paul VI "added one further personal gesture of special esteem by inviting Henri de Lubac, along with Oscar Cullmann and Jean Guitton, to dine with him the following Sunday."[8]

By the end of the Council, however, tensions were emerging among

4. Joseph Ratzinger, *Theological Highlights of Vatican II*, trans. the Missionary Society of St. Paul the Apostle (New York: Paulist Press, 1966), 43.

5. Yves Congar, OP, *My Journal of the Council*, trans. Mary John Ronayne, OP, and Mary Cecily Boulding, OP, ed. Denis Minns, OP (Collegeville, Minn.: Liturgical Press, 2012), 870.

6. Joseph Ratzinger, *Theological Highlights of Vatican II*, trans. Werner Barzel, Gerald C. Thormann, and Henry Traub, SJ (Mahwah, N.J.: Paulist Press, 2009), 260.

7. De Lubac, *At the Service of the Church*, 345.

8. Karl Heinz Neufeld, SJ, "In the Service of the Council: Bishops and Theologians at the Second Vatican Council (for Cardinal Henri de Lubac on His Ninetieth Birthday)," trans. Ronald Sway, in *Vatican II: Assessment and Perspectives: Twenty-Five Years After (1962–1987)*, vol. 1, ed. René Latourelle, SJ (Mahwah, N.J.: Paulist Press, 1988), 74–105, at 98. On the Council as an ecumenical moment, see Wolfgang Thönissen, *Ein Konzil für ein ökumenisches Zeitalter: Schlüsselthemen des Zweiten Vatikanums* (Paderborn: Bonifatius, 2012).

the theologians who at the beginning of the Council had formed a generally united front. In his journal entry of November 30, 1965, for example, Congar complains that "Küng is always very radical. He says some true things, but in which the critical research into what is true is not sufficiently tempered by concern for concrete situations."[9] More strongly, in his letter of December 1, 1965, de Lubac warns that "it will be necessary to break away from the propaganda and tendentious attempts that are already arising and that will soon be in danger of aborting the undertaking of reform and of compromising the very foundations of the faith."[10] Indeed, de Lubac notes that in the previous month he had resigned from "the governing committee of the *Concilium* journal" on the grounds that he had "observed that the orientation of the Review did not correspond to what its title had led me to expect."[11] Congar remained on the editorial board of *Concilium*, but Ratzinger also broke with *Concilium* relatively soon after the Council's conclusion. In 1967, de Lubac states bluntly that "the present doctrinal crisis" has two foundations: "a total aversion to admitting a divine revelation," and "an inability on principle to think of a transcendent order of truth."[12] Ratzinger worries already in 1966 that "renewal is mistakenly taken to mean dilution and cheapening of religion," and he notes that "here and there people seem to demand not so much truth as modernity, and they take this as the sufficient standard for behavior."[13]

Similarly, in July 1968 Congar observes that "[e]verything is being called into question at the same time," and, without losing his fundamental optimism, he adds: "The discovery of the contemporary world and of humanity's role in the world have become so dominant as to seem sometimes exclusive. The danger of *horizontalism* is not a fantasy!"[14] In his in-

---

9. Congar, *My Journal of the Council*, 861. See Christopher Ruddy, "Yves Congar and Hans Küng at Vatican II: Differing Paths of Church Reform," *Ecclesiology* 10 (2014): 159–85.

10. De Lubac, *At the Service of the Church*, 345. See also de Lubac's *Carnets du Concile*, ed. Loïc Figoureux, vol. 2 (Paris: Cerf, 2007). For background, see Loïc Figoureux, "Henri de Lubac et le concile Vatican II, espoirs et inquiétudes d'un théologien," *Cristianesimo nella Storia* 34 (2013): 249–271.

11. De Lubac, *At the Service of the Church*, 345.

12. Ibid., 348.

13. Ratzinger, *Theological Highlights of Vatican II*, 260–61.

14. Yves Congar, OP, *True and False Reform in the Church*, trans. Paul Philibert, OP (Collegeville, Minn.: Liturgical Press, 2011), 341.

structive 1979 essay "A Last Look at the Council," Congar warns against the "practice of applying the pattern 'before' and 'after' to the Council, as though it marked an absolute new beginning, the point of departure for a completely new Church."[15] He insists upon the continuity of the Council with previous Church teaching: "I was at the time [of Vatican II] and still am anxious to stress the continuity of Tradition. Vatican II was one moment and neither the first nor the last moment in that Tradition, just as Trent, Pius V and Pius X were neither the first nor the last."[16]

By 1967, Edward Schillebeeckx and others in what Jürgen Mettepenningen calls the third wave of the *nouvelle théologie* were moving strongly in the theological direction that de Lubac and Ratzinger had already sensed during the Council and about which they now expressed a growing alarm.[17] In his 1968 *God the Future of Man*, Schillebeeckx cemented his postconciliar shift by undertaking to do theology in a hermeneutical

---

15. Yves Congar, OP, "A Last Look at the Council," in *Vatican II Revisited by Those Who Were There*, ed. Alberic Stacpoole, OSB (London: Geoffrey Chapman, 1986), 337–58, at 351. See also, in the same volume, Congar's "Moving Towards a Pilgrim Church," 129–52, at 129: "Something happened at the Council and the dominant values in our way of looking at the Church were changed by the Council. That will become clear in the course of my analysis; but I am bound to stress that such a plan is simplistic. Vatican II was intentionally in continuity with the previous councils of the Church and with Tradition."

16. Congar, "A Last Look at the Council," 351. Congar goes on to say that "the current crisis [of faith] is clearly due in quite an important degree to causes that have revealed their strength since the Council. Indeed it warned against them, warding them off rather than bringing them about. Vatican II has been followed by socio-cultural change more extensive, radical and rapid and more cosmic in its proportions than any change at any other period in man's history. The Council was conscious of this great change—this is evident from the introduction to *Gaudium et Spes*—but not of all its aspects or of its violence. Many questions have arisen in the past ten or twelve years of which the Council was not aware or which it might at the most just have suspected. These include, in the sphere of thought, the collapse of metaphysics as an acceptable philosophy, the feverish pursuit of hermeneutics, the triumphant emergence of critical methods and the all-pervasive influence of the human sciences.... In the Church, we have since 1968 been passing through a crisis of the magisterium and a loss of interest on the part of many Christians, including the clergy, in what the Church is. We are increasingly absorbed by the things of this world, by politics and by Marxist categories" (ibid.). This absorption of Catholic consciousness by politics has had ill effects in the field of Vatican II studies.

17. See Jürgen Mettepenningen, *Nouvelle Théologie—New Theology: Inheritor of Modernism, Precursor of Vatican II* (London: T. & T. Clark International, 2010). To describe the *nouvelle théologie* as the "inheritor of modernism" is a mistake insofar as it implies that the *nouvelle théologie* was fundamentally modernist. The *nouvelle théologie*, like Leonine neo-scholasticism, "inherited" modernism in the sense of seeking to respond critically to it by attending to its philosophical and historical challenges to Catholic faith.

and critical key focused upon the need to reconceive doctrine in light of its eschatological consistency with the liberative praxis of Jesus. Books arguing for the need to revise dogmatic formulae proliferated, as did far-reaching calls for changes in the Church's moral teachings (including, but certainly not limited to, birth control). On the American scene, Richard McBrien separated the institutional Church from the eschatological kingdom in his 1969 *Do We Need the Church?*, and Avery Dulles's 1971 *The Survival of Dogma* sounds a strikingly different note from René Latourelle's cutting-edge work of less than a decade before. As Dulles comments in *The Survival of Dogma*: "Since Vatican II the question of the irreformability of dogma has become acute throughout the Church.... [M]any of the ancient doctrines of the Church seem to demand translation into new terms and concepts if they are to retain their intelligibility in new frameworks. In the present turmoil the guarded statements of Bouillard, which aroused such controversy twenty years ago, seem prudent and moderate."[18]

John O'Malley has emphasized the shortcomings that the "majority" allegedly felt with respect to the Council's ecclesiastical power changes: "Even before the council ended in 1965, there was a discrepancy between what the bishops hoped they had accomplished and what had happened. The majority was consistently frustrated in its efforts to make its will felt through the establishment of real structural changes."[19] By contrast, in a private letter sent to various Council participants on October 14, 1964, de Lubac observes that "the Council has long been held fast, as though hypnotized, by the question of the agreement between the primacy of the pope and episcopal collegiality. This has led to a discussion in juridical terms, claims of authority, outside the spirit that was at first affirmed in numerous interventions."[20] What de Lubac describes as a juridical hypnosis (and what O'Malley considers to have remained the central concern of "the majority," to which de Lubac belonged) fortunately did not prevent the Council from moving forward in a manner focused upon the divine

---

18. Avery Dulles, SJ, *The Survival of Dogma* (Garden City, N.Y.: Doubleday, 1971), 190.
19. John W. O'Malley, SJ, *What Happened at Vatican II* (Cambridge, Mass.: Harvard University Press, 2008), 312.
20. De Lubac, *At the Service of the Church*, 341.

revelation of the gospel of Jesus Christ. No fair reader could accuse Vatican II's Constitutions of what Congar calls "horizontalism."[21]

Attention to the opening sentences of each Constitution should make clear their Christological focus, so well exhibited by Robert Imbelli in *Rekindling the Christic Imagination*.[22] *Dei Verbum* commits the Church to "reverent attention and confident proclamation" of the word of God and expresses the goal of setting "forth authentic teaching on God's revelation and how it is communicated, desiring that the whole world may hear the message of salvation, and thus grow from hearing to faith, from faith to hope, and from hope to love" (§1).[23] *Sacrosanctum Concilium* introduces its reflections by observing that "the liturgy, through which, especially in the divine sacrifice of the Eucharist, 'the act of our redemption is being carried out,'" is "the chief means through which believers are expressing

---

21. In "A Last Look at the Council," Congar grants that "Vatican II was to some extent responsible" for the postconciliar crisis, but he notes that the actual content of the Council is not to blame even though the reforms did allow for misinterpretations to arise: "The mere fact that there was a Council and open discussion has contributed to it [the crisis]. Then there were repercussions, brought about and amplified by the modern means of communication.... The Council was open to contributions that had for so long been overlooked, excluded or condemned. It was also healthily self-critical in the light of the demands made by the Gospel and the Church's essential mission. These factors meant that the unconditional nature of the system inherited from the Counter-Reformation and the anti-revolutionary restoration of the nineteenth century was completely overcome at Vatican II. The result of the collapse of that system was that ideas and attitudes that had for too long been held at a safe distance entered the Church through the open doors and windows of the Council. And the crisis also entered that way" (Congar, "A Last Look at the Council," 351–52). Congar remains optimistic, however, that the Council has brought about a renewed ecclesiology that is rooted in believers (clergy and laity) embracing the faith with a new "personal choice motivated by deep conviction" (ibid., 353).

22. See Robert P. Imbelli, *Rekindling the Christic Imagination: Theological Meditations for the New Evangelization* (Collegeville, Minn.: Liturgical Press, 2014).

23. *Dei Verbum* §1, in *Decrees of the Ecumenical Councils*, vol. 2: *Trent to Vatican II*, ed. Norman P. Tanner, SJ (Washington, D.C.: Georgetown University Press, 1990), 971–72. As *Dei Verbum* says, our response to the word of God must be "'the obedience of faith' (see Rm 16, 26; compare Rm 1, 5; 2 Cor 10, 5–6)," and *Dei Verbum* defines faith as "a total and free self-commitment to God, offering 'the full submission of intellect and will to God as he reveals', and willingly assenting to the revelation he gives" (§5; in ibid., 973). For further discussion see Jared Wicks, SJ, "The Levels of Teaching by the Catholic Magisterium," in Wicks, *Doing Theology* (New York: Paulist Press, 2009), 237–39; see also in *Doing Theology* his analysis of "The Theologian and Magisterial Teaching," 110–15, especially in his account of how doctrine, in the act of faith, enables believers to share in "the death and resurrection of Christ to new life, a life he still lives for us and for our salvation" (Wicks, *Doing Theology*, 114). Wicks is concerned that an emphasis on the need to assent to Church doctrine not cause us to neglect the fact that doctrine directs us to an eschatological consummation in which we will see God face-to-face. Here I would underscore the mediating role of doctrine in faith's (liturgical) assent to God.

in their lives and demonstrating to others the mystery which is Christ, and the sort of entity the true Church really is" (§2).[24] Likewise, the opening sentence of *Lumen Gentium* proclaims: "Since Christ is the light of the nations, this holy synod, called together in the Holy Spirit, strongly desires to enlighten all people with his brightness, which gleams over the face of the Church, by preaching the gospel to every creature" so that the human race may "attain full unity in Christ" (§1).[25] Lastly, *Gaudium et Spes* begins with the observation that the community of believers "is composed of people united in Christ who are directed by the Holy Spirit in their pilgrimage towards the Father's kingdom and who have received the message of salvation to be communicated to everyone" (§1).[26]

Massimo Faggioli misses the mark, therefore, when he interprets the entirety of the Council as being about reforming "the institutions of the Church" so as to prepare "a ground for a world Church, able to take the tradition from its European past but unwilling to be a prisoner of its history."[27] Lacking from this perspective is an account of the Church's handing on of divine revelation (as distinct from the tradition's "European past"). It is the handing on of the true gospel of Jesus Christ that makes the Church inexhaustibly "catholic" or universal, which differs significantly from the geopolitical status suggested by the phrase "world Church." Despite the fact that Vatican II was so urgently concerned with the gospel of Christ, Faggioli's discussions of Vatican II rarely address the gospel explicitly.

The problem is that when intra-ecclesiastical power becomes the focus of historiography, Vatican II inevitably appears to be centered on community rather than on Christ, whereas in fact in the conciliar Constitutions the opposite is the case (thereby enabling the Constitutions to apprehend rightly the mystery of the Church). Maureen Sullivan concludes her *The Road to Vatican II: Key Changes in Theology* by quoting Karl Rahner's statement that "the Council was the beginning of the beginning."[28] But if

---

24. *Sacrosanctum Concilium*, §2, in *Decrees of the Ecumenical Councils*, vol. 2, 820.
25. *Lumen Gentium*, §1, in *Decrees of the Ecumenical Councils*, vol. 2, 849.
26. *Gaudium et Spes*, §1, in *Decrees of the Ecumenical Councils*, 1069.
27. Massimo Faggioli, *True Reform: Liturgy and Ecclesiology in* Sacrosanctum Concilium (Collegeville, Minn.: Liturgical Press, 2012), 144.
28. Maureen Sullivan, OP, *The Road to Vatican II: Key Changes in Theology* (New York: Paulist

the Council was truly the beginning of the beginning, then Jesus has been displaced. Paul Lakeland observes, "In an age when absolute monarchies are a thing of the past and most if not all of us live in at least some kind of democracy, our Church is the one anachronistic holdout, insisting on maintaining a structure that is directly responsible for many if not most of our ills."[29] Lakeland knows that this view cannot be squared with the Constitutions' repeated teaching that Jesus himself established the hierarchical Church, but he blames "the incompleteness of *Lumen Gentium*'s ecclesiological tradition."[30] He grants that "[w]e are immediately made aware by the Council fathers that it is Christ, not the Church, that should always be the center of our attention."[31] But in his view this means essentially that the Church has exaggerated and misunderstood its own status from the beginning. As he says, "To borrow some phrases from the work of Juan Luis Segundo, the realm of grace is 'the community of redemption,' which is the entire world, not only 'the community of revelation,' which is the Church."[32]

This sharp distinction between the world/redemption and the Church/revelation cuts against the grain of the Constitutions of Vatican II, because divine revelation—as the gospel of Jesus Christ—is never (least of all by Jesus) separated from redemption in this way. When Christ is the center, then his Body and People, the Church, will also be at the center, since he enables us to participate in him. From the perspective of Vatican II, it is not adequate to say, as Lakeland does, that "[t]he Church's mission is not to *give* grace, as if it were pouring water on a parched land, but to meet grace with grace in an embrace that pours grace on a fertile land, while at the same time the Church drinks from the wells that it encounters there."[33] Rather, Vatican II insists that the world needs Christ and his Spirit because the world

---

Press, 2007), 122, quoting Karl Rahner, SJ, "The Council: A New Beginning," in *The Church after the Council* (New York: Herder and Herder, 1966), 9–33, at 19.

29. Paul Lakeland, *A Council That Will Never End: Lumen Gentium and the Church Today* (Collegeville, Minn.: Liturgical Press, 2013), 138.

30. Ibid., 148.

31. Ibid., 152.

32. Ibid., 153, citing Segundo's *Theology for Artisans of a New Humanity: The Community Called Church*, vol. 1 (Maryknoll, N.Y.: Orbis Books, 1973).

33. Lakeland, *A Council That Will Never End*, 154.

(of which Christians are a part) is often "a parched land." The Church's mission—in the Eucharistic liturgy, in baptism and the other sacraments, in preaching, in the works of mercy—is to make Christ present in the world and thereby to renew the "parched land" that we are.

To avoid misunderstandings of the Council, it is therefore helpful to identify the main concerns that motivated the drafters of the Council's documents. I have tried to show that these concerns included most notably personal encounter with Christ as mediated to us in Scripture and Tradition, active liturgical participation in Christ's Paschal mystery, true reform of the Church so as to purify the human elements and illuminate the divine elements, and the God-given orientation of the world toward fulfillment in Christ. Within these parameters, the Council allows for plenty of leeway. A personalist view of revelation is essential, as *Dei Verbum* emphasizes, but neglect of the cognitive or propositional dimension of revelation would obscure the self-revealing God and would leave us with agnosticism rather than mystery. Active participation in the liturgy is essential, as *Sacrosanctum Concilium* insists, but the view that active participation requires facing east together remains possible. Reform of the Church is essential, as *Lumen Gentium* shows, but if such reform leads one to suppose that the Church has no divinely given constitution and that everything is changeable and depends upon who has the the power, then one has fallen afresh into a juridical ecclesiology that can produce only false reform. The profound connection of nature and grace (and world and Church) is essential, but a specific view of the natural desire for the supernatural is not required by *Gaudium et Spes*.

In his *An Unfinished Council: Vatican II, Pope Francis, and the Renewal of Catholicism*, Richard Gaillardetz helpfully affirms that the "necessary transformation of ecclesiastical structures" must not be an "accommodation to the values of the secular world" but must instead be "the necessary reform of a church that wishes to be more deeply rooted in the radical values of the Christian Gospel."[34] In the opening chapter of his book, Gaillardetz critiques five "hierocratic" pillars of the preconciliar Church: "(1) a propo-

---

34. Richard R. Gaillardetz, *An Unfinished Council: Vatican II, Pope Francis, and the Renewal of Catholicism* (Collegeville, Minn.: Liturgical Press, 2015), 155–56.

sitional theology of divine revelation, (2) a papo-centric church leadership structure, (3) a sacral priesthood, (4) a mechanistic theology of grace and the sacraments, and (5) a confrontational attitude toward the world."[35] Vatican II clearly eschews propositionalist understandings of revelation (opposed by *Dei Verbum*), papo-centrism and a hierarchical priesthood rooted only in the sanctifying office rather than also in the prophetic and royal offices (opposed by *Lumen Gentium*), mechanistic understandings of the liturgy (opposed by *Sacrosanctum Concilium*), and a condemnatory view of the world as though grace were present only in the confines of the visible Church (opposed by *Gaudium et Spes*).

Gaillardetz would do well to add, however, that Vatican II also teaches that divine revelation is propositionally intelligible (*Dei Verbum*), that the pope authoritatively interprets the gospel for the Church and can do so *in propria persona* (*Lumen Gentium*), that the hierarchical priesthood's sanctifying office and celebration of the Eucharistic sacrifice are central (*Lumen Gentium* and *Sacrosanctum Concilium*), that the sacraments cause the transformative influx of the grace of the Holy Spirit in believers (*Sacrosanctum Concilium*), and that the world is fallen and frequently stands in opposition to the gospel (*Gaudium et Spes*). One will not be able to perceive or embrace the authoritative true reform if one does not equally perceive and embrace the authoritative continuity in teaching. Similarly, Gaillardetz's concerns about the alleged resurgence of "neoclericalism" and "preconciliar triumphalism" and "confrontational rhetoric" in the pontificates of John Paul II and Benedict XVI need to be balanced by careful attention to the doctrinal and moral content that the two popes were teaching and to the close relationship of this content to the actual teachings of the four Constitutions.[36] Otherwise, misunderstandings and strawmen will take the place of real discussion, as in Gaillardetz's odd refutation of "any arrogant claim that church doctrine provides a comprehensive grasp of divine revelation in favor of a stance of receptivity toward the revealing God"—since no one actually affirms that

---

35. Ibid., 4.

36. Ibid., 69–70. See also the richly nuanced essay of Gilles Pelland, SJ, "A Few Words on Triumphalism," trans. Leslie Wearne, in *Vatican II: Assessment and Perspectives*, vol. 1, ed. René Latourelle, SJ, 106–22.

the Church's "grasp of divine revelation" is now exhaustively "comprehensive" or that the Church's "grasp of divine revelation" could be rooted otherwise than in "a stance of receptivity toward the revealing God."[37]

Gaillardetz goes on to argue that "[t]he church can claim genuine insight, drawn from revelation, without pretending it is a divinely sanctioned 'answer box' for all the world's problems," and he adds that the Church is plagued by doctrinal and moral "positions that are no longer compelling and fairly beg honest questions."[38] While of course Christ's Church must not be reduced to an "answer box," my concern here is twofold. First, believers need to be able to know what the "genuine insights" of divine revelation actually are, so that we can obey and worship the God who reveals his sav-

---

37. Gaillardetz, *An Unfinished Council*, 84–85.

38. Ibid., 86–87. In a recent essay, Gaillardetz explains further that the Council's "rich theology of revelation inserts doctrine within the broader framework of God's sharing of God's self with humanity. This recontextualization of doctrine invites a form of doctrinal humility.... This doctrinal humility is evident in the Council's insistence that Revelation not be treated as a divine answer book providing definitive solutions to all the questions of our time.... [T]he Council introduced a crucial distinction [via the notion of the "hierarchy of truths"] between the *content* of divine revelation, understood as God's self-communication in Christ by the power of the Spirit, and those church doctrines that, in varying degrees, *mediate* that content. In this context, doctrinal humility means recognizing that, although church doctrine may mediate divine revelation, it never exhausts it" (Gaillardetz, "The Pastoral Orientation of Doctrine," in *Go into the Streets! The Welcoming Church of Pope Francis*, ed. Thomas P. Rausch, SJ, and Richard R. Gaillardetz [New York: Paulist Press, 2016], 125–40, at 128). Gaillardetz's strong distinction between the "content" of divine revelation and "doctrines that, in varying degrees, *mediate* that content" is not sufficiently precise to capture the actual teaching of *Dei Verbum*, since Gaillardetz's way of phrasing it risks bypassing the cognitive dimension of the personal "content" of divine revelation, and thus of the *intrinsic* bond between mediating doctrines and the actual divine revelation. Of course, as Gaillardetz says, "the church must always be open to the possibility that a doctrine may need to be reformulated in ways that better express its deep meaning and that are more conducive to its proper communication in the modern age" (Gaillardetz, "The Pastoral Orientation of Doctrine," 127). When Gaillardetz responds to those who hope that Pope Francis will "reverse this or that controverted church teaching" by stating that "history shows that doctrine changes when pastoral contexts shift and new insights emerge such that particular doctrinal formulations no longer mediate the saving message of God's transforming love" (Gaillardetz, "The Pastoral Orientation of Doctrine,", 137), the consequences of sharply separating "doctrine" from the "content" of revelation are manifest, since the fundamental question is whether "doctrinal formulations" are true. In fact, the content of the "saving message" and of "God's transforming love" was spelled out in great detail in the apostolic period, and there never was a "saving message" without this cognitive content. Furthermore, the claim that "doctrinal formulations no longer mediate the saving message" raises the issue of whether they ever did: are we dealing here with development of doctrine or with doctrinal corruption? With regard to such "doctrinal formulations," Gaillardetz gives the example of usury, but he does not clarify whether he thinks that the Church taught definitively about usury along lines that now the Church definitively rejects.

ing Word. The standard for such faith-knowledge must be more than the determination that certain teachings are for many people "no longer compelling." The fact that Gaillardetz is known for his work on the Church's Magisterium makes the looseness of his formulations here particularly troubling. Second, what is the status of the specific doctrinal and moral teachings of the four Constitutions of Vatican II? Should *they* command the obedient assent of believers, and if so, on what grounds? Or can the Council's teachings about the doctrinal and moral requisites of following Jesus Christ be placed, if one disagrees with these teachings, among what Gaillardetz calls "the many compromises made to mollify the conservative minority"?[39] For example, must Catholics affirm in faith the teaching of *Lumen Gentium* that "[t]hrough this sense of faith which is aroused and sustained by the Spirit of truth, the people of God, under the guidance of the sacred magisterium to which it is faithfully obedient, receives no longer the words of human beings but truly the word of God (see 1 Th 2:13)"?[40]

Gaillardetz is right to appreciate the Council's "noncompetitive account of the relationship between pope and bishops."[41] But what happens if or when a number of bishops in one country or region begin to take pastoral steps that have moral and doctrinal import, and other bishops from other countries and regions deny that these steps accord with true holiness and true discipleship to Jesus Christ? If the pope intervenes against (or favors) one group of bishops over the other, will not the spurned group of bishops find the pope's exercise of authority to be negatively "competitive"? Gaillardetz similarly dodges the real issue when he observes, "Revelation, the council teaches, begins not with a collection of doctrines but with God's Word. This Word is offered as an event of divine self-communication."[42] In

---

39. Gaillardetz, *An Unfinished Council*, 96.
40. *Lumen Gentium*, §12, in *Decrees of the Ecumenical Councils*, vol. 2, 858.
41. Gaillardetz, *An Unfinished Council*, 96.
42. Ibid., 99. In his "The Pastoral Orientation of Doctrine," Gaillardetz notes that the "more formal, propositional language inevitably puts doctrine at several degrees of abstraction from the gospel as it is experienced concretely in the life of discipleship" (Gaillardetz, "The Pastoral Orientation of Doctrine," 132), but the key is what "several degrees of abstraction" means. If it means that a doctrinal truth (for example, "the Son is consubstantial with the Father") is separate from believers' concrete experience of the saving reality that it describes (in this case, the divine Son), then this would be a misunderstanding of the way in which doctrine, in the act of faith, serves to unite the believer concretely to saving realities.

fact, an "event of divine self-communication" must include ideas that are communicated, and indeed this is what "a collection of doctrines" fundamentally is.

Even if not intentionally, Gaillardetz helps us to see that the Church has a problem regarding divine revelation and its authority that no amount of ecclesiastical power-restructuring can resolve. Modern people know that Scripture is the product of many human authors and redactors from a wide array of time periods and worldviews, culminating in the eschatological fervor of the late Second Temple period. Modern people also understand that the Church has existed in many different cultures, has changed significantly over time in terms of its practices and doctrines, and has suffered from strife and divisions. Why then should modern people accept the teaching of Scripture and the Church as the authoritative word of God for their lives?[43] This is the problem facing Christianity in many areas of the world today.

Fortunately, the Second Vatican Council addressed this problem in profoundly helpful ways. The reforms mandated by the Council assist modern people in perceiving that the gospel of Jesus Christ—as liturgically mediated in Scripture and Tradition by the Church—is true and life-giving. The four Constitutions insist upon the reality and authority of divine revelation. It is this salvific content of faith, expressive of the Person of Jesus Christ, that therefore should be central in books on the Council.

Drawing upon the homilies of Pope Francis, Robert Imbelli reminds us: "The church's distinctive mission is its witness and call to the world to find its deepest transformation and true life in Christ for the greater Glory of God—the glory revealed fully on the Face of Jesus Christ."[44] Our shar-

---

43. In his *By What Authority? A Primer on Scripture, the Magisterium, and the Sense of the Faithful*, Gaillardetz suggests his affinity for the view that "the irreversibility of certain of the Church's teachings" flows from "the exercise of infallibility as an exceptional instance in which elements of church tradition, understood in the literal sense, are excluded from the possibility of dramatic reversal" (Gaillardetz, *By What Authority? A Primer on Scripture, the Magisterium, and the Sense of the Faithful* [Collegeville, Minn.: Liturgical Press, 2003], 51). Even if Vatican II's Constitutions counted as such an "exceptional instance," Gaillardetz's position does not exude confidence in the fidelity of the contemporary Church's mediation of divine revelation.

44. Imbelli, *Rekindling the Christic Imagination*, 96.

ing in this glory revealed in Christ, who forgives and heals our sinfulness and opens up the very life of the triune God to us, is what the Constitutions of Vatican II are ultimately about. This is the test of every interpretation of the Council: the ongoing theological event of Vatican II, as an event of the Church's faithful handing on of the apostolic gospel, must have Jesus Christ at its center. "For no other foundation can any one lay than that which is laid, which is Jesus Christ" (1 Cor 3:11).

BIBLIOGRAPHY

Alberigo, Giuseppe, ed. *History of Vatican II*. 5 Vols. English version edited by Joseph A. Komonchak. Leuven: Peeters, 1995–2006.

———. *A Brief History of Vatican II*. Translated by Matthew Sherry. Maryknoll, N.Y.: Orbis Books, 2006.

Alberigo, Giuseppe, and James Provost, eds. *Synod 1985: An Evaluation*. Edinburgh: T. & T. Clark, 1986.

Antonelli, Cesare. *Il dibattito su Maria nel Concilio Vaticano II. Percorso redazionale sulla base di nuovi documenti di archivio*. Padova: Edizioni Messaggero di Sant' Antonio, 2009.

Aubry, Augustin-Marie. *Obéir ou assenter? De la "soumission religieuse" au magistère simplement authentique*. Paris: Desclée, 2015.

Barth, Karl. *Ad Limina Apostolorum: An Appraisal of Vatican II*. Translated by Keith R. Crim. Edinburgh: The Saint Andrew Press, 1969.

Bea, Augustin. *The Word of God and Mankind*. Translated by Dorothy White. London: Geoffrey Chapman, 1967.

Beal, Rose M. *Mystery of the Church, People of God: Yves Congar's Total Ecclesiology as a Path to Vatican II*. Washington, D.C.: The Catholic University of America Press, 2014.

Benedict XVI, Pope. "Ad Roman Curiam ob omnia natalicia." *Acta Apostolicae Sedis* 98 (6 January 2006): 40–53.

———. "A Proper Hermeneutic for the Second Vatican Council." In *Vatican II: Renewal within Tradition*, edited by Matthew L. Lamb and Matthew Levering, ix-xv. Oxford: Oxford University Press, 2008.

Berkouwer, G. C. *The Second Vatican Council and the New Catholicism*. Translated by Lewis B. Smedes. Grand Rapids, Mich.: Eerdmans, 1965.

Blanchard, Shaun. "'Proto-Ecumenical' Catholic Reform in the Eighteenth Century: Lodovico Muratori as a Forerunner of Vatican II." *Pro Ecclesia* 25 (2016): 71–89.

Blondel, Maurice. *The Letter on Apologetics and History and Dogma*. Translated by Alexander Dru and Illtyd Trethowan. Grand Rapids, Mich.: Eerdmans, 1994.

Boeve, Lieven. *Interrupting Tradition: An Essay on Christian Faith in a Postmodern Context*. Leuven: Peeters, 2003.

Böttigheimer, Christoph, ed. *Zweites Vatikanisches Konzil. Programmatik—Rezeption—Vision*. Freiburg im Breisgau: Herder, 2014.

Bouyer, Louis. *The Paschal Mystery: Meditations on the Last Three Days of Holy Week*. Translated by Mary Benoit. Chicago: Regnery, 1950.

———. Où en est le Mouvement liturgique?" *La Maison-Dieu* 25 (1951): 34–46.

———. *Liturgical Piety*. Notre Dame, Ind.: University of Notre Dame Press, 1955.

———. *Le rite et l'homme: Sacralité naturelle et liturgie*. Paris: Cerf, 1962.

———. *The Liturgy Revived: A Doctrinal Commentary of the Conciliar Constitution on the Liturgy*. Notre Dame, Ind.: University of Notre Dame Press, 1964.

———. *Liturgy and Architecture*. Notre Dame, Ind.: University of Notre Dame Press, 1967.

———. *Eucharist: Theological and Spirituality of the Eucharistic Prayer*. Notre Dame, Ind.: University of Notre Dame Press, 1989.

———. *The Memoirs of Louis Bouyer: From Youth and Conversion to Vatican II, the Liturgical Reform, and After*. Translated by John Pepino. Kettering, Ohio: Angelico Press, 2015.

Boyer, Mark G., *The Liturgical Environment: What the Documents Say*. 2nd ed. Collegeville, Minn.: Liturgical Press, 2004.

Braine, David. "The Debate between Henri de Lubac and His Critics." *Nova et Vetera* 6 (2008): 543–90.

———. *Language and Human Understanding: The Roots of Creativity in Speech and Thought*. Washington, D.C.: The Catholic University of America Press, 2014.

Cessario, Romanus, OP. *A Short History of Thomism*. Washington, D.C.: The Catholic University of America Press, 2005.

Chantraine, Georges, SJ. "The Supernatural: Discernment of Catholic Thought according to Henri de Lubac." In *Surnaturel: A Controversy at the Heart of Twentieth-Century Thomistic Thought*, edited by Serge-Thomas Bonino, OP, translated by Robert Williams with Matthew Levering, 21–40. Ave Maria, Fla.: Sapientia Press, 2009.

Chenu, Marie-Dominique, OP. "A Council for All Peoples." In *Vatican II Revisited by Those Who Were There*, edited by Alberic Stacpoole, OSB, 19–23. London: Geoffrey Chapman, 1986.

Cimorelli, Christopher, and Daniel Minch. "Views of Doctrine: Historical Consciousness, Asymptotic Notional Clarity, and the Challenge of Hermeneutics as Ontology." *Louvain Studies* 37 (2013): 327–63.

Comte, Bernard. "Le père de Lubac, un théologien dans l'Église de Lyon." In *Henri de Lubac: La rencontre au coeur de l'Église*, edited by Jean-Dominique Durand, 35–89. Paris: Cerf, 2006.

Congar, Yves, OP. *Vraie et fausse réforme dans l'Église*. Paris: Cerf, 1950.

———. "The Church: The People of God." In *The Church and Mankind: Dogma*, edited by Hans Küng and Edward Schillebeeckx, OP, 11–37. Concilium, Vol. 1. Glen Rock, N.J.: Paulist Press, 1964.

———. "Conquering Our Enmities." In *Steps to Christian Unity*, edited by John A. O'Brien, 100–109. New York: Doubleday, 1964.

———. *Situation et taches présentes de la théologie*. Paris: Cerf, 1967.

———. *Tradition and Traditions: An Historical and Theological Essay*. Translated by Michael Naseby and Thomas Rainborough. New York: Macmillan, 1967.

———. "The Council as an Assembly and the Church as Essentially Conciliar." Translated by Alain Woodrow. In *One, Holy, Catholic and Apostolic: Studies on the Nature and Role of the Church in the Modern World*, edited by Herbert Vorgrimler, 44–88. London: Sheed and Ward, 1968.

———. "Le chrétien, son présent, son avenir et son passé." *Lumiere et vie* 21/108 (1972): 72–82.

———. "What Belonging to the Church Has Come to Mean." Translated by Frances M. Chew. *Communio* 4 (1977): 146–60.

———. *Église catholique et France moderne*. Paris: Hachette, 1978.

———. *Le Concile de Vatican II. Son église: Peuple de Dieu et corps du Christ*. Paris: Beauchesne, 1984.

———. "A Last Look at the Council." In *Vatican II Revisited by Those Who Were There*, edited by Alberic Stacpoole, OSB, 337–58. London: Geoffrey Chapman, 1986.

———. "Moving Towards a Pilgrim Church." In *Vatican II Revisited by Those Who Were There*, edited by Alberic Stacpoole, OSB, 129–52. London: Geoffrey Chapman, 1986.

———. *I Believe in the Holy Spirit*. 3 vols. Translated by David Smith. New York: Crossroad, 1997.

———. *True and False Reform in the Church*. Translated by Paul Philibert, OP. Collegeville, Minn.: Liturgical Press, 2011.

———. *My Journal of the Council*. Translated by Mary John Ronayne, OP, and Mary Cecily Boulding, OP. Edited by Denis Minns, OP. Collegeville, Minn.: Liturgical Press, 2012.

Cullmann, Oscar. *Vatican Council II: The New Direction*. New York: Joanna Cotler Books, 1968.

Cunningham, Lawrence S. *The Meaning of Saints*. San Francisco: Harper and Row, 1980.

Danneels, Gottfried. "The Ongoing Agenda: A Council Unlike Any Other." In *The Second Vatican Council: Celebrating Its Achievements and the Future*, edited by Gavin D'Costa and Emma Jane Harris, 19–34. London: Bloomsbury, 2013.

D'Costa, Gavin. *Vatican II: Catholic Doctrines on Jews and Muslims*. Oxford: Oxford University Press, 2014.

———. "*Nostra Aetate*." In Lamb and Levering, *Reception of Vatican II*.

Denysenko, Nicholas E. *Liturgical Reform after Vatican II: The Impact on Eastern Orthodoxy*. Minneapolis, Minn.: Fortress Press, 2015.

Douthat, Ross. "A Crisis of Conservative Catholicism." *First Things*, no. 259 (January 2016): 21–28.
De Chirico, Leonardo. *Evangelical Theological Perspectives on Post–Vatican II Roman Catholicism*. New York: Peter Lang, 2003.
de La Potterie, Ignace. "Interpretation of Holy Scripture in the Spirit in Which It Was Written (*Dei Verbum* 12c)." Translated by Leslie Wearne. In *Vatican II: Assessment and Perspectives; Twenty-Five Years After (1962–1987)*. Vol. 1, edited by René Latourelle, SJ, 220–66. Mahwah, N.J.: Paulist Press, 1988.
de La Soujeole, Benoît-Dominique, OP. *Introduction to the Mystery of the Church*. Translated by Michael J. Miller. Washington, D.C.: The Catholic University of America Press, 2014.
de Lubac, Henri, SJ. *Surnaturel*. Paris: Aubier, 1946.
———. "Le problème du développement du dogme." *Recherches de science religieuse* 35 (1948): 130–60.
———. "Le Mystère du surnaturel." *Recherches de science religieuse* 36 (1949): 80–121.
———. *The Splendor of the Church*. Translated by Michael Mason. New York: Sheed and Ward, 1956.
———. *The Mystery of the Supernatural*. Translated by Rosemary Sheed. New York: Herder and Herder, 1967.
———. "The Church in Crisis." *Theology Digest* 17 (1969): 312–25.
———. "L'Église dans la crise actuelle." *Nouvelle revue théologique* 91 (1969): 580–96.
———. *L'Église dans la crise actuelle*. Paris: Cerf, 1969.
———. *La Révélation Divine*. 3rd ed. Paris: Cerf, 1983.
———. *A Brief Catechesis on Nature and Grace*. Translated by Richard Arnandez, FSC. San Francisco: Ignatius, 1984.
———. *Entretien autour de Vatican II. Souvenirs et reflections*. Paris: Cerf, 1985.
———. *Catholicism: Christ and the Common Destiny of Man*. Translated by Lancelot C. Sheppard and Elizabeth Englund. San Francisco: Ignatius Press, 1988.
———. *At the Service of the Church: Henri de Lubac Reflects on the Circumstances That Occasioned His Writings*. Translated by Anne Elizabeth Englund. San Francisco: Ignatius Press, 1993.
———. *The Drama of Atheist Humanism*. Translated by Edith M. Riley, Anne Englund Nash, and Marc Sebanc. San Francisco: Ignatius Press, 1995.
———. "The Mystery of the Supernatural." Translated by Anne Englund Nash. In Henri de Lubac, *Theology in History*, 281–316. San Francisco: Ignatius Press, 1996.
———. *The Mystery of the Supernatural*. Translated by Rosemary Sheed. New York: Crossroad, 1998.
———. *Augustinianism and Modern Theology*. Translated by Lancelot Sheppard. New York: Crossroad, 2000.
———. *Carnets du Concile*. Edited by Loïc Figoureux. 2 vols. Paris: Cerf, 2007.
———. "The Total Meaning of Man and the World." Translated by D. C. Schindler. *Communio* 35 (2008): 613–41.

———. *Vatican Council Notebooks*. Vol. 1. Translated by Andrew Stefanelli and Anne Englund Nash. San Francisco: Ignatius Press, 2015.

Duffy, Eamon. *The Stripping of the Altars: Traditional Religion in England, 1400–1580*. 2nd ed. New Haven, Conn.: Yale University Press, 2005.

Dulles, Avery, SJ. *The Survival of Dogma*. Garden City, N.Y.: Doubleday, 1971.

———. "The Reception of Vatican II at the Extraordinary Synod of 1985." Appendix to *The Reception of Vatican II*, 349–63. Edited by Giuseppe Alberigo, Jean-Pierre Jossua, and Joseph A. Komonchak. Translated by Matthew J. O'Connell. Washington, D.C.: The Catholic University of America Press, 1987.

———. "Yves Congar: In Appreciation." *America* 173 (15 July 1995): 6–7.

———. "Church, Ministry, and Sacraments in Catholic-Evangelical Dialogue." In *Catholics and Evangelicals: Do They Share a Common Future?*, edited by Thomas P. Rausch, SJ, 101–21. New York: Paulist Press, 2000.

———. "Nature, Mission, and Structure of the Church." In *Vatican II: Renewal within Tradition*, edited by Matthew L. Lamb and Matthew Levering, 25–36. Oxford: Oxford University Press, 2008.

Echeverria, Eduardo J. "The Essentialist versus Historicist Debate about the Truth Status of Dogmatic Formulations: A Critique of the Cimorelli/Minch Proposal." *Louvain Studies* 38 (2014): 356–69.

Evennett, H. Outram. *The Spirit of the Counter-Reformation*. Edited by John Bossy. Cambridge: Cambridge University Press, 2008.

Faggioli, Massimo. *True Reform: Liturgy and Ecclesiology in* Sacrosanctum Concilium. Collegeville, Minn.: Liturgical Press, 2012.

———. *A Council for the Global Church: Receiving Vatican II in History*. Minneapolis, Minn.: Fortress Press, 2015.

———. *Pope Francis: Tradition in Transition*. Translated by Sean O'Neill. New York: Paulist Press, 2015.

———. "Vatican II: The History and the Narratives." In *50 Years On: Probing the Riches of Vatican II*, edited by David G. Schultenover, 61–81. Collegeville, Minn.: Liturgical Press, 2015.

Famerée, Joseph. *L'ecclésiologie d'Yves Congar avant Vatican II. Analyse et reprise critique*. Louvain: Louvain University Press, 1992.

Feingold, Lawrence. *The Natural Desire to See God according to St. Thomas Aquinas and His Interpreters*. 2nd ed. Ave Maria, Fla.: Sapientia Press, 2010.

Ferrone, Rita. *Liturgy*: Sacrosanctum Concilium. New York: Paulist Press, 2007.

Figoureux, Loïc. "Henri de Lubac et le concile Vatican II, espoirs et inquiétudes d'un théologien." *Cristianesimo nella Storia* 34 (2013): 249–71.

Flannery, Austin, OP, ed. *Vatican II: The Liturgy Constitution*. Dublin: Scepter Books, 1964.

———, ed. *Vatican Council II*. Vol. 1, *The Conciliar and Post Conciliar Documents*. Rev. ed. Northport, N.Y.: Costello Publishing, 1996.

Flynn, Gabriel. "*Mon Journal du Concile*: Yves Congar and the Battle for a Renewed

Ecclesiology at the Second Vatican Council." *Louvain Studies* 28 (2003): 48–70.

———. "Epilogue: Yves Congar's Theology in the New Millennium." In *Yves Congar: Theologian of the Church*, edited by Gabriel Flynn, 459–61. Leuven: Peeters, 2005.

———, ed. *Yves Congar: Theologian of the Church*. Leuven: Peeters, 2005.

Fisichella, Rino, ed. *Gesù rivelatore. Teologia fondamentale*. Casale Monferrato: Piemme, 1988.

Fouilloux, Étienne. "Friar Yves, Cardinal Congar, Dominican: Itinerary of a Theologian." Translated by Christian Yves Dupont. *U.S. Catholic Historian* 17 (1999): 63–90.

Frein, Brigid Curtin. "Scripture in the Life of the Church." In *Vatican II: The Continuing Agenda*, edited by Anthony J. Cernera, 71–87. Fairfield, Conn.: Sacred Heart University Press, 1997.

Gaillardetz, Richard R. *By What Authority? A Primer on Scripture, the Magisterium, and the Sense of the Faithful*. Collegeville, Minn.: Liturgical Press, 2003.

———. *An Unfinished Council: Vatican II, Pope Francis, and the Renewal of Catholicism*. Collegeville, Minn.: Liturgical Press, 2015.

———. "The Pastoral Orientation of Doctrine." In *Go into the Streets! The Welcoming Church of Pope Francis*, edited by Thomas P. Rausch, SJ, and Richard R. Gaillardetz, 125–40. New York: Paulist Press, 2016.

Gaillardetz, Richard R., and Catherine E. Clifford. *Keys to the Council: Unlocking the Teaching of Vatican II*. Collegeville, Minn.: Liturgical Press, 2012.

Galot, Jean. "Christ: Revealer, Founder of the Church, and Source of Ecclesial Life." Translated by Leslie Wearne. In *Vatican II: Assessment and Perspectives: Twenty-Five Years After (1962–1987)*. Vol. 1, edited by René Latourelle, 385–406. Mahwah, N.J.: Paulist Press, 1988.

Garrigou-Lagrange, Réginald, OP. *De Revelatione per Ecclesiam catholicam proposita*. 2 Vols. Rome: F. Ferrari, 1950.

George, Timothy. "*Unitatis Redintegratio* after Fifty Years: A Protestant Reading." *Pro Ecclesia* 25 (2016): 53–70.

Gertler, Thomas. *Jesus Christus—Die Antwort der Kirche auf die Frage nach dem Menschsein*. Leipzig: St. Benno-Verlag, 1986.

Gilson, Étienne. *Being and Some Philosophers*. 2nd ed. Toronto: Pontifical Institute of Mediaeval Studies, 1952.

Grummett, David. "De Lubac, Grace, and the Pure Nature Debate." *Modern Theology* 31 (2015): 123–46.

Guarino, Thomas G. "Analogy and Vatican II: An Overlooked Dimension of the Council?" *Josephinum Journal of Theology* 22 (2015), forthcoming.

Gy, Pierre-Marie, OP. *The Reception of Vatican II Liturgical Reforms in the Life of the Church*. Milwaukee, Wisc.: Marquette University Press, 2003.

Haight, Roger, SJ. *Christian Community in History*. 2 vols. New York: Continuum, 2004–2005.

Hanvey, James, SJ. "Vatican II: For the Life of the World." In *The Second Vatican*

Council: Celebrating Its Achievements and the Future, edited by Gavin D'Costa and Emma Jane Harris, 45–68. London: Bloomsbury, 2013.

Healy, Nicholas J., Jr. "Henri de Lubac on Nature and Grace: A Note on Some Recent Contributions to the Debate." *Communio* 35 (2008): 535–64.

———. "*Dignitatis Humanae.*" In Lamb and Levering, *Reception of Vatican II.*

Hinojosa, Clara Dina. "Full, Conscious and Active Participation." In *Full, Conscious and Active Participation: Celebrating Twenty-Five Years of Today's Liturgy*, edited by Michael R. Prendergast, 5–11. Portland, Ore.: Pastoral Press, 2003.

Hünermann, Peter, and Bernd Jochen Hilberath, eds. *Herders theologischer Kommentar zum Zweiten Vatikanischen Konzil.* 5 Vols. Freiburg im Breisgau: Herder, 2004–2006.

Hütter, Reinhard. *Dust Bound for Heaven: Explorations in the Theology of Thomas Aquinas.* Grand Rapids, Mich.: Eerdmans, 2012.

Imbelli, Robert P. "The Reaffirmation of the Christic Center." In *Sic et Non: Encountering Dominus Iesus*, edited by Stephen J. Pope and Charles Hefling, 96–106. Maryknoll, N.Y.: Orbis Books, 2002.

———. *Rekindling the Christic Imagination: Theological Meditations for the New Evangelization.* Collegeville, Minn.: Liturgical Press, 2014.

———. "The Christocentric Mystagogy of Joseph Ratzinger." *Communio* 42 (2015): 119–43.

———. "Benedict and Francis." In *Go into the Streets! The Welcoming Church of Pope Francis*, edited by Thomas P. Rausch, SJ, and Richard R. Gaillardetz, 11–27. New York: Paulist Press, 2016.

———. "The Identity and Ministry of the Priest in the Light of Vatican II: The Promise and Challenge of *Presbyterorum Ordinis.*" *Josephinum Journal of Theology*, forthcoming.

Jackson, Pamela. *An Abundance of Graces: Reflections on* Sacrosanctum Concilium. Chicago: Hillenbrand Books, 2004.

John Paul II, Pope. *Crossing the Threshold of Hope.* Translated by Jenny McPhee and Martha McPhee. Edited by Vittorio Messori. New York: Alfred A. Knopf, 1995.

Kasper, Walter. *The Methods of Dogmatic Theology.* Translated by John Drury. Glen Rock, N.J.: Paulist Press, 1969.

Kieckhefer, Richard. *Theology in Stone: Church Architecture from Byzantium to Berkeley.* Oxford: Oxford University Press, 2004.

Knop, Julia, Magnus Lerch, and Bernd J. Claret, eds. *Die Wahrheit ist Person: Brennpunkte einer christologisch gewendeten Dogmatik. Festschrift für Karl-Heinz Menke.* Regensburg: Verlag Friedrich Pustet, 2015.

Koch, Kurt. *Das zweite Vatikanische Konzil: Eine Bilanz. Die Hermeneutik der Reform.* Augsburg: Sankt Ulrich Verlag, 2012.

Komonchak, Joseph A. *Foundations in Ecclesiology.* Chestnut Hill, Mass.: Boston College, 1995.

———. "Thomism and the Second Vatican Council." In *Continuity and Plurality* in *Catholic Theology: Essays in Honor of Gerald A. McCool, SJ*, ed. Anthony J. Cernera, 53–73. Fairfield, Conn.: Sacred Heart University Press, 1998.

———. "Le valutazioni sulla *Gaudium et Spes*: Chenu, Dossetti, Ratzinger." In *Volti di fine concilio. Studi di storia e teologia sulla conclusion del Vaticano II*, edited by Joseph Dore and Alberto Melloni, 115–63. Bologna: Il Mulino, 2000.

———. "Vatican II as an 'Event.'" In *Vatican II: Did Anything Happen?*, edited by David G. Schultenover, SJ, 24–51. New York: Continuum, 2007.

———. "Benedict XVI and the Interpretation of Vatican II." In *The Crisis of Authority in Catholic Modernity*, edited by Michael J. Lacey and Francis Oakley, 93–110. Oxford: Oxford University Press, 2011.

Lakeland, Paul. *A Council That Will Never End:* Lumen Gentium *and the Church Today*. Collegeville, Minn.: Liturgical Press, 2013.

Lamb, Matthew L. "Vatican II after Fifty Years: The Virtual Council versus the Real Council." In *The Second Vatican Council: Celebrating Its Achievements and the Future*, edited by Gavin D'Costa and Emma Jane Harris, 7–17. London: Bloomsbury, 2013.

Lamb, Matthew L., and Matthew Levering, eds. *The Reception of Vatican II*. Oxford: Oxford University Press, forthcoming.

Langevin, Dominic M., OP. *From Passion to Paschal Mystery: A Recent Magisterial Development concerning the Christological Foundation of the Sacraments*. Fribourg: Academic Press Fribourg, 2015.

Latourelle, René, SJ. *Theology of Revelation*. New York: Alba House, 1966.

———, ed. *Vatican II: Assessment and Perspectives: Twenty-Five Years After (1962–1987)*. Vol. 1. Mahwah, N.J.: Paulist Press, 1988.

Lawler, Michael G., Todd A. Salzman, and Eileen Burke-Sullivan. *The Church in the Modern World:* Gaudium et Spes *Then and Now*. Collegeville, Minn.: Liturgical Press, 2014.

Lehner, Ulrich L. *The Catholic Enlightenment: The Forgotten History of a Global Movement*. Oxford: Oxford University Press, 2016.

———. *On the Road to Vatican II: German Catholic Enlightenment and Reform of the Church*. Minneapolis, Minn.: Fortress Press, 2016.

Levering, Matthew. *Engaging the Doctrine of Revelation: The Mediation of the Gospel through Church and Scripture*. Grand Rapids, Mich.: Baker Academic, 2014.

———. *Engaging the Doctrine of the Holy Spirit: Love and Gift in the Trinity and the Church*. Grand Rapids, Mich.: Baker Academic, 2016.

Lindbeck, George A. "The Second Vatican Council." *Concordia Theological Monthly* 34 (January 1963): 19–24.

Long, Steven A. "Obediential Potency, Human Knowledge, and the Natural Desire for the Vision of God." *International Philosophical Quarterly* 37 (1997): 45–63.

López, Antonio, FSCB. "Vatican II's Catholicity: A Christological Perspective on Truth, History, and the Human Person." *Communio* 39 (2012): 82–116.

Malloy, Christopher J. "De Lubac on Natural Desire: Difficulties and Antitheses." *Nova et Vetera* 9 (2011): 567–624.

Mannion, Gerard. "Re-engaging the People of God." In *Go into the Streets! The Welcoming Church of Pope Francis*, edited by Thomas P. Rausch, SJ, and Richard R. Gaillardetz, 57–75. New York: Paulist Press, 2016.

Marchetto, Agostino. *The Second Vatican Ecumenical Council: A Counterpoint for the History of the Council*. Translated by Kenneth D. Whitehead. Scranton, Penn.: University of Scranton Press, 2010.

Marshall, Bruce D. "Reckoning with Modernity." *First Things*, no. 258 (December 2015): 23–30.

Martinez, Raul Berzosa. *La Teología del Sobrenatural en los Escritos de Henri de Lubac: Estudio Historico-Teologico (1931–1980)*. Burgos: Aldecoa, 1991.

McDermott, John M., SJ. "Did That Really Happen at Vatican II? Reflections on John O'Malley's Recent Book." *Nova et Vetera* 8 (2010): 425–66.

Meszaros, Andrew. "Revelation in George Tyrrell, Neo-Scholasticism, and *Dei Verbum*." *Angelicum* 91 (2014): 535–68.

———. "Vatican II as Theological Event and Text according to Yves Congar." *Josephinum Journal of Theology*, forthcoming.

Mettepenningen, Jürgen. *Nouvelle Théologie—New Theology: Inheritor of Modernism, Precursor of Vatican II*. London: T. & T. Clark International, 2010.

Miccoli, Giovanni. *La chiesa dell'anticoncilio: I tradizionalisti alla riconquista di Roma*. Rome: Laterza, 2011.

Miller, Charles E. *Liturgy for the People of God*. Vol. 1, *Foundations of Vatican II Liturgy*. Staten Island, N.Y.: Alba House, 2000.

Miller, Vincent J. *Consuming Religion: Christian Faith and Practice in a Consumer Culture*. New York: Continuum, 2004.

Moulins-Beaufort, Eric de. "Henri de Lubac, Reader of *Dei Verbum*." *Communio* 28 (2001): 669–94.

Neufeld, Karl Heinz. "In the Service of the Council: Bishops and Theologians at the Second Vatican Council (for Cardinal Henri de Lubac on His Ninetieth Birthday)." Translated by Ronald Sway. In *Vatican II: Assessment and Perspectives: Twenty-Five Years After (1962–1987)*. Vol. 1, edited by René Latourelle, 74–105. Mahwah, N.J.: Paulist Press, 1988.

Nichols, Aidan, OP. *Yves Congar*. London: Geoffrey Chapman, 1989.

———. "A Tale of Two Documents: *Sacrosanctum Concilium* and *Mediator Dei*." In *A Pope and a Council on the Sacred Liturgy*, edited by Alcuin Reid, OSB, 9–27. Farnborough, U.K.: Saint Michael's Abbey Press, 2002.

———. *Reason with Piety: Garrigou-Lagrange in the Service of Catholic Thought*. Naples, Fla.: Sapientia Press, 2008.

Norwood, Donald W. *Reforming Rome: Karl Barth and Vatican II*. Grand Rapids, Mich.: Eerdmans, 2015.

Oakes, Edward T. "The *Surnaturel* Controversy: A Survey and a Response." *Nova et Vetera* 9 (2011): 626–56.

Oakley, Francis. "History and the Return of the Repressed in Catholic Modernity:

The Dilemma Posed by Constance." In *The Crisis of Authority in Catholic Modernity*, edited by Michael J. Lacey and Francis Oakley, 29–56. Oxford: Oxford University Press, 2011.

O'Collins, Gerald, SJ. *Living Vatican II: The 21st Council for the 21st Century.* New York: Paulist Press, 2006.

———. "*Ressourcement* and Vatican II." In *Ressourcement: A Movement for Renewal in Twentieth-Century Catholic Theology*, edited by Gabriel Flynn and Paul D. Murray, 372–91. Oxford: Oxford University Press, 2012.

———. *The Second Vatican Council: Message and Meaning*. Collegeville, Minn.: Liturgical Press, 2014.

O'Malley, John W., SJ. "Reform, Historical Consciousness, and Vatican II's Aggiornamento." *Theological Studies* 32 (1971): 573–601.

———. "Vatican II: Historical Perspectives on Its Uniqueness and Interpretation." In *Vatican II: The Unfinished Agenda. A Look to the Future*, edited by Lucien Richard, OMI, Daniel Harrington, SJ, and John W. O'Malley, SJ, 22–32. Mahwah, N.J.: Paulist Press, 1987.

———. *Tradition and Transition: Historical Perspectives on Vatican II*. Wilmington, Del.: Michael Glazier, 1989.

———. *What Happened at Vatican II*. Cambridge, Mass.: Harvard University Press, 2008.

———. *Catholic History for Today's Church: How Our Past Illuminates Our Present*. Lanham, Md.: Rowman and Littlefield, 2015.

Ouellet, Marc. *Relevance and Future of the Second Vatican Council: Interviews with Father Geoffroy de la Tousche*. Translated by Michael Donley and Joseph Fessio, SJ. San Francisco: Ignatius Press, 2013.

Paul VI, Pope. "Address at the Solemn Opening of the Second Session of the Second Vatican Council, 29 September 1963." In *Council Daybook: Vatican II, Session I, 1962, and Session II, 1963*, edited by Floyd Anderson, 143–50. Washington, D.C.: National Catholic Welfare Service, 1965.

Pelland, Gilles. "A Few Words on Triumphalism." Translated by Leslie Wearne. In *Vatican II: Assessment and Perspectives: Twenty-Five Years After (1962–1987)*. Vol. 1, edited by René Latourelle, 106–22. Mahwah, N.J.: Paulist Press, 1988.

Pesch, Otto Hermann. *Das Zweite Vatikanische Konzil: Vorgeschichte—Verlauf—Ergebnisse—Nachgeschichte*. Ostfildern: Matthias Grünewald, 2001.

Philips, Gérard. *L'Église et son mystère au IIe Concile du Vatican. Histoire, texte et commentaire de la Constitution* Lumen Gentium. 2 vols. Paris: Desclée, 1967–1968.

Portier, William L. "What Kind of a World of Grace? Henri Cardinal de Lubac and the Council's Christological Center." *Communio* 39 (2012): 136–51.

Power, David M., OMI. *Unsearchable Riches: The Symbolic Nature of Liturgy*. New York: Pueblo, 1983.

Quisinsky, Michael, and Peter Walter, eds. *Personenlexikon zum Zweiten Vatikanischen Konzil*. Freiburg: Herder, 2012.

Rahner, Karl, SJ. "The Council: A New Beginning." In *The Church after the Council*, 9–33. New York: Herder and Herder, 1966.

———. "Towards a Fundamental Theological Interpretation of Vatican II." *Theological Studies* 40 (1979): 716–27.

Ramage, Matthew. "*Unitatis Redintegratio*." In Lamb and Levering, *Reception of Vatican II*.

Ratzinger, Joseph. *Theological Highlights of Vatican II*. Translated by the Missionary Society of St. Paul the Apostle. New York: Paulist Press, 1966.

———. *Principles of Catholic Theology: Building Stones for a Fundamental Theology*. Translated by Mary Frances McCarthy, SND. San Francisco: Ignatius Press, 1987.

———. "Chapter 1: Revelation Itself." In *Commentary on the Documents of Vatican II*. Vol. 3, edited by Herbert Vorgrimler, 170–80. New York: Crossroad, 1989.

———. "Dogmatic Constitution on Divine Revelation: Origin and Background." Translated by William Glen Doepel. In *Commentary on the Documents of Vatican II*. Vol. 3, edited by Herbert Vorgrimler, 155–66. New York: Crossroad, 1989.

———. "Part I, Chapter I." Translated by W. J. O'Hara. In *Commentary on the Documents of Vatican II*, edited by Herbert Vorgrimler. Vol. 5, *Pastoral Constitution on the Church in the Modern World*, 115–63. New York: Herder and Herder, 1989.

———. *Gospel, Catechesis, Catechism: Sidelights on the* Catechism of the Catholic Church. San Francisco: Ignatius Press, 1997.

———. *Milestones: Memoirs 1927–1977*. Translated by Erasmo Leiva-Merikakis. San Francisco: Ignatius Press, 1998.

———. *The Spirit of the Liturgy*. Translated by John Saward. San Francisco: Ignatius Press, 2000.

———. *Jesus of Nazareth: From the Baptism in the Jordan to the Transfiguration*. Translated by Adrian J. Walker. New York: Doubleday, 2007.

———. "Biblical Interpretations in Conflict: On the Foundations and the Itinerary of Exegesis Today." Translated by Adrian Walker. In *Opening Up the Scriptures: Joseph Ratzinger and the Foundations of Biblical Interpretation*, edited by José Granados, Carlos Granados, and Luis Sánchez-Navarro, 1–29. Grand Rapids, Mich.: Eerdmans, 2008.

———. *Theological Highlights of Vatican II*. Translated by Werner Barzel, Gerald C. Thormann, and Henry Traub, SJ. Mahwah, N.J.: Paulist Press, 2009.

Rausch, Thomas P., SJ, and Richard R. Gaillardetz, eds. *Go into the Streets! The Welcoming Church of Pope Francis*. New York: Paulist Press, 2016.

Reese, Thomas J., SJ, ed. *The Universal Catechism Reader: Reflections and Responses*. New York: HarperCollins, 1990.

Routhier, Gilles, Philippe J. Roy, and Karim Schelkens, eds. *La théologie catholique entre intransigeance et renouveau. La reception des mouvements préconciliaires à Vatican II*. Leuven: College Erasme / Universiteitsbibliotheek, 2011.

Roy, Philippe J. *Bibliographie du Concile Vatican II*. Vatican City: Libreria Editrice Vaticana, 2012.

Ruddy, Christopher. "'In my end is my beginning': *Lumen Gentium* and the Priority of Doxology." *Irish Theological Quarterly* 79 (2014): 144–64.

———. "Yves Congar and Hans Küng at Vatican II: Differing Paths of Church Reform." *Ecclesiology* 10 (2014): 159–85.

———. "The Local and Universal Church." In *Go into the Streets! The Welcoming Church of Pope Francis*, edited by Thomas P. Rausch, SJ, and Richard R. Gaillardetz, 109–24. New York: Paulist Press, 2016.

Rush, Ormond. *Still Interpreting Vatican II: Some Hermeneutical Principles*. New York: Paulist Press, 2004.

Sarah, Robert, et al. *Christ's New Homeland—Africa: Contribution to the Synod on the Family by African Pastors*. Translated by Michael J. Miller. San Francisco: Ignatius Press, 2015.

Scarisbrick, J. J. "An Historian's Reflections on Yves Congar's *Mon Journal du Concile*." In *Yves Congar: Theologian of the Church*, edited by Gabriel Flynn, 249–75. Leuven: Peeters, 2005.

Schenk, Richard, OP. "*Gaudium et Spes*: The Task before Us," *Nova et Vetera* 8 (2010): 323–35.

Schillebeeckx, Edward, OP. "Questions on Christian Salvation of and for Man." In *Toward Vatican III: The Work That Needs to Be Done*, edited by David Tracy, Hans Küng, and Johann B. Metz, 27–44. New York: Seabury Press, 1978.

———. *Church: The Human Story of God*. Translated by John Bowden. New York: Crossroad, 1990. First published in Dutch, 1989.

Schindler, David L., and Nicholas J. Healy, Jr. *Freedom, Truth, and Human Dignity: The Second Vatican Council's Declaration on Religious Freedom: A New Translation, Redaction History, and Interpretation of Dignitatis Humanae*. Grand Rapids, Mich.: Eerdmans, 2015.

Schloesser, Stephen. "Against Forgetting: Memory, History, Vatican II." *Theological Studies* 67 (2006): 275–319.

Segundo, Juan Luis, SJ. *Theology for Artisans of a New Humanity: The Community Called Church*. Vol. 1. Maryknoll, N.Y.: Orbis Books, 1973.

Smith, Innocent, OP. "Ecclesial Authorship, the Council, and the Liturgy: Reflections on a Debate between Ratzinger and Lefebvre." *Angelicum* 92 (2015): 93–113.

Sullivan, Maureen, OP. *The Road to Vatican II: Key Changes in Theology*. New York: Paulist Press, 2007.

The Synod of Bishops. "'Final Report,' December 7, 1985." In *The Extraordinary Synod—1985: Message to the People of God*, 37–68. Boston, Mass.: St. Paul Editions, 1986.

Tanner, Norman P., SJ, ed. *Decrees of the Ecumenical Councils*. Vol. 2, *Trent to Vatican II*. Washington, D.C.: Georgetown University Press, 1990.

Taylor, Charles. *The Language Animal: The Full Shape of the Human Linguistic Capacity*. Cambridge, Mass.: Harvard University Press, 2016.

Thiel, John E. *Senses of Tradition: Continuity and Development in Catholic Faith*. Oxford: Oxford University Press, 2000.

Thompson, Augustine, OP. *Cities of God: The Religion of the Italian Communes, 1125–1325*. 2nd ed. University Park: Pennsylvania State University Press, 2006.
Thompson, Daniel Speed. *The Language of Dissent: Edward Schillebeeckx on the Crisis of Authority in the Catholic Church*. Notre Dame, Ind.: University of Notre Dame Press, 2003.
Thönissen, Wolfgang. *Ein Konzil für ein ökumenisches Zeitalter: Schlüsselthemen des Zweiten Vatikanums*. Paderborn: Bonifatius, 2012.
Tilley, Terrence W. *Inventing Catholic Tradition*. Maryknoll, N.Y.: Orbis Books, 2000.
———. *The Disciples' Jesus: Christology as Reconciling Practice*. Maryknoll, N.Y.: Orbis Books, 2008.
Tück, Jan-Heiner, ed. *Erinnerung an die Zukunft. Das Zweite Vatikanische Konzil. Werweiterte und aktualisierte Auflage*. Freiburg im Breisgau: Herder, 2013.
Turbanti, Giovanni. *Un concilio per il mondo moderno. La redazione della constituzione pastorale "Gaudium et spes" del Vaticano II*. Bologna: Il Mulino, 2000.
van Beeck, Frans Jozef, SJ. *Catholic Identity after Vatican II: Three Types of Faith in the One Church*. Chicago: Loyola University Press, 1985.
Vereb, Jerome-Michael. *"Because He Was a German!" Cardinal Bea and the Origins of Roman Catholic Engagement in the Ecumenical Movement*. Grand Rapids, Mich.: Eerdmans, 2006.
Vide, Vicente, and José R. Villar, eds. *El Concilio Vaticano II: Una perspectiva teologica*. Madrid: San Pablo, 2013.
Vismara, Paola. "Lodovico Antonio Muratori (1672–1750): Enlightenment in a Tridentine Mode." In *Enlightenment and Catholicism in Europe: A Transnational History*, edited by Jeffrey D. Burson and Ulrich L. Lehner, 249–68. Notre Dame, Ind.: University of Notre Dame Press, 2014.
von Balthasar, Hans Urs. *The Office of Peter and the Structure of the Church*. Translated by Andrée Emery. San Francisco: Ignatius Press, 1986. First published in German, 1974
Vorgrimler, Herbert, ed. *Commentary on the Documents of Vatican II*. 5 Vols. New York: Herder and Herder, 1967–1969.
Vosko, Richard S. *God's House Is Our House: Re-imagining the Environment for Worship*. Collegeville, Minn.: Liturgical Press, 2006.
Wahlberg, Mats. *Revelation as Testimony: A Philosophical-Theological Study*. Grand Rapids, Mich.: Eerdmans, 2014.
Walter, Peter. "Kontinuität oder Diskontinuität? Das II. Vaticanum im Kontext der Theologiegeschichte." In *Das II. Vatikanische Konzil und die Wissenschaft der Theologie*, edited by Ansgar Kreutzer and Günther Wassilowsky, 11–31. Frankfurt: Peter Lang, 2014.
Weigel, George. *Evangelical Catholicism: Deep Reform in the 21st-Century Church*. New York: Basic Books, 2013.
Wenzel, Knut. *Das Zweite Vatikanische Konzil: Eine Einführung*. Freiburg: Herder, 2014.

White, Thomas Joseph, OP. "The Tridentine Genius of Vatican II." *First Things*, no. 227 (November 2012): 25–30.

———. "Imperfect Happiness and the Final End of Man: Thomas Aquinas and the Paradigm of Nature-Grace Orthodoxy." *The Thomist* 78 (2014): 247–89.

———. *The Incarnate Lord: A Thomistic Study in Christology*. Washington, D.C.: The Catholic University of America Press, 2015.

———. "*Gaudium et Spes*." In Lamb and Levering, *Reception of Vatican II*.

Wicks, Jared, SJ. "Dei Verbum Developing: Vatican II's Revelation Doctrine, 1963–1964." In *The Convergence of Theology: A Festschrift Honoring Gerald O'Collins, S.J.*, edited by Daniel Kendall, SJ, and Stephen T. Davis, 109–25. New York: Paulist Press, 2001.

———. "Pieter Smulders and Dei Verbum." 5 Parts. *Gregorianum* 82 (2001): 247–97; 82 (2001): 559–93; 83 (2003): 225–67; 85 (2004): 242–77; 86 (2005): 92–134.

———. "Dei Verbum under Revision, March–April 1964: Contributions of Charles Moeller and Other Belgian Theologians." In *The Belgian Contribution to the Second Vatican Council*, edited by Doris Donnelly, Joseph Famerée, Mathijs Lamberigts, and Karim Schelkens, 460–94. Leuven: Peeters, 2008.

———. "More Light on Vatican Council II." *Catholic Historical Review* 94 (2008): 75–101.

———. "Six Texts by Prof. Joseph Ratzinger as *Peritus* before and during Vatican Council II." *Gregorianum* 89 (2008): 233–311.

———. *Doing Theology*. New York: Paulist Press, 2009.

———. "Further Light on Vatican Council II." *Catholic Historical Review* 95 (2009): 546–69.

———. "Vatican II on Revelation—From behind the Scenes." *Theological Studies* 71 (2010): 637–50.

———. "Cardinal Willebrands's Contributions to Catholic Ecumenical Theology." *Pro Ecclesia* 20 (2011): 6–27.

———. "Vatican II's Turn in 1963: Toward Renewing Catholic Ecclesiology and Validating Catholic Ecumenism." *Josephinum Journal of Theology* 19 (2012): 1–13.

———. "Vatican II Taking Hold of Its (and Pope John's) Council Goals, September 1962–May 1963." *Josephinum Journal of Theology* 19 (2012): 172–86.

———. "Lutheran-Catholic Dialogue: On Foundations Laid in 1963–64." *Concordia Theological Journal* 39 (2013): 296–309.

———. "Vatican II in 1964: Major Doctrinal Advances, but Also Fissures on Addressing the Modern World." *Josephinum Journal of Theology* 20 (2013): 4–19.

———. "Tridentine Motivations of Angello Roncalli/Pope John XXIII before and during Vatican II." *Theological Studies* 75 (2014): 847–62.

———. "Scripture Reading Urged Vehementer (Dei Verbum No. 25): Background and Development." In *50 Years On: Probing the Riches of Vatican II*, edited by David G. Schultenover, SJ, 365–90. Collegeville, Minn.: Liturgical Press, 2015.

Wintz, Jack, and John Feister. "Road Map for the Future: Teachings of Vatican II." In *Vatican II Today: Calling Catholics to Holiness and Service*, edited by Judy Ball and Joan McKamey, 1–9. Cincinnati, Ohio: St. Anthony Messenger Press, 2005.

Wojtyła, Karol. *Sources of Renewal: The Implementation of the Second Vatican Council*. Translated by P. S. Falla. San Francisco: Harper and Row, 1980.

Wood, Susan K., SCL. "Henri de Lubac and the Church-World Relationship in *Gaudium et Spes*." In *The Legacy of Vatican II*, edited by Massimo Faggioli and Andrea Vicini, 226–47. Mahwah, N.J.: Paulist Press, 2015.

INDEX

abortion, 161
Abraham, 42
Acerbi, Antonio, 186n38
active participation, 6, 10–13, 18, 50–51, 53–54, 59–64, 67–72, 74–80, 206–7, 216
Adam, 152; as type of Christ, 152
Ad Gentes, 12, 115n109, 159, 208
aggiornamento, 19, 174n1, 178–79, 184n31, 187, 191n53, 209
Alberigo, Giuseppe, 14, 15n30, 177, 185, 187, 189, 191, 193
altar: freestanding, 53n13
analogy of faith, 42, 194n60
Anointing of the Sick, 73, 113
anthropology: christological, 170; theological, 11, 200
Antonelli, Cesare, 126n120
apostles: commissioning of, 43, 65, 116; as witnesses of revelation, 28, 31, 34
Apostolicam Actuositatem, 12, 121n116, 208
Aristotle, 145
atheism, 8, 135, 151, 169
Aubry, Augustin-Marie, 118n112
Augustine, 151

Baius, Michael, 144
baptism, 66, 75, 91, 110–12, 114, 117, 122, 216; of infants, 73
Barth, Karl, 17n35, 171n72, 202n82
Bea, Augustin, 22n6
Beal, Rose, 81
beatific vision, 125, 139, 141–43, 146, 213n23
Beauduin, Lambert, 51
Bellarmine, Robert, 205

Benedict XVI, Pope, 3n10, 9, 180, 184–87, 188n43, 189–94, 196–97, 203, 204n87, 217
Berkouwer, G. C., 17n35
Bernard of Clairvaux, 141
Berzosa Martinez, Raul, 137n10
birth control, 212
Blanchard, Shaun, 13n25
Blondel, Maurice, 19n38, 192, 196
Boeve, Lieven, 24
Bologna Schools, 189
Borromeo, Charles, 101n73
Bouillard, Henri, 212
Bouyer, Louis, 10, 12, 51–64, 65n64, 67, 69, 71–72, 75–79
Boyer, Charles, 140n24
Boyer, Mark G., 53n13
Braine, David, 46n64, 137n11
Bugnini, Annibale, 77n74
Burke-Sullivan, Eileen, 172n76, 194n60

Cajetan, 139, 145
capitalism, 163
Casel, Odo, 51
Catechism of the Catholic Church, 20–21
Cessario, Romanus, 100n68
Chantraine, Georges, 137n10
Chenu, Marie-Dominique, 198
Church: as body of Christ, 13, 81, 86, 89, 91, 93, 110, 119, 215; as bride of Christ, 89, 91, 93, 109; Christ-given authority to teach, 2n3; heavenly, 8; hierarchical constitution of, 8, 87, 92, 95, 106–7, 114, 116, 128–30, 182, 205, 208, 215; holiness of, 89–90,

239

Church: as body of Christ, (cont.) 92–96, 98, 107–8, 111, 122–24, 127, 129, 132; infallibility of, 93, 96–97; as interpreter of Scripture, 42; marks of, 129; as Mystical Body, 11, 66, 94, 109–10, 204; as people of God, 3n10, 39, 42, 55, 81, 85, 89, 95, 98, 111–15, 133, 149, 215, 219; as *perfecta societas*, 204; as personal reality, 40; reforming the Church's external structure, 2n3, 3, 6, 216; as sacrament of salvation, 9, 92, 124; as sacrament of the world, 171; as sacrament of unity, 78, 107, 112; as temple of the Spirit, 81, 91, 112, 116
Church-state relations, 165
Christus Dominus, 7, 12, 114n106, 116n110, 119n113, 208
Chrysostom, John, 42
Cimorelli, Christopher, 132n140
Clifford, Catherine, 7–9
collegiality. *See* episcopal collegiality
Comte, Auguste, 169
Comte, Bernard, 137n10
Confirmation, 73, 112
Congar, Yves, 4n12, 5, 10, 12, 16, 17n35, 19n37, 48n70, 81–107, 109, 117, 128–32, 136, 179n13, 180n14, 183n28, 186n38, 188, 193, 198, 201n80, 209–13
Constitution on the Sacred Liturgy. *See Sacrosanctum Concilium*
continuity. *See* doctrinal continuity
contraception. *See* birth control
covenant, 25, 55, 67, 91, 99, 112, 120, 160
Cross, 11, 31–32, 37, 53n13, 54, 66, 71, 107, 123, 127, 154, 169, 172
Cullman, Oscar, 2n3, 17n35, 209
culture: legitimate autonomy of, 163
Cunningham, Lawrence, 208
curia, 7n18, 16n33

Daniélou, Jean, 30
Danneels, Godfried Cardinal, 177
D'Costa, Gavin, 7n18
deacons, 120; permanent diaconate, 120
death, human, 37, 150, 156
debitum naturae, 141
De Chirico, Leonardo, 17n35
deification, 35, 108
Dei Filius (Vatican I), 23, 25, 29n36
Dei Verbum, 6–8, 10–11, 13n25, 14, 20–25,
33–49, 177–78, 181–82, 193, 213, 217, 218n38
De Lubac, Henri, 3n10, 4n12, 5, 10, 12, 16, 22n6, 30, 53n14, 126n120, 129, 134–47, 152, 168–72, 179n13, 182, 184, 197–98, 202n82, 207–12
De Moulins-Beaufort, Eric, 178n10
Denysenko, Nicholas, 19, 50n1
deposit of faith, 27, 47, 91, 99, 104, 106–7, 118, 188n44
Descoqs, Pedro, 140n24
development of doctrine, 48n70, 96, 116, 134n2, 181n19, 204, 218n38
Dignitatis Humanae, 7, 12, 122n118, 165n57, 208
direction of liturgical prayer, 10, 53, 56–58, 60–62, 64, 76–80, 216; facing East, 56–58, 61, 64, 76, 78–80, 216; facing the people, 10, 53, 60–62, 77
discontinuity. *See* doctrinal rupture
divine revelation. *See* revelation
Divini Cultus (Pius XI), 51
divorce, 160
doctrinal continuity, 4n12, 5, 187–88, 190, 192–94, 203–4, 211n15, 217
doctrinal rupture, 4n12, 5, 47–48, 191, 194, 196, 218n38
dogma, 24, 48, 86–88, 96, 98, 130, 133, 179, 207, 212; adequation to revelation, 24, 132n140; irreformability of, 212
Dogmatic Constitution on Divine Revelation. *See Dei Verbum*
Dogmatic Constitution on the Church. *See Lumen Gentium*
domestic church, 113
Dominus Iesus (Congregation for the Doctrine of the Faith), 175n2
Douthat, Ross, 201n80
Duffy, Eamon, 60n48, 62n54
Dulles, Avery, 4n12, 5, 83n7, 86, 180, 186, 188, 212

Ecclesiam Suam (Paul VI), 1, 3, 178n11
ecclesiology: *communio* ecclesiology, 3n10; ecclesiological horizontalism, 7n16, 210, 213; ecclesiology of communion, 185, 196; missiological ecclesiology, 195; political decentralization in, 194–97, 206
Echeverria, Eduardo J., 132n140

economy of salvation, 8, 25, 147
ecumenical dialogue. *See* ecumenism
ecumenism, 7n18, 12, 17, 100n70, 104, 167, 184, 195–97
episcopacy, 116–19, 123, 133, 158, 219; as successors of the apostles, 116–17. *See also* power distribution between pope and bishops
episcopal collegiality, 3n10, 116, 117–18, 212
Erasmus, 100
Eucharist, 11, 34, 53n13, 54–55, 57–62, 64, 66–67, 71, 80, 107–8, 110, 112, 114–15, 119–20, 124, 155, 181n19, 182, 205, 213, 217; communion under both kinds, 64, 72; frequency of reception of, 60, 64, 72; sacrifice of, 53n13, 57–58, 64, 66–67, 71, 76, 107, 112, 115, 120, 125, 213, 217; tabernacle, 75
Eucharistic adoration, 54
Eucharistic prayer, 10, 53n13, 61–64, 72, 80
evangelical counsels, 122–23
Evangelii Gaudium (Pope Francis), 3
evangelization, 3, 16, 115
Evennett, H. Outram, 106n97
exegesis: historical-critical, 193
extrinsicism, 143

facing the people. *See* direction of liturgical prayer
Faggioli, Massimo, 12, 174–75, 184–99, 205–6, 214
faith, 3, 66, 91–92, 109, 114, 117, 122, 129, 152, 205, 213; invitation to, 3; obedience of, 8, 47, 205, 213n23; and reason, 34
the fall, 36
Famerée, Joseph, 82n5
Feingold, Lawrence, 137n11
Feister, John, 76
Fessard, Gaston, 30
Feuerbach, Ludwig, 169
Figoureux, Loïc, 136n6, 210n10
First Vatican Council, 23, 34, 45, 116, 188n44
Flynn, Gabriel, 6, 82n4, 85
Fouilloux, Étienne, 100n70
Francis, Pope, 3, 83n9, 184–85, 195, 218n38, 220
Frein, Brigid Curtin, 24n16

French Revolution, 191n53, 200n78
fundamental theology, 11

Gaillardetz, Richard, 7–9, 47–48, 171n72, 216, 218–20
Galot, Jean, 14n26
Garrigou-Lagrange, Réginald, 29
Gaudium et Spes, 6–11, 14n26, 17n14, 134–137, 147–69, 181–83, 194, 198–200, 211n16, 214, 217
genocide, 166
George, Timothy, 17n35
Gertler, Thomas, 17n34, 171n76
Gilson, Étienne, 141n26
grace, 6, 10, 12, 14, 36–37, 94–95, 98, 114–15, 126–27, 133–35, 137–47, 150–51, 153–60, 162–64, 166–68, 171, 183, 207, 215, 217; means of, 94–95, 98; nature and, 134–35, 137–39, 147, 153, 161, 164, 171–72, 207, 216; state of, 158
Gravissimum Educationis, 12, 163n56, 208
Gregorian chant, 74
Gregory the Great, 59, 61
Grillmeier, Alois, 84
Grummett, David, 137n11
Guardini, Romano, 51
Guarino, Thomas G., 19n37
Guitton, Jean, 209
Gy, Pierre-Marie, 51

Haight, Roger, 198n74
Hanvey, James, 203–5
Healy, Nicholas J., Jr., 7n18, 48n70, 137n11
hermeneutic of continuity. *See* doctrinal continuity
Hilberath, Bernd Jochen, 14
Hinojosa, Clara Dina, 76n71
historical consciousness, 11, 13, 184, 193
history of salvation, 12
Holy Orders, sacrament of, 73, 113, 116, 120
Holy Spirit: gifts of, 110, 113; guidance of, 1, 39, 47, 194n60; inspiration of, 1; sending of, 8, 37–38, 43, 91, 109, 181
Honorius, Pope, 97
Humanae Vitae (Paul VI), 175n2
humanism, 162, 169
human nature, 10, 12, 14, 161–62; as fallen, 14
Hünermann, Peter, 14
Hütter, Reinhard, 137n11, 198n74

INDEX 241

iconography, 62
image of God, 141, 150, 152–53; soul as image of the Trinity, 141
Imbelli, Robert P., 3n10, 12, 174–86, 190, 196–97, 199–200, 205, 213, 220
infallibility. *See* Church. *See also* papal infallibility
Inter Mirifica, 12, 121n117, 148, 208
interreligious dialogue, 7n18, 12, 167, 195–97
Islam, 115
Israel, 13, 24, 36, 49

Jackson, Pamela, 51, 76n71
Jesus Christ: ascension of, 65; aversion to the revelatory primacy of, 180; death of, 45, 51, 57, 66, 71, 73, 109, 126, 153, 175n2, 181, 213n23; earthly ministry of, 26; as goal of history, 8; Incarnation of, 38, 42–43, 91, 110–11, 127, 170; as Jewish Messiah, 36, 46, 55–56, 180; as mediator, 36, 125, 127; Paschal Mystery of, 11, 13–14, 45, 54, 64–66, 76–77, 80, 105–6, 152, 207, 216; Passion of, 57, 65, 73, 95; priestly office, 11, 66, 121; prophetic office, 11, 121; Resurrection of, 14, 37, 54, 65, 71, 73, 95, 109, 122, 153–54, 161, 175n2, 181, 192n56, 213n23; royal office, 11, 121; sacrifice of, 10, 55, 120, 127, 205; as Suffering Servant, 46; as Word, 14, 29, 34–37, 90, 127, 151, 159, 170, 181
Jewish people, 13, 115
John Paul II, Pope, 3n10, 4, 9, 135, 187, 189–90, 198n74, 217
Johnson, Luke Timothy, 180
John XXIII, Pope, 2–3, 14, 16, 48, 60, 82–83, 135, 174, 178n11, 187, 197, 209; decision to call the Council, 16, 82
Jossua, Jean-Pierre, 82n4
Journet, Charles, 96
Judaism. *See* Jewish people
Jungmann, Josef, 51
justification, 34

Kasper, Walter, 198n74
Kieckhefer, Richard, 77
kingdom of God, 43, 94, 109, 124, 155; inauguration of, 43
Koch, Kurt, 204n87

Komonchak, Joseph, 4, 19n37, 129n122, 171n70, 179n13, 189n46, 191, 198n74
Küng, Hans, 186, 208, 210

Ladaria, Luis, 14n28
laity: dignity of, 120; work of, 8, 121–22
Lakeland, Paul, 215
Lamb, Matthew L., 184n31, 195n62
Langevin, Dominic M., 65n64
La Poterie, Ignace de, 24n16
La Soujeole, Benoît-Dominique de, 111n103
Latourelle, René, 10, 12, 24–33, 45, 212
Lawler, Michael G., 172n76, 194n60
Lefebvre, Marcel, 188n44, 208
Léger, Paul-Émile, 83n9
Lehner, Ulrich L. 13n25
Leo XIII, Pope, 17n35
Liberius, Pope, 97
Lindbeck, George A., 17n35
Liturgical Movement, 50–52, 64, 71, 76n71, 105–6
liturgy, 6, 8, 14, 16, 26, 50n1, 51–52, 54–55, 59, 61–72, 75–80, 87, 96, 104–5, 125, 128, 163, 178, 195, 206, 213, 216–17, 220; changes to the rites of, 69–76, 117; clericalization of, 60–61, 63–64, 77–79; devotional practices and, 54, 62, 67; Eastern, 62; eternal liturgy, 19, 80; inculturation of, 71, 74, 96, 103; as source and summit of Christian life, 8; synagogue-church transition as pertaining to, 54–59; use of Latin, 96
Liturgy of the Hours, 73, 76
Long, Steven A., 137n11
López, Antonio, 168
Lumen Gentium, 6–8, 10–11, 13n25, 14n26, 81–84, 86, 90, 107–33, 171, 177, 181–82, 194, 214–15, 217
Luther, Martin, 91n38, 100, 102–3

Magisterium, 8, 40, 89, 102, 160, 200, 211n16, 219; dissent from, 194, 196; ordinary, 192n56
Malloy, Christopher J., 137n11
Mannion, Gerard, 3n10
Marchetto, Agostino, 189
Mariology, 13
marriage, 73, 113, 160–61, 194n60
Marshall, Bruce D., 201n80, 203n85

242 INDEX

Marx, Karl, 169
Marxism, 151, 211n16
Mary, 13n25, 74, 84, 92, 94–95, 114, 125–27; cooperation with Christ in work of salvation, 126–27; devotion to, 128; as icon of the Church, 92, 126, 128; inclusion of in *Lumen Gentium*, 126, 219; as mother of God, 114, 127; as new Eve, 126; as virgin, 114, 127
matrimony. *See* marriage
McBrien, Richard, 212
McDermott, John M., 15n29
Mediator Dei (Pius XII), 51–52, 72
Meszaros, Andrew, 5n13, 23n13, 86n18, 132n135, 195n65
metaphysics, 211n16
Mettepenningen, Jürgen, 211
Miccoli, Giovanni, 190n49
Michel, Virgil, 51
Miller, Charles E., 67n66, 76n73
Miller, Vincent J., 80n91
Minch, Daniel, 132n140
mission. *See* evangelization
Modernism, 104, 211n17
modern world, 8, 11, 13–14, 158, 170, 176, 195, 197–98, 200n78, 201n80
Moeller, Charles, 84
Monotheletism, 97
Moses: experience at Sinai, 26
Muratori, Lodovico, 13n25
Murray, John Courtney, 83n9
Mystici Corporis (Pius XII), 205

natural beatitude, 140
natural desire: to see God, 135–36, 137n11, 142–46, 216; for the supernatural, 137n11, 144, 146, 216
natural knowledge of God, 38
nature. *See* human nature
Neufeld, Karl Heinz, 136n9, 209
Neuhaus, Richard John, 186, 187n41
Newman, John Henry, 4n12, 97, 181n19
Nicea, Council of, 49
Niceno-Constantinopolitan Creed, 192n56
Nichols, Aidan, 29n35, 51, 52n8, 82n5
Nietzsche, Friedrich, 169
1985 Extraordinary Synod of Bishops, 2, 21, 180n14, 185–86
Norwood, Donald W., 17n35

Nostra Aetate, 7, 12, 115n108, 167n59, 208
nouvelle théologie, 16, 86n21, 176, 197, 203, 205, 208–9, 211
Novak, Michael, 186
nuclear weapons, 166

Oakes, Edward T., 137n11
Oakley, Francis, 188n44
obediential potency, 145–46
O'Collins, Gerald, 23, 86n21, 175n2, 177, 181n19
O'Malley, John W., 4n12, 7n16, 14–16, 83n9, 84–85, 191, 192n56, 202n81, 212
Optatam Totius, 12, 120n114, 208
Orientalium Ecclesiarum, 12, 113n105, 117, 208
original sin, 151
Ottaviani, Alfredo, 83
Ouellet, Marc, 17–18

papacy, 16n33, 113, 116–18, 133, 191n53, 205, 212, 217, 219. *See also* power distribution between pope and bishops
papal infallibility, 34, 96, 116–18
Paschal II, Pope, 97
Pastoral Constitution on the Church in the Modern World. *See Gaudium et Spes*
Paul (apostle), 40, 49, 133
Paul VI, Pope, 1, 2n3, 3, 14, 16, 60, 126n120, 175, 178n11, 184, 186n38, 188n44, 209
Pelland, Gilles, 217n36
Penance, sacrament of, 73, 113
people of God. *See* church
Perfectae Caritatis, 12, 208
periti: role of, 16n31
Pesch, Otto Hermann, 15
Philips, Gérard, 15, 84, 131n131
Pié-Ninot, Salvador, 14n28
Pius V, Pope, 211
Pius VII, Pope, 97
Pius X, Pope, 50, 67n66, 200n78, 211
Pius XI, Pope, 51, 72, 200n78
Pius XII, Pope, 51, 72, 205
pluralism, 11; religious, 196
pneumatology: of *aggiornamento*, 4n12
polygamy, 160
pope. *See* papacy
Portier, William, 170
Power, David M., 53n14

INDEX 243

power distribution between pope and bishops, 3n10, 7n18, 16n33, 17, 82, 85, 205–6, 214, 219–20
predestination, 94
Presbyterorum Ordinis, 12, 120n114, 208
priesthood: of all believers, 50n1, 68, 80, 85, 112, 181n19
priests, 10, 44, 53, 58–64, 68–73, 78–80, 97, 115, 120, 123, 130, 158, 181n19, 182; priestly identity, 181n19
Protestant liberalism, 202n82
Protestant Reformation, 90, 97, 101
Prügl, Thomas, 14n28
pure nature, 139–40, 142
purgatory, 125

Rahner, Karl, 83n9, 84, 198, 214
Ramage, Matthew, 7n18
Ratzinger, Joseph, 4n12, 5, 20–23, 24n16, 79, 84, 179n13, 180, 187, 189, 191, 193n58, 194, 196–203, 209–11; role as *peritus*, 192
Reconciliation. *See* Penance, 113
Redemptor Hominis (John Paul II), 198n74
Reformation. *See* Protestant Reformation
Regnon, Théodore de, 139
religious freedom, 7n18, 13, 48, 165, 184, 201n80
religious liberty. *See* religious freedom
religious life, 44, 73, 85n16, 121–24, 208
ressourcement, 19, 104n89, 105, 174n1, 178–79, 181–82, 191n53
revelation, 2n3, 9–13, 21–47, 49, 132, 176, 178–79, 181–82, 192–93, 197, 202, 208, 210, 214–20; as communicating God's Word, 26–27, 29, 219; as event, 26; as personal encounter, 9–12, 22–25, 27–44, 46–47, 49, 182, 216, 218n38; as propositional, 6, 9–12, 22–28, 30–44, 46–47, 49, 216–17, 218n38, 219n42; transmission of, 8, 26, 33–34, 38–40
Richard of Chichester, 175n2
rights, human, 156–57
Rousselot, Pierre, 139
Roy, Philippe J., 14n27
Ruddy, Christopher, 3n10, 6n15, 182n24, 210n9
rupture. *See* doctrinal rupture
Rush, Ormond, 4n12, 48n72

sacramentals, 72–73, 76
sacraments, 11, 54, 58, 65–66, 71–73, 76, 83, 88–92, 96, 98–99, 107–10, 114, 116, 119, 122, 129, 205, 207, 216–17
sacrifice, 54–57
Sacrosanctum Concilium, 6–8, 10–11, 13n25, 14n26, 16, 50–54, 62, 64–77, 80, 181–82, 194, 198, 213, 214n24, 217
Salzman, Todd A., 171n76, 194n60
Sarah, Robert, 83n9
Scarisbrick, J. J., 85n14
Schenk, Richard, 15n30
Schillebeeckx, Edward, 84, 129, 130n127, 171, 188n44, 211
Schindler, David L., 7n18, 48n70, 136n7
Schlosser, Marianne, 14n28
Schnackenburg, Rudolph, 84
Scripture: adequacy to revelation, 24; canon of, 40; human authors of, 40–42; inspiration of, 8, 33, 40–41; interpretation of, 8, 33, 40, 42; in the life of the Church, 33, 43; as soul of sacred theology, 44
Second Vatican Council: American neo-conservative interpretation of, 186–87, 191; Christological interpretation of, 176; evangelistic task of, 1, 13, 115, 180, 214; historicist reception of, 175–76, 187–88, 192–93, 196–97, 198n74, 206; liberal narrative of, 186; traditionalist narrative of, 186; true and false reform in, 12, 196, 217
Segundo, Juan Luis, 215
Semmelroth, Otto, 16, 84
sensus fidei, 8, 113
Sermon on the Mount, 45
sexual revolution, 201n80
sin, 37
Smedt, Émile de, 84
Smith, Innocent, 131n131
Smulders, Pieter, 16, 84
socialism, 163
Son: as consubstantial with the Father, 49; sending of, 8, 14n26
Suárez, Francisco, 141n26
subsistit in, 8, 110, 111n103
Suenens, Léon-Joseph, 84
Sullivan, Maureen, 131–32, 214
supernatural, 134, 140–41, 149

Syllabus Errorum (Pius IX), 200n78
synod of bishops, 130

Taylor, Charles 46n64
Theobald, Christoph, 177
Thiel, John, 47, 48n70
Thomas Aquinas, 140, 145–46
Thompson, Augustine, 60n48, 62n54
Thompson, Daniel Speed, 188n44
Thönissen, Wolfgang, 209n8
Tillard, Jean-Marie, 186n37
Tilley, Terrence W., 48n70, 48n72, 188n44
Toletus, Francisco, 139
Torrell, Jean–Pierre, 22n6
Tradition, 1, 4n12, 8, 20, 24, 26, 28, 38–40, 42, 47–49, 54, 88, 103–5, 131, 178, 187, 188n44, 191–92, 194, 205–8, 211, 214, 216, 220; Church as living subject of, 104; historicization of, 187
Trent, Council of, 34, 82n5, 87, 90, 101n73, 106n97, 211
Trinity, 29, 34, 36, 91, 124–25, 128, 141, 156, 179, 181, 221
triune God. *See* Trinity
Turbanti, Giovanni, 134n2

Unitatis Redintegratio, 7, 12, 115n107, 167n58, 208
universal call to holiness, 3n10, 8, 12–13, 78, 82–83, 122, 182

usury: revision of doctrinal formulation of, 218n38

Van Beeck, Frans Jozef, 182n25
Vatican I. *See* First Vatican Council
Vatican II. *See* Second Vatican Council
Vereb, Jerome-Michael, C.P., 7n18
Vismara, Paola, 13n25
vision of God. *See* beatific vision
Von Balthasar, Hans Urs, 21, 30, 85n16
Vonier, Anscar, 95
Vorgrimler, Herbert, 14
Vosko, Richard, 77–78

Wahlberg, Mats, 9n22, 46–47
Walter, Peter, 188n43
Weigel, George, 82n5, 186
Wenzel, Knut, 15
White, Thomas Joseph, 19n37, 82n5, 129n124, 137n11
Wicks, Jared, 14, 16n31, 17n35, 82n5, 86n20, 115n107, 134n2, 135n5, 171n70, 174n1, 177, 213n23
Wintz, Jack, 76
Wojtyła, Karol, 4, 186
Wood, Susan, 134

year, liturgical, 73–74; Good Friday, 74; Holy Saturday, 74; Lent, 74

An Introduction to Vatican II as an Ongoing Theological Event was designed in Garamond, with Scala Sans and Garda Titling display type, and composed by Kachergis Book Design of Pittsboro, North Carolina. It was printed on 60-pound Natural Recycled and bound by McNaughton & Gunn of Saline, Michigan.

www.ingramcontent.com/pod-product-compliance
Lightning Source LLC
Chambersburg PA
CBHW031412290426
44110CB00011B/354